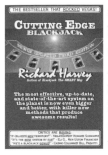
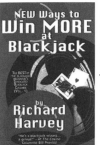

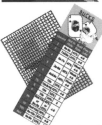

Other Books From Mystic Ridge Books

Baring It All, compiled and edited by Layla Shilkret ($14.95): 20 Explicit true stories of how 20 women attained spiritual and loving heights through great lovemaking. *Romantic.* Great *ideas. Foreplay!*
A Woman In Ecstasy by Jeffrey Adamson (Spring 2009, $16.95): For men. A celebrated lover of women shares his unique lovemaking insights & methods. To make the woman you fancy desire you *forever.*

New Children's Early Reader Books from MRB Kidz

Rebecca & The Great Goat Getaway by "Professor" Christopher Furfur ($15.95): The antidote to the chant: "I'm bored!" A young girl becomes a hero and discovers the meaning of life after saving animals in need.
The Fuzzy Escape Artists by Michael Isaacs ($15.95): All-too-clever pound puppies confound their owner with their wily escapades in this hilarious and *interactive* picture book. Kids and teachers love it!
How Should I Care For My Doggy? by "Professor" Christopher Furfur with Dr. George Abernathy (Fall 2009, $16.95): A beloved vet teaches kids to be caring pet owners and achieve happiness with their pet.

Blackjack
The SMART Way
by
Richard Harvey

GOLD (FOURTH) EDITION

MYSTIC RIDGE BOOKS

Farmington, Connecticut

Blackjack The SMART Way by Richard Harvey

MYSTIC RIDGE BOOKS, 222 MAIN STREET #142, FARMINGTON, CT 06032
Find us on the World Wide Web at: **http://www.blackjacktoday.com**.
MYSTIC RIDGE BOOKS is a division of Mystic Ridge Productions, Inc.

First Edition Printed February 1999.
Second Edition Printed June 1999.
Millennium Edition Printed November 1999.
Third Edition (previously called The Millennium Edition) Printed June 2000.
Third Edition Second Printing September 2001.
Revised Third Edition First Printing August 2002.
Revised Third Edition Second Printing June 2003.
Revised Third Edition Third Printing December 2004.
Revised Third Edition Fourth Printing September 2005.
Revised Third Edition Fifth Printing September 2006.
Gold (Fourth) Edition First Printing April 2009.
Gold (Fourth) Edition Second Printing November 2009.
Gold (Fourth) Edition Third Printing July 2011.

ISBN-13: 978-0-9742845-1-4

Legal Disclaimer:
This book's purpose is to prepare you to deal well with the blackjack environment and to make you a smart, conservative, winning player. NO book should guarantee winnings every time because you're dealing with the vagaries of cards and other variables including your temperament and skills and differing casino rules, restrictions and practices. There are rarely huge jackpots to be won in any one sitting and blackjack is unlikely to make you a millionaire. Discipline is key. You must never bet or play beyond your limit. If you become obsessed with or addicted to gambling, contact Gambler's Anonymous and AVOID casinos entirely.

PRINTED AND BOUND IN THE UNITED STATES OF AMERICA.

Library of Congress Cataloging-in-Publication Data

Harvey, Richard, 1960-
  Blackjack the smart way / by Richard Harvey. — Gold (fourth) ed.
     p. cm.
  Includes index and glossary.
  ISBN 978-0-9742845-1-4 (alk. paper)
  1. Blackjack (Game) I. Title.
  GV1295.B55H39 2009
  795.4'23—dc22
                                              2009011285

Contents

Publisher's Note For The Gold (Fourth) Edition

And see the many advantages of buying this book NEW on page 278!

All of us at Mystic Ridge Books are very proud to bring you this new Edition of *Blackjack The SMART Way*. It's no fluke that three prior Editions (and many Printings) have sold out and tens of thousands of copies have been sold. There are *many* reasons why.

No other book has the leading-edge information you now hold in your hands. *Blackjack The SMART Way* gives you:

✔ A comprehensive system, born of exciting discoveries about card behavior and previously unknown blackjack phenomena uncovered in Richard Harvey's own cutting-edge computer studies. *It is jam-packed with information that you will find nowhere else.* Most other books rely upon computer research done more than 40 years ago and rehash old ideas produced by others.

✔ A casino-tested-and-proven, uniquely successful new approach to winning. The author, who is not just a researcher, but is first and foremost an expert player, field tested all aspects of his system at many different casinos in many different locales. These tests — conducted by several expert players — proved that this system is highly successful, with a very high winning rate.

✔ Skills most players are unaware they must possess, essential to becoming a consistent winner.

✔ Detailed explanations for *every* strategy move the author recommends. He doesn't ask you to take his word for it. He *shows* you *why* the *Blackjack The SMART Way* system makes so much sense. Read this book and you will understand the logic that rules the game.

✔ A system the author uses himself to achieve a win rate of over 85%. He puts his money where his mouth is.

✔ A system that has produced great results for tens of thousands of players. We at Mystic Ridge Books *know* this, because of the feedback we've received from countless readers. These results can be duplicated by you as others have done before you. This system *works;* it's been hailed by players and insiders alike.

✔ A system that is designed specifically for the realities you'll face at *today's* casinos — not for the casinos of 10 or 20 years ago.

It's all of this and more!

Now, once you've mastered all of the information in this book, check out the companion Compact Disc audio book, *Richard Harvey's Blackjack PowerPrep Session*, and then you will want to read *Cutting Edge Blackjack*, Richard Harvey's second bestseller, which gives you crucial information on an even higher level. Not only does it contain the author's historic breakthrough method to identify players' facedown cards at single and double deck tables but it also unveils a mammoth amount of powerful state-of-the-art discoveries and methods you can use to increase your winning rate to the max, to great profit, from the author's most recent computer studies! Then, there's Richard Harvey's newest book, *NEW Ways To Win MORE at Blackjack*, with unique information culled from the author's syndicated columns.

And there are always Mr. Harvey's popular blackjack seminars (see page 276). They're not held very often, though, so if you're interested, sign up now! They sell out fast! And now you must be a member of our New Books Club to attend — so act now (see pages 277-278)!

Enjoy!

From Everyone at

Mystic Ridge Books

Farmington, Connecticut

ii

Author's Note For The New Fourth (Gold) Edition

It's been more than 10 years since I wrote the First Edition of *Blackjack The SMART Way* but a whirlwind of events since then makes it seem like 100 years. Since then I finished yet another large-scale multi-year blackjack research project and this newest Edition has been updated and rewritten not just to include some of my latest discoveries and innovations but also with the changes in the casino world.

You see, they've read my books, too, and have made some changes in a vain attempt to thwart the methods introduced in my books. (I laughed out loud when I saw the first 5-player table outside Binion's in downtown Vegas, for instance. I knew right away they'd read my second book, *Cutting Edge Blackjack*.) I take all that as a supreme compliment.

Can you believe it? Since this book was first published in 1999, three Editions have sold out! It makes me proud to see how much blackjack players love this book. Critics have hailed it too — it's gotten *countless* great write-ups for the unique contribution it has made to the blackjack world.

Another nice thing is that I've been asked to do hundreds of book events, talk show appearances, seminars and other speaking engagements nationwide. I have been featured on the cover of gaming magazines, asked to write articles, and I've even become a blackjack columnist, by invitation!

Looking back, I must admit that I was a bit nervous when I did my first book events in the gaming capital of the world, Las Vegas. With the sophistication of players there, I thought perhaps I'd run into a little resistance to something new. But, no! I am proud to say that the excitedly positive response during my two book Vegas tours was *amazing*. Las Vegas gaming expert Howard Schwartz was among the many insiders who praised my books for "blazing new territory."

And indeed the nicest thing to come from all of this has

iii

been the awesome feedback I've gotten from a gazillion readers. Good reviews are one thing, but *reader* reaction, to me, is the most important thing, and, universally, players who've read *Blackjack The SMART Way* have said they've gained a much better understanding of the game and have gone on to win as they never had before.

But, let's talk about *you*. No matter what level you're on, you will benefit from the winning strategies in this book. If you are a beginner or an intermediate player, you will appreciate the fact the methods revealed in this book will equip you to win most of the time and have fun without risking the house payment. You will also like the fact that this system is on the leading edge (having been born of my own unique card-based computer research) yet easy to understand.

If you are an advanced player, you will be thrilled with the cutting edge skills you will acquire that will enable you to play with a precision you never thought possible. But I think you'll find you must rethink the whole game. I was able to make discoveries overlooked by prior researchers because their studies were based upon what I call phony blackjack (computer simulations produced by random number generators), whereas my research began with actual cards, dealt, collected and shuffled in the exacting way it's done at a casino.

(By the way, you might want to consider obtaining the companion CD audio book, *Richard Harvey's Blackjack Power Prep Session,* which works great as a pre-casino practice session. And you'll eventually want to move up to *Cutting Edge Blackjack* and *NEW Ways to Win MORE at Blackjack,* for powerful state-of-the-art methods that'll blow your mind. And check out **blackjacktoday.com** for free blackjack tips!)

After making tens of thousands of players consistent, happy winners, I look forward to doing the same for you.

Best Wishes,
Richard Harvey

A ♣

YOUR MONEY
IS
ON THE LINE

Blackjack is a great game, and you're about to learn a fantastic new way to beat the house consistently; not EVERY time, but MOST times. Here's a game where they *pay* you to have a good time! Even at the low stakes tables, which most players prefer, you could win up to $400 or more within two hours while having fun playing cards! Not bad.

Now, it's unlikely that you will become a millionaire from blackjack if you play at the low stakes tables. (You win what you put on the table.) This is not like a megabucks state lottery. It is much more winnable, however!

By the end of the year the "little returns" you gain from each casino trip can easily add up to *thousands* of dollars, even for the casual player. That is, *if* you are a good student of *Blackjack The SMART Way.* I am assuming, though, you understand that anything worth doing requires a little effort. That being said, countless readers before you have found the journey to be both pleasant and rewarding.

Nothing Comes From Nothing

Blackjack is deceptive, in that it seems like a simple game, but it is most definitely NOT. Casinos have been effective in conning great numbers of otherwise smart people into believing the line that "if you can count to 21, you can play blackjack." That popular casino come-on has led many down the road to disaster.

No. Blackjack is a *challenging* game, much like the game of Bridge. If it weren't, casinos would be packed with wealthy, happy winners.

But I will make your job simple by giving you the tools and the rules you need to win. I will make it as easy as possible for you to understand the ins and outs of blackjack from a *winner's* perspective. You hold in your hands the key to fun and profit.

The First Principles Of Winning at Blackjack

Do you want to know what the First Principle of Winning at

Blackjack is? *Be happy with your gains – no matter how modest they might be. Never throw back your winnings.*

The Second Principle of Winning at Blackjack is the flip side of the First: *Know when it's one of those times when you should cut your losses and leave.*

If you keep your losses on any one occasion below what you usually win on average on any one trip to the casino, you won't wipe out the winnings you've earned in the majority of your trips to the casino.

Makes sense, right? Well, these principles might sound, on the surface, *obvious* to you; perhaps even unnecessary to mention. But they are obviously NOT. If these principles were easy to implement, casinos would be loaded with winners.

What I'm talking about is *knowing when to leave.* You need more than a vague recognition of this necessary skill in order to put it into action at the casino. Many players say they understand this principle but then go out and either throw back all the winnings they have made on good days or accrue huge losses on losing days. Because they play *too long,* whether up or down.

In later chapters, you will acquire the necessary skills so that you will never again throw back your winnings or leave a big loser.

This is NOT Your Father's Blackjack Game

There are many things you must know if you want to win at casino blackjack. First, you must realize that the game has changed since the father of Old School Blackjack strategy, Edward Thorp, wrote the first computer-driven blackjack tome *Beat The Dealer* in 1962 and Lawrence Revere wrote his improvement upon that, *Playing Blackjack As A Business,* in 1969.

In fact, the complexion of the average casino has changed in just the past *10* years alone and — many of the players who have taken my seminars say they have noticed this — it *is* a bit harder to beat the house now. That is, playing the <u>old</u> way.

Don't worry. *Blackjack The SMART Way* will get you through the morass that is the modern casino environment.

New Challenges

Why the radical change over the years?

Number one — there has been a veritable explosion in the construction of new casinos in recent years (almost all of the 50 states now allows casino gambling in some form or another). Unfortunately, many of these casinos are either unregulated or under-regulated. That is, many lie in regions where there is little or no governmental oversight. (There have been Congressional hearings investigating this shortcoming with an eye toward possibly imposing Federal regulations but that appears unlikely.) This presents a possible danger the player should be aware of in picking the right casinos to play in.

Number two — casinos have gotten very sophisticated about targeting winners for countermeasures. Countermeasures include frequent shuffling, dealer changes, and bringing in new cards, which can spoil your game. (We'll discuss this in detail in Chapter 11.) And there have been game changes made in reaction to the innovations in my books! (Not to worry. They don't work.)

And finally, aside from casino countermeasures, which are legal but unfair, there are a small minority of casinos and dealers who are resorting to dirty tricks that make winning all but impossible. By dirty tricks I mean casino cheating. While this is not the norm by any means, I estimate that you might run into this about 10 percent of the time if you play at as many casinos as I do.

That's why you especially need to read this book from cover to cover. You need to understand the modern challenges you're facing at today's casinos and learn how to respond to them to protect yourself against losses that might be caused not by your card strategy but by outside forces. Sometimes you will be playing not just against the game but against the house as well.

An Object Lesson

You can lose a lot more than your money if you are unaware of all of this. For instance, there was a tragic story I became aware of while being interviewed on a Las Vegas talk show. On the wall, behind the interviewer, was an article with a headline that read "High Roller Shoots Dealer," or something to that effect.

It seems this high roller was playing at a casino somewhere in Asia (I don't remember where — Singapore?) and he was losing hand after hand. Yet, he continued to play! HE WENT ON TO LOSE NEARLY 50 HANDS IN A ROW! Convinced he had been cheated (ya think?!), he then pulled out a revolver and killed the dealer! Later on, he told a reporter he regretted killing her, but he "couldn't help himself."

There are a number of lessons to be learned here (other than the fact that being a "high roller" doesn't necessarily mean being a smart player). First: yes, there is some cheating going on out there. Second: you need to know how to detect and avoid it. Finally: shooting the dealer is just...*wrong!*

Blackjack Is Still Fun and Profitable

Given all of this, it should be obvious that today's blackjack player must be much more knowledgeable and skilled than players of the past. Just knowing a good card strategy won't cut it.

And so I will teach you the extra skills you will need, to avoid falling victim to any unfair modern blackjack practices.

I win the great majority of times with my methods, and you can too (that is, if you devote yourself to learning). That's why I can write this book in good conscience. If I can win, so can you.

Good players can still win consistently but they need a new approach. A lot goes into winning aside from knowing state-of-the-art card and betting strategies (and we'll get into that).

Blackjack is still a great game. It offers the excitement of uncertainty and possible risk, and yet, with the right method and an awareness of the minefields to avoid, it can be approached with the confidence of one who knows he or she will beat the house on most occasions and make a nice bit of money over time. It's a game of wits that requires keen thinking, which is exhilarating to card game fanatics who love the thrill of winning.

The Concepts Today's Blackjack Player Needs to Learn

There are a number of important concepts a player needs to understand in order to come out a winner:

♣ CARD STRATEGY: This is the process of choosing which of the options available to you would give you the best odds of winning in any given card situation. (Actually, in some cases, you will be facing a *losing* situation, no matter what you do; in those cases you must pick the move that loses a lesser percentage of times than other possible moves.) *Blackjack The Smart Way* is special in that it explains the mathematical reasoning behind each recommended move — so you come to understand the WHYs behind the game. Plus, the winning card strategy found here is unique to this book.

♣ MONEY MANAGEMENT: This includes deciding how much you should bet on a particular hand; how much money you should bring to the table; how to keep any losses to a minimum; and how to leave with your winnings intact. Having a good money management system is as important as having a good card strategy. My **3-Level, Notch-Up, Notch-Down Bet Management System** tips the odds in your favor. It gets your bet up to a good level when the cards are good for you, and lowers your bet to a minimum amount when the cards are not, so that even if you win only about 50% of the hands played (typical of a Basic Strategy player), it greatly increases your odds of coming away a winner.

♣ KNOWING HOW TO PICK A GOOD CASINO: This is an essential skill you must perfect. Few players seem aware that there are good and bad casinos. Learning this often-neglected skill will spare you many heartaches. *The more discriminating you become, the higher your winning rate will be.*

♣ KNOWING WHEN TO LEAVE A CASINO: Whether you are winning or losing, you need to know when to call it quits.

Staying too long is one of the most common habits of the perpetual loser. This might just be the most important concept you will learn here.

♣ KNOWING HOW TO PICK A GOOD TABLE WITHIN A CASINO: This is crucial. It will save you hundreds, if not thousands of dollars, in unnecessary losses. All tables are not alike, as you will learn.

♣ KNOWING WHEN TO LEAVE A TABLE: This also is immensely important. It gives you a lot of power in counteracting losing streaks and possible dirty tricks; it also protects your gains. Most players get rooted to the first table they find. Why? I'll teach you when it's wise to get up and find a better table.

♣ THE **X FACTOR:** This is one of my inventions. It's a measure of how well the cards are breaking for you, versus the dealer. Getting a handle on this is necessary to making critical decisions such as those you must make in betting. You will use the **X Factor** to assess, in quantitative terms, whether the table you are playing at is bad, neutral, good or great. It's an entry-level way to take advantage of the scientific discoveries that have come from my research.

♣ KEEPING TRACK OF THE CARDS: By paying attention to what cards have been played, you can take advantage of the predictability of the game. You can do this either by card counting or, better yet, by using my entry-level card analysis method, **Card Observation**. This approach, similar to one used effectively by Bridge players, is based on easy-to-understand math and will help to maximize your gains.

♣ KNOWING HOW TO DETECT CASINO COUNTERMEASURES: This will protect you when you have been targeted for unfair practices designed to make you lose and will enable you to leave with your winnings intact.

♣ KNOWING HOW TO SPOT THE ROGUE "DIRTY DEALER":

This will keep you from falling victim to a cheater that, although not common, is out there. This will spare you huge losses.

♣ KNOWING HOW TO DETECT RIGGED CARDS: This will keep you away from the minority of casinos who play dirty.

♣ KEEPING TRACK OF YOUR FELLOW PLAYERS: This will enable you to respond to the threats posed by players who sit out some bets or otherwise vary the number of bets they place; players who enter the game or leave the table; and, people who pretend to be players but who are actually casino employees (shills)!

I will teach you all of this and more.

Who Should NOT Play Blackjack

That being said, blackjack is *not* a game for those who lack the determination and desire to learn how to play correctly. You cannot win consistently if you are relying upon your hunches to guide you. And since blackjack involves real money – YOUR money – promise me right now that you will treat this "game" with respect and study what I am about to teach you.

Dumb Luck

By the way, there IS such as thing as DUMB luck. That is, there are players who occasionally win without having a clue about what they're doing. I have witnessed it.

In the mid-1990s, I was at a new casino in Ruidoso, New Mexico, a lovely winter resort town; at the time, it was chock full of drunk tourists on vacation – some of the WORST blackjack players I'd ever seen. One guy was splitting 10s (I'll explain this faux pas later). The gal next to me was betting a fortune no matter how well she was doing. In fact, everyone seemed intent on impressing the others with how much money they were risking. Miraculously though – and you won't see this very often – the

8

dealer busted and lost more than is normal, and some of these fools actually were ahead when I got up to leave. (I was ahead by about $75 after an hour of choppy action.) That's *dumb luck!*

Another time, I was at an Atlantic City casino where a pretty blonde was making such hopelessly stupid moves everyone at the table was groaning but, in spite of herself, she won hand after hand! Of course, I didn't see how much money she actually left with. Like most others who go unprepared, she undoubtedly played until all her money was gone.

I promise you, YOU won't win in the long run through dumb luck. It may work once in a blue moon, but not in a string of trips to the casino. You certainly don't want to rely on it, because then you WILL find out why they affix the word "dumb" to it.

Don't Be A Big Shot

And please don't try to compete with the reckless big shots that "grace" every casino. You know the type: the boisterous fools who toss around black chips ($100 chips) or pink chips ($1000 chips) for effect, unaware they are demonstrating (to those in the know) how little they know about the game. They crave attention and sometimes get it with a lucky win or two. But these are the people you read about later, the ones who bet wildly until they inevitably lose everything; in desperation, some even then commit suicide in similar dramatic fashion. Watch them long enough and you'll witness their painful downfall.

Don't emulate them. It's YOUR money. Treat it with respect. The truly <u>smart</u> players never make a show of it. They *seek* anonymity. They win quietly and only make bets that won't set them back terribly if they lose.

Learning My Strategy Requires Practice

If you decide you want to learn how to play intelligently and try my strategy, you must first study not just the text but the charts as well AND THEN PRACTICE, PRACTICE, PRACTICE.

Practice at home, with <u>cards</u>. I perfected my system and practiced applying my methods at home before subjecting myself to risk. Make your mistakes at home. You can make it fun by inviting friends over to play with you if you wish, each player taking turns being the dealer. Make practice fun!

Blackjack Requires an Analytical Approach

Now there are four factors that make blackjack very winnable:

❶ Its relative predictability (much like the game of Bridge).
❷ Its adherence to mathematical principles.
❸ The *personality* of each of the dealer's up cards.
❹ The *personality* of the cards (my studies have uncovered the existence of <u>repeating phenomena</u> due to the fact that casino shuffling does not reorder the cards much)

By predictability I mean your ability to figure out what type of card is likely to be dealt next and what the dealer's hole card (facedown card) is likely to be, among other things.

By mathematical principles I mean all of the card behavior-related factors that enable you to get a handle on the probability of your winning a particular hand.

By the personality of the dealer up cards I mean the unique behavior of each of the up cards. Each has a different propensity toward reaching a winning score and busting, for example. You must get to know each one like you know the back of your hand.

By the personality of the cards, I am including the reality that certain card mixes are consistently good or bad for the player. Your ability to identify how good the cards are is crucial to winning.

I will give you the tools you need to win but then you need to apply that knowledge in a constantly changing environment. How you handle your bets, for instance, cannot be scripted before-hand. With the information I will give you, you must then analyze what's going on at your table at a particular point in time and adjust to the realities of the moment to maximize your gains. I will give you guideposts, concepts, methods and strategies developed through years of research and experience, but in the end you must be able to apply what you've learned.

You might run into a difficult table or casino, and then you will have to decide whether it's time to change tables or casinos, or hang in there and battle it out. You will encounter challenging card situations you must think through. No one else can do that for you. There's no getting on a cell phone and calling or text messaging someone for advice.

Don't sweat it. I'm going to make everything as simple to understand as possible. But what I'm trying to say is that you need to do your homework. Blackjack is a fun, winnable game, but it's not a simple game like tic-tac-toe. You must study this book fully and then practice, practice, practice until you are confident you are able to use this system and win.

It's a Game of Ups 'n Downs

Now, one thing you must understand is that *blackjack is a game of swings — up-and-down cycles.* Like the wind, the **flow of the cards** blows hot and cold, with no one holding up a sign to let you know how long the current breeze, good or bad, will last.

And I'd particularly like to dispel the notion that it's possible with the right system to win a *predictable* amount of money each hour. That's not how the game works. I have proven through my research that your ability to accumulate gains depends not just on your skill level but also on the quality of the cards you're being dealt. Each card mix you'll encounter will show different characteristics, overall and *per each betting spot.*

Sometimes down cycles will right themselves. Sometimes they *won't.* Sometimes up cycles will last through many shuffles. Sometimes they *won't.* I will teach you to make sense of all this.

Beware Loser's Traps

Whatever you do — never, never throw good money after

bad. My advice on money management and words to the wise on when to leave a table or casino will protect you from this hazard IF you practice what I'm about to preach.

Willpower and discipline are an important part of this equation. I've seen way too many players throw away their winnings because they have no self-control. This is totally unnecessary. I'll give you simple guidelines to help you avoid this major pitfall.

Playing The Percentages

Now, before I teach you Basic Strategy (which is for beginners only), there's something you must know. *You will sometimes lose hands in spite of making the right moves.*

There is no way to play any card situation (except if you draw a Blackjack) such that you will win 100% of the time, nor has there ever been a player who has ever come close to doing this. Even when you have what seems like a great hand, like a hand of 20 points, you will still lose a certain amount of times when the dealer draws a 21 or a Blackjack! And you will sometimes merely push (or tie) with the dealer when you hold 21 points.

*What you must do is **play the percentages.** That is, you must make the move that will cause you to win the highest percentage of times (or, with losing hands, choose the move that loses least).* That's a very important concept to understand. I'm going to call this the Third Principle of Winning at Blackjack.

It's not winning every hand that makes a player a great player or a winner. It's the player's ability to pick the moves that *make the most mathematical sense* (as with the moves that simply limit your losses in no-win situations).

Losing a certain number of hands is part of the game. So, don't get blown away by the times that my strategy, proven highly successful in casino tests, doesn't win for you with a particular hand in a particular card situation.

Now, inevitably, there will be times where you make the correct move but you'll lose and some bully — ignorant of the wisdom of your move — will accuse you of playing poorly. DON'T

BE INTIMIDATED! Don't let jerks make you afraid to do what's right and protect your money.

After I explain the underlying math to you, you won't have any doubt that my system is the way to go about things. Plus, you will witness the results at the casino.

Don't Waffle – Stick To This Strategy

The corollary to this is: You must stick to your guns and make the card moves you know are correct, no matter how controversial. If, for instance, you know you should surrender with a 16 against the dealer's up card of 10 but you sometimes get so overwhelmed by the fear that someone will criticize you that you choose instead to hit or stand, you're going to wind up *losing* more of your hard earned money over time than you would have had you played the percentages and made the right move. Some dealers are trained to make you feel stupid for surrendering a hand. Get used to it. There is always some dumbo telling you how to play. Get used to it.

Think about it: If I tell you to play a hand a certain way because it wins, let's say, 62% of the time (conversely *losing* 38% of the time), do you really want to be scared or cajoled instead into making a different move when that choice would cause you to LOSE 62% of the time?

For instance, if you ignore my advice and instead you routinely stand on a point total of 13 versus the dealer's 10, you will only win a minority of times — when the dealer busts. The few times that happens might delude you into thinking you made the right move. But you'll *lose* roughly 80% of the time!!! That's an example of playing the wrong side of the percentages!

The beautiful thing is you can learn to predict how card situations will play out over time through the insights that have come from my research. There's no need to read tea leaves or consult the bully sitting next to you. Stick to what is tested and proven successful.

This bears repeating, because so many players get blown

away by momentary events: *don't get upset about the hands you lose, in the normal course of the game, if you're playing correctly* (that is, unless you're sitting at a horrible table; but that's a different matter). That's part of the game. *How you do over the course of time is what we're concerned about.*

My Warnings Come from Observations

Examples of wrong-headed thinking abound. Not long ago, I met a seemingly intelligent fellow who said he was a recreational blackjack player. He then related some very astute observations about situations he'd run into. But he then drew the wrong conclusions.

For example, he noticed that the dealer at one particular casino never seemed to lose when he showed weak up cards. So what did this recreational player do? He *changed his playing strategy!* He began to take cards when he knew he shouldn't! Not only that – he told me *he now does that at ALL casinos!*

That's akin to changing your golf stroke to a ridiculous one because the last time you hit the ball you lost your balance, made a faulty swing, yet you lucked out, getting a hole in one. Don't fall into this common trap! It will lead to disaster!

Once you acquire the knowledge contained in this book, you will know how to deal with the sort of problem this player ran into. You will be capable of analyzing each situation intelligently and responding appropriately. Perhaps he should have left the casino (the dealer might have been cheating). Perhaps he should have left the table (the card mix might have been bad). Perhaps he should have lowered his bets (the card action might have been choppy but not altogether bad). The one response he should never have considered was to change his card strategy (assuming he was using a good one) to suit one unique situation!

Don't Play 'Til You Drop!

Another example of faulty thinking is seen everyday at every casino: witness the players who play until they drop from exhaustion or, finally, the lack of money.

One of my friends once said to me, "your system doesn't address the situation where someone might want to play for many hours at a time." He's right. Because that's a stupid thing to do and a good way to become a perpetual loser.

This bears repeating. Please – especially at first – *limit the amount of time you play to no more than one or two hours at any one casino.* You'll be mentally exhausted after two hours of concentrating on everything to which you must pay attention and you'll begin to make costly mistakes if you go over that limit. And there are other reasons why playing marathons inevitably leads to losses; this will be made clear to you in later chapters.

There will, in fact, be times when you should leave a casino *before* an hour or two is through, whether you are up or down in chips. I will teach you how to recognize these situations.

That reminds me of the first time I went to a casino, in Atlantic City. Playing at a $25 minimum bet table, I won more than $450 in 20 minutes! I had driven nearly four hours to get there, so I had to pry myself away from that table, but I had the foresight to know the winning cycle was over and it was time to leave. That's why I came away a winner and continue to do so.

When You Should Choose NOT To Play Casino Blackjack

One last thing – and please keep this in mind – there are times when you should not even consider playing. NEVER go to a casino when:

- ♣ You're ill and can't concentrate.
- ♣ You've forgotten the rules or your card strategy.
- ♣ You've had alcohol. You'll make big mistakes! Why else do some casinos love providing you with free booze? You should hear the stories I'm told of players who drop thousands of dollars after having one too many.
- ♣ You're depressed, pessimistic or worried. You're not in the right frame of mind.

15

- ♣ You've gotten obsessed and you've lost your perspective of blackjack being a form of *entertainment,* to be played in moderation. You play too often, when you know you shouldn't.
- ♣ You've gotten "greedy" and it's no longer fun. I can't quite explain it to you, but you will tend to *lose* when you find you have lost the "fun" and the normal gains from blackjack no longer seem to please you. Plus, it's a sign that you're entering dangerous psychological territory.
- ♣ You've just come off a losing session and you're upset. Your emotions are clouding your thinking. (Poker players call this "steaming.") Take a day or two off.

You can only win at blackjack if you stay *disciplined.* Blackjack is a game, but it's an adult game. Your money is on the line.

Debunking Cherished Myths

Now, one final word. I have not been surprised to see that this book has been somewhat provocative, because it debunks myths that some would prefer you believe are true. New theories and inventions are often the focus of skepticism from competing writers intent on preserving the old way of doing things. Often, in fact, they have a *financial* interest in doing so, such as those who are puppets for the casino industry or those who sell systems based on old ideas.

Happily, though, I am proud to say that those who have no interest in living in the past, namely, today's blackjack *players* and a good number of gutsy and impartial gaming *insiders,* have overwhelmingly greeted *Blackjack The SMART Way's* new concepts and methods with excitement and praise. (And in addition, all I need to point to are the attempted casino countermeasures that have been made in response to my books; the ultimate *proof* of my accomplishments!)

OK. Let's talk next about smart blackjack card strategy! ***You are not ready yet to enter a casino.***

BASIC
CARD
STRATEGY

There is something important you need to understand before you go any further. *There is NOT one mutually-agreed-upon Basic Strategy that we all would be wise to follow.* There are, in fact, many different opinions as to what Basic Strategy should be.

The myth that there is just one Basic Strategy handed down from on High is not as dangerous, however, as the myth that blackjack is a simple game, and that one chart is all you need to become a winner. Nothing could be further from the truth, as you will see. This myth has kept many from becoming great players.

That being said, let's look at what makes *Blackjack The SMART Way* Basic Strategy a good starting point — *for beginners*.

It's Simple, Really: Win, Lose or "Push"

In casino blackjack, you're playing against the dealer — not the other players. How do you win? Usually in one of two ways:

❶ By getting a higher point total than the dealer without busting (losing by going OVER 21).

❷ If the *dealer* busts (goes over 21) and you haven't busted.

If you beat the dealer, the dealer will pay you the same amount of chips as you placed as your bet. If you lose, the dealer will take your bet. If you "push" (tie), you will not make any money, but you won't lose any, either — you get to keep your bet.

There's one special situation that works differently, from whence comes the name of the game: If you are dealt an Ace and a 10 or a face card, you now possess a *Blackjack,* and, unless the dealer has a Blackjack, you're an instant winner, AND you are paid one-and-a-half times the amount you placed as your bet. If the dealer also has a Blackjack, it's considered a push. (You have a little-known option of taking Even Money when the dealer shows an Ace, however. In that case, you are paid only the amount you placed as your bet; but, you avoid the possible push in the event the dealer has a Blackjack. We'll discuss this later.)

Now, if the *dealer* has a Blackjack, players who do not also have a Blackjack lose instantly — without playing out their hands.

The best situation is when the dealer busts. No matter what your score is, you WIN — UNLESS you busted beforehand. The trouble is *you don't have the luxury of waiting to see if the dealer is going to bust before deciding whether you should draw an extra card that might make your hand bust.* This quandary is one of the factors that makes the game so challenging. There will be times, where you know the dealer is most likely to bust, when you should not risk busting by taking any more cards.

No sweat. This book will teach you the mathematical logic behind the game of blackjack, so that you will understand when the dealer is most vulnerable to busting, and then know how to respond. As you will see, your move will often depend upon what the dealer's up card is.

(FYI: In blackjack, the Jacks, Queens and Kings are no more important than the 10s; they all count for 10 points. And so, from now on, I will simply refer to them all as the "10s" or the "10-pointers.")

The Ace Has A Powerful Advantage

One more thing: the Ace has a <u>dual</u> nature, which makes it quite desirable. It can count as one or 11 points. Dealers have restrictions in how they must count their Aces, but you don't.

Dealers must count their Aces as 11 points if that creates a total of 17 to 21 points (with one possible exception — some casinos require their dealers to continue taking cards if they have a "soft 17," a 17-point hand where the Ace counts for 11 points).

Unlike the dealer, you can often *choose* what you want your Ace to be. For example, you might decide to stand on a hand of Ace-7, counting your Ace as an 11, which would give you a score of 18. Or, in some situations, you might want to take more cards, which might then necessitate counting your Ace as a 1 point card. Of course, if you draw an Ace to a hand that totals 11 points or more, you will have no choice but to consider that

Ace a 1 point card (otherwise, you'd bust).

Everything Starts With The Dealer Up Card

OK. Now, *Blackjack The SMART Way* Basic Strategy is based upon two things: *first, what dealer up cards indicate about the dealers' relative strength, vis a vis what their eventual point totals are likely to be; and, second, how dealers must play their cards.*

(Later, as an advanced player, your strategy will also be based on what the dealer's hole card and your hit card are likely to be.)

Dealers give themselves one face-up card (their up card) and one facedown card (their *hole* card).

Now, blackjack dealers are required to pull cards until they get to a total of at least 17. (Except, as noted before, at the casinos where dealers must draw a card to their hand of Ace-6, also known as a "soft 17," because of the Ace's ability to count either as a 1 point or 11 point card.   This is a move that favors the house, by the way.   It tends to lead to stronger dealer scores.)

This reality of how dealers must play their cards means that YOU SHOULD ALWAYS STAND ON HANDS THAT TOTAL 17 OR MORE (assuming your hand doesn't include an Ace, which, as you'll see soon, you might want to count as 1 point in some situations).

Here's How Your Strategy Will Work

One of the many ways *Blackjack The SMART Way* is unique is that card strategy is based upon the differing *personalities* of the dealer up cards.

The up card gives us very important information. Every dealer up card behaves differently, depending on what its point value is. For example, they arrive at different average winning scores over time, and have different busting rates.

So, for instance, if you have a hand that totals less than 17 points and you know the dealer's up card is very strong, you might very well choose to take more cards until you reach a score of 17 to 21 points.

If, instead, you're facing one of the dealer's weaker up cards, which is more likely to make the dealer bust, you might then decide to stand pat with your original two cards — even if you have a non-winning point total of 12, 13, 14, 15 or 16. It depends upon what particular up card the dealer has, and how weak it is. We'll examine that in a second.

The point is, if you have a hand that is known as a "stiff" (a hand of 12 through 16, which puts you in danger of busting if you take one more card), you will sometimes want to STAND, to avoid the risk of busting, in the hope that you'll win simply because the dealer might bust.

The only times you'll have *no* decision to make are when you either get a Blackjack, or when you have achieved a total of 17 to 21 points — hands upon which you would always stand.

HARD and SOFT Hands

The first thing you should do when your first two cards are dealt is assess whether your point total makes your hand HARD or SOFT.

A HARD hand is one that contains no Ace.

As you might have surmised, hard hands that total more than 12 points pose a risk. You have the danger of busting if you need to "hit" those cards — that is, take more cards to improve your score. Examples of hard hands are shown on the following page, in **Illustration 2-1** (these are by no means the only possible hard hand combinations, however).

A SOFT HAND is a hand that contains at least one Ace.

Since an Ace can count for either 1 point or 11, a soft hand is one that cannot bust if you hit it — that is, if you ask the dealer for another card in the hope of bettering your score. Soft hands are great because they often offer you the lucrative option of doubling your bet, when it's allowed, and when it's desirable. So, in this sense, some of these hands might seem somewhat more desirable than hard hands of the same point totals.

Illustration 2-1:

Examples of Hard Hands

The Blackjack The Smart Way (Conservative) 3-Level, Notch-Up, Notch-Down Bet Management System

© 2009 by *Richard Harvey*.

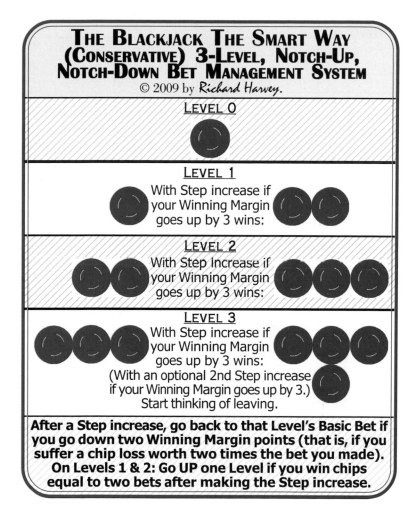

Level 0

Level 1

With Step increase if your Winning Margin goes up by 3 wins:

Level 2

With Step Increase if your Winning Margin goes up by 3 wins:

Level 3

With Step increase if your Winning Margin goes up by 3 wins:
(With an optional 2nd Step increase if your Winning Margin goes up by 3.)
Start thinking of leaving.

After a Step increase, go back to that Level's Basic Bet if you go down two Winning Margin points (that is, if you suffer a chip loss worth two times the bet you made). On Levels 1 & 2: Go UP one Level if you win chips equal to two bets after making the Step increase.

COLOR-CODED
Blackjack The SMART Way
BASIC STRATEGY CHART

	2	3	4	5	6	7	8	9	10	A
4-8	H	H	H	H	H	H	H	H	H	H
9	H	D	D	D	D	D	H	H	H	H
10	D	D	D	D	D	D	D	H	H	H
11	D	D	D	D	D	D	D	D	H	H
12	H	H	S	S	S	H	H	H	H	H
13	S	S	S	S	S	H	H	H	H	H
14	S	S	S	S	S	H	H	H	H	SUR/H*
15	S	S	S	S	S	H	H	H	SUR/H*	SUR/H*
16	S	S	S	S	S	H	H	SUR/H*	SUR/H*	SUR/H*
17+	S	S	S	S	S	S	S	S	S	S
PAIR 2S	SP	SP	SP	SP	SP	SP	H	H	H	H
PAIR 3S	H	SP	SP	SP	SP	SP	H	H	H	H
PAIR 4S	H	H	H	H	H	H	H	H	H	H
PAIR 5S	D	D	D	D	D	D	D	H	H	H
PAIR 6S	H	SP	SP	SP	SP	SP	H	H	H	H
PAIR 7S	SP	SP	SP	SP	SP	SP	H	H	H	SUR/H*
PAIR 8S	SP	SP	SP	SP	SP	SP	SP	SP	SP	SP
PAIR 9S	SP	SP	SP	SP	SP	S	SP	SP	S	S
PAIR 10S	S	S	S	S	S	S	S	S	S	S
PAIR AS	SP	SP	SP	SP	SP	SP	SP	SP	SP	SP
A2-A5	H	H	D	D	D	H	H	H	H	H
A6	H	D	D	D	D	H	H	H	H	H
A7	S	D	D	D	D	S	S	H	H	S
A8,A9,BJ	S	S	S	S	S	S	S	S	S	S

*SUR/H = SURRENDER IF POSSIBLE; HIT IF NOT

On the next page, in **Illustration 2-2**, you will see some examples of SOFT HANDS.

You will soon see that you'll have to play your hard hands differently than your soft hands.

Hard And Soft Totals

Now, a **hard _total_** is a bit different than a hard <u>hand</u>. A hard total *can* contain an Ace, but only if the Ace must count as 1 point. A hard total can include more than two cards, too. It is the sum of a player or dealer's cards, where there is only one possible total. So, if there is an Ace, it's in situations where the other cards total more than 11 and the Ace must be a 1-point card.

A **soft total** is a total that always includes one or more Aces, where those Aces can count either as 1 point or 11 — and these totals refer to hands of two or more cards which have the ability of accepting an extra card without busting. This distinction will be important to you, when deciding how to play your cards.

A Word About "Stiffs" And Your Emotions

Now, certain types of hard hands tend to drive players crazy —I'm especially referring to the class of hands known as "stiffs" (hands that total between 12 and 16 points, which are in danger of busting with an extra card). Some players actually groan when they are dealt a stiff.

In fact, many players moan when they get anything less than a Blackjack or two 10s. Yes, those are marvelous. But, on occasion, even those 10s might only give you a push (a tie with the dealer, without gain), or, the two 10s might even *lose,* if the dealer has 21 points total, or a Blackjack.

What I'm cautioning you against is getting *emotional* with every hand that is dealt. Often, the results will turn out far differently than you had expected. More than anything else, letting your feelings get the better of you — especially negative feelings — will only hurt your game. Negative emotions will only

Illustration 2-2:

Examples of Soft Hands

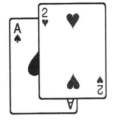
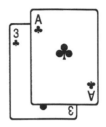

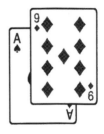

cloud your thinking, and, ultimately, wear you out prematurely.

The reality is twofold: many stiffs become winning hands -- sometimes with and sometimes without extra "hit cards;" and, you *will* lose a number of hands, every time. Get used to it.

Your Options

OK, now, let's look at the options you have, in playing your hands. You may choose to do any one of the following moves:

HIT — That means to take another card. (HIT is denoted by an "H" in the strategy charts.)

STAND — That means you <u>don't</u> want to take another card; you want to stick with the cards you have. (Indicated by an "S" in the strategy charts.)

DOUBLE DOWN or DOUBLE — This is where you're allowed to raise your initial bet by up to the same amount of chips you placed as your original bet, and then you're given just one extra card. You might do this in two situations: first, if your initial hand of 2 cards has a lot of potential to draw to a strong winning total with just one more card, so you want to get more money on the table; or second, if you're pretty certain the dealer will bust, and you have a hand that won't bust with the acceptance of one more card. You have the option in most casinos of "doubling" with an extra amount of chips that's *less* than your original bet, but, hey, if it's a situation where it's worth doubling down, go *all* the way. *Double* your bet. (See **Illustration 2-3** on page 27, for a demonstration of how to double down.) (Represented by a "D" in the strategy charts.)

SPLIT — This is where you have a pair of cards of the same point value and you want to separate them, to play them out as two individual hands (or more – if the dealer places a card on top of the split cards that's the same point value, you can RE-split *those* too, in most casinos, into two separate hands; many casinos allow this to be done until you reach a limit of four hands). The dealer then places a card upon one of your split cards, which you then play out like a normal hand. After you're through playing out the first of the two split hands, you do the same, then, with your second split card. The one *exception* to this is when you split a pair of Aces. Then, you often have the limitations of getting one extra card upon each, and splitting only one time. Aces are so strong, often producing winning totals in combination with 8 of the 13 cards (the 6s through the 10s) that you shouldn't mind those limitations. There's a demonstration of splitting in **Illustration 2-4** on p. 28. (Abbreviated as "Sp" in the strategy charts.)

SURRENDER — This option allows you to give up your hand without playing it out if you think it's a definite loser. The dealer then gives you half of your bet back, while taking the other half. What do you gain? You spare yourself the loss of half your bet. Surrender, unfortunately, is not offered at every casino. And surprisingly, while it gives a big advantage to the player, few players avail themselves of it when it is offered! They're either unaware of it, too shy to do it, or not certain how and when to do it! If you're not allowed to surrender, by the way, you should do the alternative moves I suggest — either HIT (indicated by "Sur/H") or SPLIT (noted by "Sur/Sp" in the charts).

INSURANCE OR EVEN MONEY — If the dealer has an Ace as the up card, the dealer will ask "Insurance?" That means you can place an amount of chips equal to HALF your initial bet in the Insurance section of the table, and, if, after the dealer checks the hole card and it's a 10, for a Blackjack, you will essentially achieve a push (Insurance has historically paid 2-to-1 but some casinos are cutting back on the bonus, paying 6-to-5). If the dealer does NOT have a Blackjack, you lose your Insurance bet and play on. When wise, I suggest instead that beginners ask for *"Even Money." When the dealer says "Insurance?" say "Even Money" and the dealer instantly pays off your Blackjack. You won't get the usual Blackjack bonus, but an amount equal to your bet.* It's quicker that way and it helps prevent payoff mistakes.

Illustration 2-3:

HOW TO DOUBLE DOWN

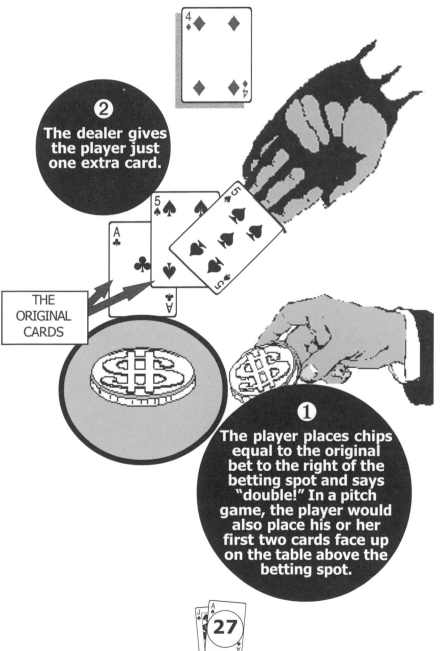

② The dealer gives the player just one extra card.

THE ORIGINAL CARDS

① The player places chips equal to the original bet to the right of the betting spot and says "double!" In a pitch game, the player would also place his or her first two cards face up on the table above the betting spot.

Illustration 2-4:

How To Split Your Cards

② The dealer then deals cards to each of the split cards, one at a time, the player playing them as two new hands - except in the case of Aces where (at most casinos) players are dealt just one extra card.

① The player says "split" and places more chips (equal to the original bet) besides the betting spot. When playing a pitch game, the player also separates his or her cards into two hands. In a shoe game the dealer does so.

28

How To Signal The Dealer

To do any of the moves listed on the prior pages, you must usually use hand signals. (Your moves are being recorded by the "eye in the sky" — a hidden camera above the table — in case disputes arise later.) Let's review how this is done.

Signaling is done a little differently at the 1– and 2-deck tables, where you hold your cards in one hand, than at the multi-deck tables, where cards are placed, face-up, in front of you and you're not allowed to touch them.

Signaling At 1- & 2-Deck Tables

At 1- & 2–deck tables — also known as "pitch game" tables, because the cards are pitched, or tossed to you — here's how you do it (first wait for your turn to arrive, of course!):

To HIT, gently stroke or scratch your cards on the table, toward you. The dealer will give you a card, face up. If you want yet another card, repeat this process.

To STAND, slip your cards face down under your bet. You can do this as soon as you decide to stand — you don't have to wait until it's your turn. The dealer will simply pass by you when he or she sees your cards under your bet, and move on to the next player.

To DOUBLE DOWN, lay your cards face up on the table, above your betting spot. Then, place an amount of chips equal to your bet to the right of your betting spot, and say "double!" The dealer will then give you one extra card, face down under your bet. (You may peek at it if you like, but then leave it where it was placed.)

To SPLIT, as with doubling, separate your cards and place them face up, above your betting spot, a few inches apart. Then, place an amount of chips equal to your bet to the right of your betting spot, and say "split!" You will now be playing two different hands. The dealer will then place one card upon the card to your right. If you want to HIT that hand, hit the table gently or make a rubbing motion on the table, toward you. To stand on that hand, wave your hand back and forth in a "no thank you!" motion. The dealer will then place a second card on the other card you had split, and you will play out that hand, with the same procedure.

(By the way, if your second cards on either of those split cards are of the same point value, you can split those, too, at most casinos. To do so, place another pile of chips equal to your original bet on the table and say "split!")

To SURRENDER, deposit your cards face up on the table and say "surrender!" The dealer will then take half your bet, and leave the other half in your betting spot for you to take, or to use in the next round.

For EVEN MONEY, place your Blackjack face up in front of your bet and say "Even Money!" when the dealer draws an Ace up card and asks "Insurance?" The dealer will usually pay off your Blackjack immediately (with an amount equal to your bet).

For INSURANCE, place an amount of chips equal to half your bet in the circular zone that says INSURANCE, when the dealer draws an Ace up card and asks "Insurance?" Also, if you have a Blackjack, lay down your cards, face up, in front of your bet. An Insurance bet rides separately from your original bet. You will LOSE your Insurance bet if the dealer checks and finds that he or she does NOT have a Blackjack. However, if the dealer *does* have a Blackjack, you will be paid TWICE the amount you placed in the Insurance spot but — unless you have a Blackjack — you will lose your original wager (so you will essentially achieve a push).

(By the way — few players seem to realize that it is some-times advisable to take Insurance even if you do NOT have a Blackjack. I recommend that move only for advanced players, though. We'll talk about that in Chapter 10.)

Be very careful when you want to double, split or surrender, by the way. <u>DO NOT move your hands</u> when you verbally tell the dealer what you want to do. You might end up with an unwanted card that will create controversy at the table, if not wind up against your favor. If the dealer gives you that extra card by mistake, he or she will then have to interrupt the game and call for a casino boss to come to the table to resolve the dispute. Often, they'll resolve the disagreement in your favor. Sometimes not.

Signaling At Multi-Deck Tables

OK — here's how you signal at tables with more than 2-decks, more commonly known as "shoe" game tables (so named for the device that holds the cards), where the cards are dealt face up.

(You're not allowed to touch your cards at these tables. The casinos are afraid of cheaters who, if allowed to touch the cards, might "mark" them for the purpose of cheating.)

To HIT, either gently hit the table with your open hand, or stroke the table lightly with a short motion that is directed toward you. The dealer then gives you one more card. Repeat this process for every extra card you want.

To STAND, wave your hand back and forth in a standard "no thank you" signal.

To DOUBLE DOWN, place an amount of chips equal to your bet to the right of your betting spot while saying "double!" The dealer then places one card, face up, on your hand.

To SPLIT, place an amount of chips equal to your bet to the right of your betting spot, while saying "split!" The dealer will then separate your cards into two new hands, place one card upon the split card to your right, and you will play that hand first, and then the other. At most casinos, you can split again if you're dealt a like card on either of the split cards. To do that, follow the same procedure as before.

To SURRENDER, don't move at all (careful!) — simply say "surrender!" The dealer then takes half your bet, and leaves the other half for you to use as you'd like.

For EVEN MONEY, say "Even Money!" and the dealer will usually pay off your Blackjack immediately (with an amount equal to your bet).

For INSURANCE, place an amount of chips equal to half your bet in the circular zone that says INSURANCE.

Blackjack The SMART Way Basic Strategy

OK. How do you know how to play your cards? *How you play your cards has less to do with what you have than what the dealer's up card is, and therefore, what you assume the dealer's point total will be.* For example, if the hand below is your hand (a soft total of 18 or 8), you might want to STAND, HIT, or DOUBLE DOWN. *It depends upon what the dealer has.* (See the charts on the color insert after page 22, and on pages 50-54.)

The dealer's strongest up cards — the ones that will beat you most often — are the 9, 10, and Ace. Upon seeing those, you should assume they will achieve a winning score — and a high winning score at that. As you will see shortly, you should then HIT your Ace-7 combination (seen above) against the dealer's 9 and 10, to try to improve your score. Your 18 won't beat the dealer's anticipated 19, 20 or 21.

However, against the dealer's Ace, strange though it may seem, you'd be wise to STAND. Follow my thinking here — if the dealer doesn't have a Blackjack, you now know the hole card is not one of the four 10-point cards. The dealer, therefore, only has a 2 in 9 chance (a small, 22% probability) of having a card in the hole that would beat you (of the 9 possible non-10 cards, only an 8 or 9 would give the dealer an immediate win over you). That leaves your 18 looking pretty good, and so you STAND.

(See how probability rules the game? See how *Blackjack The SMART Way* strategy is based upon a rock-solid mathematical foundation? This is just one example of how you'll be weighing the probabilities affecting each of your moves. You will soon understand that there are often other considerations that will affect your odds of winning any one hand, which you will need to factor into your probability calculations.)

OK, now, against the dealer's 2, 7 or 8, you would also be wise to STAND. The dealer's 2, as you'll see shortly, doesn't bust enough for you to risk doubling down on with your Ace-7; but your 18 will beat or push with the 2 more often than not. With the up card of 8, my studies have shown the dealer's resultant score will most often be 17 or 18, or a bust. If the dealer has a 7 showing, you'd assume the dealer to have just 17 points, because my research shows that, more than not, the dealer will draw to a 17 or bust with 7 as the up card. So, with the dealer's 2, 7 or 8, you'll STAND on your Ace-7, because your 18 will do well against the dealer's 2 and 8 — at least holding its own, a majority of times — and will beat the dealer's 7 most times.

If the dealer has up cards of 3 through 6, however, you'd DOUBLE DOWN holding that hand of Ace-7. That's because they're the dealer's weakest up cards, often causing the dealer to bust. So, you'd want to double, to get more money on what will probably be a winning hand for you.

"Your" Cards vs. The "Dealer's" Cards

The dealer's up card tells you your relative likelihood of winning any hand. Some are best for the player, some for the dealer.

We'll call the dealer's 3 through 6 YOUR CARDS (for now — we'll add one more card later):

That is, if the dealer shows these cards, you should quietly get excited. These are the cards that most often cause the dealer to bust (typically in the range of 40% of the time). With these cards showing, you'll do most of your doubling down and splitting, since you believe the dealer is likely to bust. These are your "money" cards.

You should stay sharp to take notice of these cards — a bell should go off in your head, so you can take advantage of every opportunity these cards afford you to double down and split your cards when appropriate. That way, you'll get as much money on the table as you can in probable winning situations.

We'll call the dealer's up cards of 9, the 10s and Ace the DEALER'S CARDS (for now — we'll add one more card later):

As indicated before, the dealer wins more often than not with the up cards of 9, 10 and Ace, and so you must play more cautiously when they appear.

(Notice how dealers seem to have more up cards in their favor than players do. Another thing you might notice is that the 8 is not included here. This is because, contrary to popular thinking, it is not a strong card for the dealer, nor is it such a bad card for the player, as I will explain later. You will come to understand that the 8 is off in its own category.)

Now, about the dealer's up cards of 2 and 7 — there will be a separate chapter, called "The Tricky 2s & Silent 7s," on these.

You will see, with regard to these up cards (contrary to what most of you have been taught), that the dealer's 2 behaves more like a "dealer's card," and the dealer's 7 often behaves like a "player's card." But let's save this discussion for Chapter 4.

Why Three Different Charts?

To learn how to play each of your hands, refer to the charts on pages 50-54 that spell out your recommended Basic Strategy moves. You will want to memorize these moves, so that they are second nature to you by the time you go to the casino. However, I will explain the *logic* behind each move, so that if you momentarily forget how to play a particular card situation in the heat of action at the blackjack table, you might at least remember what your *reasoning* should be, so that you might be able to think it through and make the right move. That's the benefit of being taught the WHYs behind the *Blackjack The SMART Way* system.

As is standard, I've divided up the game into three different charts, for the three different types of hands and card situations you will encounter, based upon the first two cards you will be dealt. The first chart will tell you how to play your first two cards, if they are HARD hands (hands which contain no Aces). The second chart will tell you how to play your first two cards if they are SOFT hands (hands with at least one Ace). The last chart will tell you how to play hands with *two like cards*.

To be super accurate about proper Basic Strategy moves, you'd need different charts for each game variation -- for 1-deck games, 2-deck games, etc. However, I feel the small degree of added accuracy gained by such an approach does not justify the possibility for confusion, nor the added degree of difficulty.

Basic Strategy: How To Play HARD HANDS

OK. Let's discuss what you should do if your first two cards are hard hands, from the point of view of what your point total is (please refer to CHARTS 1A & 1B on pages 50 and 51):

♣ **With totals of 4 through 8, you will always HIT**.
   You cannot bust by taking extra cards; so do so.

♥ **With a total of 9, DOUBLE DOWN if the dealer has an up card of 3 to 7. Otherwise, HIT.**
Your 9 is just large enough to make a nice total if you get one of the 10s or an ACE (which account for 38% of the cards). You will want to DOUBLE to get more money on the table when the dealer shows the weakest up cards.

♠ **With a total of 10, DOUBLE DOWN against the dealer's 2 through 8. Otherwise, HIT.**
Since you have a greater than 50% chance of improving your 10 to a winning point total with one hit card, and the dealer's 2 through 8 statistically don't achieve as many high winning scores as the 10, here's where you want more money on the table to capitalize on your mathematical advantage. (Plus -- in doubling, you won't bust; but, the *dealer* will, and you'll win every time that happens.)

♦ **With a total of 11, DOUBLE against the dealer's 2 through 9. Otherwise HIT.**
Oh boy! Eleven is a great total, because my research indicates it tends to draw to high winning scores and causes you to bust rather infrequently. Plus — eight of the 13 possible hit cards you might get in *doubling* will produce a winning score — the 6, 7, 8, 9, and 10-pointers. So, with a strong total like that, by all means, get more money on the table by doubling — EXCEPT against the dealer's strongest cards, the 10 and Ace, against which you should simply HIT your 11. This might be controversial in some circles, but — those cards produce strong winning totals for the dealer. The dealer is likely to outscore you with the 10 and Ace if you restrict yourself to taking just one extra card. (See Chapter 5 for details.)

♣ **With a total of 12 STAND if the dealer's up card is 4 through 6. HIT against all other up cards.**
A hand of 12 is tricky. You have to hit against the dealer's stronger cards and try to better your score. The only cards that will cause your 12 to bust are the 10s, which make up about 31% of the deck. So, 69% of the time — the great majority of the time — you'll do well to hit your 12. If the dealer shows a 4 through 6, though, the dealer is most likely to bust, so you'll STAND to avoid your 31%

risk of busting. Let the dealer bust.

♥   **With a total of 13 it's similar to a total of 12 except you also STAND versus the dealer's 2 and 3.**
Since 5 possible cards — the 9s through the 10-pointers, or approximately 38% of the possible hit cards you might draw will cause you to bust on this total, you'll want to STAND versus the up cards that bust the most: the 2 through the 6.

♠   **With totals of 14 through 16, STAND against the dealer's 2 through 6. Otherwise HIT, <u>unless</u> SURRENDER is allowed. SURRENDER your: 14-16 against the dealer's Ace; 15 and 16 against the 10; and, 16 against the 9.**
When your total is up in this range, you are very likely to bust when taking another card to better your score (around 50% or better). So STAND when the dealer is most likely to bust. You must HIT when the dealer is most likely to score a winning total, EXCEPT when the dealer has such a strong up card that your best option is to surrender (if allowed) and take the smallest possible loss (while at the same time getting back half your bet). Surrender is a very advantageous option for you. Don't be too shy to use it!   If SURRENDER is not allowed by the casino, HIT those hands.

♦   **With a hard total of 17 or more, always STAND.**
Since the dealer must stand on all hard 17s and above, you are now in winning territory. The odds are high that you will bust if you draw another card to your hard hand total of 17 or greater, so you should never consider doing so. (Of course, the only way you can *beat* the dealer with a 17 is if the dealer busts — it's the lowest winning total. So if you get a score of 17 don't be unhappy if you simply push with the dealer.)

♣   **With a Blackjack, you win instantly and are paid a bonus (some casinos pay 3-to-2, others 6-to-5) UNLESS the dealer has a Blackjack too. Then you'd push. In the isolated case where the player has a Blackjack and the dealer shows an Ace, I suggest beginners take EVEN MONEY (see page 26).**

This is usually a no-brainer. You STAND on a Blackjack! But, for beginners, who lack advanced skills, whose win rate is lower than advanced players', and who might be disappointed if they push here, this might be the best way to go. It blows a tiny percentage of gains over time, but, psychologically, it gives the beginner a much-needed boost, and it raises their winning rate. (NOTE: Advanced Players might want to take Even Money if they know the dealer has a Blackjack!!)

(NOTE: Some casinos have restrictions on what cards you can double down on, and some do not allow surrendering. In many casino locales, however, you can find a casino that offers these desirable options *without* limitations. Try to avoid the casinos with rules that hamper your game. See Chapter 3 for more information on how to pick a good casino.)

What To Do After You've Hit Your Hand

OK. Now, what if you've HIT your first two cards, as recommended above, but you are still below 17 points?

Easy. Just refer to CHART 1B (page 51). (Your totals are listed in the column on the far left; the dealer's up cards are shown in the top row.)

Basic Strategy: How to Play SOFT HANDS

When your hand is SOFT — it contains at least one Ace — here's how you should play it (please refer to CHART 2, page 52):
- ♠ **If you have an Ace-2 through Ace-5 DOUBLE DOWN when the dealer has a 4 through 6. Otherwise HIT.** Since you're dealing with weak point totals of 16 or less, you want to play it safe and only double here when you're pretty certain the dealer will bust.
- ♣ **If you have an Ace-6, DOUBLE DOWN against the dealer's 3 through 6. Otherwise, HIT.**

Although you always stand on a HARD 17, that's **not** true of a SOFT 17. You NEVER stand on a soft 17 (and that includes 3-, 4- or more-card soft 17s.) There are two reasons for this. First — since 8 out of 13 possible hit cards (Ace, 2, 3, 4, 10, J, Q, and K) would give you winning totals — you have extremely favorable odds in DOUBLING DOWN against the dealer's weakest cards (when the dealer is most likely to bust) and in getting a good card when HITTING against the dealer's stronger cards, with the hope of beating the dealer's likely strong total). Second — 17 is the weakest winning score possible, and, with the flexibility of the Ace (to be a 1-point card if necessary) the odds are in your favor if you hit this hand with the hope of improving it.

♥ **If you have an Ace-7, DOUBLE when the dealer shows a 3 through 6. STAND on a 2, 7, 8 or Ace. HIT against the 9s and 10s.**

This is the most complicated Ace combination in terms of remembering what to do. Since Ace-7 is a pretty good total of 18 points, STAND against the dealer's Ace or 2, rather than risk ruining your respectable total (nor would you want more money down against those cards, which are dealer's cards). You should also stand against the dealer's 7 and 8, but for a different reason — you expect to win or push here. However when faced with the dealer's 9, and 10, which will usually produce very strong totals of 19 through 21 you must try to better your score. Otherwise, you'll take a beating in terms of losses. Plus, more than half of the time, you will get a hit card that will either improve your Ace-7 (if it's an Ace, 2 or 3), or, at the very least, not hurt you (if it's a 10, J, Q or K).

♦ **ALWAYS STAND with Ace-8 and Ace-9.**

These point totals — 19 and 20 — are too good to HIT or DOUBLE on. They're often winners. You don't want to risk making these weaker with a hit card.

♠ **Ace-10 is a Blackjack. (See bottom of page 37.)**

♣ **If you get two Aces, ALWAYS SPLIT THEM** (for now).
The great thing about splitting Aces is that 8 of the possible 13 cards you might get upon each of those Aces

would provide you with *two potentially winning hands* (the 6, 7, 8, 9 and the 10s would help each of the Aces achieve nice scores —— 62% of the cards). Go for it! Remember, though, you will have two restrictions when splitting Aces: at nearly all casinos, you will only be given one card upon each of your Aces; and, you may only split them once. We will take this into consideration, in Chapter 10, on Advanced Strategy. In fact, in Chapter 5, you will learn about one particular situation when, as an advanced player, you will choose NOT to split Aces. This is yet another unique aspect of *Blackjack The SMART Way*. Most other books will tell you that you should always split Aces, even as advanced players. NOT so — not if you're smart!

As with your hard hands, if my recommendation for your soft hand was to HIT and, after hitting your hand, your total is still below 17, then refer to CHART 1B (page 51) for what to do.

The Rules of Splitting

Splitting your hand into two new hands when you have a pair of cards of the same point value is often a good thing to do. There are various reasons for doing so. Sometimes your pair of like cards add up to a poor, substandard total that might bust with a hit card, and, by splitting them, you might create the possibility of getting two hands that would have a better chance to achieve winning totals. Sometimes your pair of like cards are individually so strong —— in spite of their already achieving a good total —— that they would both be highly likely to outscore the dealer's up card. Or, perhaps you simply might want to get more money down in a probable winning situation, where the dealer appears likely to bust (and, by the way, you should DOUBLE after splitting if your new hand is a total worth doubling on; most casinos allow this). And, then there are times where your pair of like cards are losers no matter what you do, but, by splitting them, you will lose the least, over the course of time. This is often the case, for example, with pairs of 8s. Any of these reasons is sufficient to cause you to want to split.

Please refer now to CHART 3A (page 53). This shows you the method you'll use in splitting, at most casinos at which you'll play — where you can DOUBLE DOWN after splitting, and re-split if you get another like card upon one of the original cards.

(Review CHART 3B, on page 54, on your own. You should try not to play at casinos that limit your game with the restrictions referred to in that chart; they work against you and require you to use a new strategy, as you can see. You really don't want to memorize yet another chart, nor accept limitations that cut into your winnings, do you?)

OK, so here's how you will handle the different types of pairs of like cards you might get:

♦ **If you have a pair of 2s, SPLIT them against the dealer's 2 through 7. Otherwise — HIT. With 3s, SPLIT them against the *3* through 7. Otherwise, HIT.**

Two 2s equal 4, and two 3s equal 6, which are not great point totals. Against the 4 through 6, it's a no-brainer — those are the dealer's weakest cards. Plus, my research shows the dealer's 2, 3 and 7 will outperform your unsplit hands of 4 and 6 points. If you split them you create two new hands that are less likely to bust. Plus, your split cards would then be more likely to achieve winning point totals AND outperform the dealer's up cards listed above. But, against the dealer's stronger up cards of 8 through Ace, you'd be smart to HIT your pairs of 2s and 3s, because you're likely to lose whether or not you split them, and so, save your money. Exception: your split 3s don't fare well against the 2. HIT them instead.

♣ ***NEVER split two 4s or 5s. HIT the 4s. DOUBLE DOWN on the 5s against a dealer's 2 through 8, and HIT against the dealer's 8, 9, 10 and Ace.***

Two 4s equal 8, which is not a bad total. If you were dealt a 9, you'd have 17 points. If your hit card was one of the four 10-point cards, you'd have 18 points. With an Ace you'd have 19. With a 2 you'd have 10 points; with

41

a 3, you'd have 11 points — good totals to build upon. The alternative — splitting those 4s — would be bad. You'd have two hands of 4 points. According to my re search, those new hands would bust more than 40% of the time, and up to 60%, depending on the **flow of the cards** (we'll get into that concept in Chapter 10)! Now, with your pair of 5s, that's a total of 10 points; it provides a great foundation upon which you will often build strong totals! That's better than splitting and then hitting individual 5s, which often draw to stiff totals that bust a lot. So, keep the 5s together, and play them like you would any other hand of 10 points.

♥ **With two 6s, SPLIT them against the dealer's 3 through 7. HIT them against all other up cards.** This hand totals 12. Not great. With a 10, you'd bust. Two hands of 6 are better — versus the dealer's weakest cards, that is. Plus, it lets you get more money on the table when the dealer is most likely to bust (although the dealer's 7 doesn't bust a lot, interestingly enough, my data shows that it draws to lower scores than the dealer's 6!).

♠ **With two 7s, SPLIT them against the dealer's 2 through 7. HIT them against all other up cards.** Very similar to your pair of 6s. Two 7s equal 14. Not a great total. You might bust with 6 of the possible 13 hit cards. Two hands of 7 each offer more hope of achieving two winning hands, when facing the dealer's 2 through 7. The dealer's 8, 9,10 and Ace, however, are too strong to split against, with your resultant split hands of 7 apiece, but you still have a better than even chance of pulling a card that won't bust your 14 (and might help) if you HIT. Understand that, in hitting your 14 versus the dealer's strong up cards, you will experience high losses. None- theless, it is the move that will cause you to incur the fewest losses.

♦ **ALWAYS SPLIT 8s** (for now). Two 8s equals 16, *the worst possible total.* If you split them, you will have two hands of 8, which are much more promising — 62% of the possible 13 cards you might now get (Ace, 2, 3, 9 and the 10s) would give each of your new hands more hopeful totals. Understand, though that your individual 8s will not stack up well against the dealer's strongest cards. You will lose nearly 50% of the time if you split once, and progressively more with each extra split. However, any of your other options will only lose more for you.

♣ **SPLIT Two 9s, UNLESS the dealer has a 7, 10 or an Ace, when you should STAND.**
Two 9s equals 18, which isn't bad at all. So, you DON'T split this against the dealer's up card of 7, because *Blackjack The SMART Way* research shows that the 7 most often busts or scores 17 points for the dealer — therefore you've already beaten that; you should not split the 9s and potentially mess that up! You DON'T split 9s against the dealer's 10 or Ace because my research shows the 10 and Ace usually reach higher totals than your 9 (plus both cards bust less!). You don't want to lose two hands! However, since the numbers from my studies indicate that your 9 draws to an 18 or higher the majority of times, you are on the right side of mathematical probability if you split against the other up cards — the dealer's 2 through 6 have weak results vs. the 9; the dealer's 8 draws to lower totals, on average, than your 9; and, when facing the strong dealer's 9, it's wise to split, because your two 9s (totaling 18) will usually be out-scored by the dealer's 9 and will not be enough to win. In splitting them, you will actually lower your odds of LOSING. This, unfortunately, is an unavoidable losing situation for you.

♦ **NEVER EVER SPLIT 10s. STAND.**
You've got a great point total here: 20. That 20 will win for you most of the time. You're likely to spoil that strong total by splitting. The 10s make up less than a third of the deck. The odds are 69% that you'll spoil EACH of those 10s with lower hit cards if you split them. Plus — if you do this move, you'll send the other players at your table scurrying to other tables to get away from you, or YOU might have to run for cover!

♠ **ALWAYS SPLIT Aces** (for now; see page 39).

A Practical Example

Now, let's see if you know how to read the Basic Strategy Charts, starting on page 50. Take a moment to review them, and then we'll do an example.

OK— let's say you were dealt the cards below, and the dealer's up card is a 7:

That's a poor total of 7. Go to CHART 1A (page 50), look up your 7 on the left column and move your finger over to the dealer's 7 column (the up cards are across the top). It says "H" for HIT... OK, but what if you hit and then get a three?:

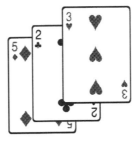

Now look at CHART 1B (page 51). You have a 10 against the dealer's 7. The chart says you HIT a 10 against the dealer's 7. OK, so you HIT again, and, guess what? You get another 3!:

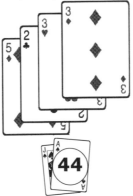

Uh oh! You've got a 13, and CHART 1B tells you to HIT a total of 13 against a 7.

So you HIT...and you get. . .

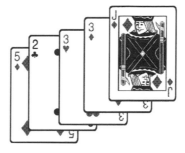

...a JACK, a 10-pointer! Oops! You busted! (Get used to it!)

The point I am trying to make here is -- you will bust on a certain number of hands every time you play. You will never win every hand — not nearly! So, do yourself a favor and keep your emotions in check when you do bust.

How To Place A Bet

OK, now let's discuss how you get into the action. (If there's an ongoing round being played, wait until it is completed.)

In front of your seat, drawn on the green felt top of the blackjack table, will be a small circle, square or other geometric shape designating your betting spot (see DIAGRAMS A & B, pages 55 and 56). Place your bet, in chips, in that spot, before the dealer starts to deal the next round. (You can purchase chips from the dealer between rounds.)

Here's how you stack your chips, if you have a wager composed of different denominations — you're supposed to stack your chips in reverse order to their monetary value, going from highest to lowest, with the highest chips on the bottom.

The dealer will then deal you two cards — your *hand*.

(You can usually place bets at more than one betting space to play more than one hand at a time, but many casinos require that each bet then be TWICE the table minimum. Really, though, beginners and intermediates should not even consider this. It's hard enough to decide how to handle one hand. There are a lot of things to keep track of and numbers to remember, and that easily gets forgotten if you start going back and forth between hands to make appropriate decisions for the different circumstances that affect each hand. Plus — you tend to attract too much unwanted attention when you take more than one betting spot. You'll understand why you will want to avoid being scrutinized by casino personnel, when you read Chapter 11.)

The Dealer Commences Action

Now, here's how the play goes at a typical casino:

The dealer shuffles the cards when the dealer reaches the plastic reshuffle card (although at some casinos the dealer does this at his/her discretion!). When the cards are shuffled, a player is then handed the reshuffle card to "cut" the cards, and the card below that marker then becomes the top of the pile; the cards above the marker are moved to the bottom (you can refuse to cut the deck if you so choose, by the way). The dealer then usually puts the reshuffle card about 40% up from the bottom of the card pile and "burns" (discards) the top card, or, in some casinos, the dealer burns as many cards as there are players, WITHOUT showing you those cards. (It makes card tracking more difficult. Do not EVER play at casinos that burn more than one card!).

The dealer waits for all bets to be made — the players placing their bet of chips in their betting spot(s). Then, the dealer deals two cards to each player and themselves, one card at a time. The dealer's first card is turned up (either immediately or after the dealer has dealt everyone their first two cards), and the dealer's second card will be the "hole card," kept face down under the first card until it's the dealer's turn to play out his or her hand (see DIAGRAM A, page 55). (At a very few casinos, the dealer turns the *second* card up to become the up card; whatever the policy, it should be done in a standard fashion.) Players then take their turns, starting with the player to the left of the dealer.

After all players have played their hands, the dealer then turns the hole card over and takes more cards if necessary, until he or she reaches a total of 17 or more points OR busts (except, or course, in casinos where dealers must hit their soft 17s). Players that beat the dealer in points, or simply win because the dealer busted and they did not, get paid in chips an amount equal to their bet, or 1.5 times their bet if they have a Blackjack.

If the dealer gets an up card of an Ace, they immediately ask players if they want Insurance. If you do, you place an amount of chips equal to half your bet within the horseshoe shaped Insurance area in front of your bet (see DIAGRAM A, page 55). If you have a Blackjack and would prefer even money, say "Even Money," and the dealer will pay you an amount equal to your bet. The dealer then slides the hole card over an electronic device which tells them whether they have a Blackjack or not. Typically, one light lights up if the answer is "no" and play continues. Two lights means "yes," and all players lose except for those who also had a Blackjack, who *push,* unless they took Even Money or Insurance.

By the way, dealers at most casinos also check 10s in this fashion, to make sure they don't have a Blackjack. They do NOT offer Insurance in that case, however.

A Word About Mistakes

OK, so now you know a ground-floor way to play EVERY hand against every dealer up card, and you've been practicing with cards at home, and what do you find?

You always forget something! Perhaps you also make a few mistakes in the course of playing. Get used to this. I'm still kicking myself for not doubling with an 8 against the dealer's 5 the other night, *knowing* that 10s were coming. I indeed got a 10 and won, but I could have won twice as much if I had only acted on my correct determination and doubled down.

Every blackjack player goofs and makes wrong moves from time to time. No big deal. You can survive making occasional minor card strategy mistakes. Like an Olympic skater, you can get up from a fall on the ice once in awhile, and still go on to become a winner.

However, *you must NEVER make costly errors in handling your bets or your money.* In that regard, the following chapters will be even more important to you than this one.

Let Me Spare You Some Grief

Before we move on to a different topic, I need to address a common question. That is: "If the dealer's drawing cards to a total of at least 17 points, that means if I stand on stiffs I will frequently lose; so, shouldn't I play the way the dealer plays?"

No! You should never adopt a strategy akin to the way the dealer plays. Some players insist on learning the hard way why it's not wise to play your cards using the same "strategy" as the dealer's, drawing a card on every hand until you reach a total of at least 17. DON'T try this foolish method!

The reason you will lose more than the dealer playing this way is this: you must play your hand BEFORE THE DEALER. Therefore, you must pull a card using this strategy whether or not the dealer is likely to bust (where you might win the most times by *standing* on one of your stiffs). When you bust YOU lose your money. When the dealer busts, the dealer personally loses nothing.

Wouldn't it be wiser to learn to stand on some of your more dangerous, bustable hands in situations where the dealer is likely to give you a win by busting?

Trust me — I will only recommend that you stand on a stiff when it is mathematically in your favor. Sometimes, though, this means it will cause you to LOSE less than you would by hitting your stiff hand. (This brings to mind a common player misconception. A lot of players think that if they follow a recommendation and it loses more hands than it wins that it is the wrong move. Not necessarily. Some moves *will* cause you to lose more than you win. But, the alternatives will cause you to suffer worse losses. So, to clear up any possible future misunderstandings, you must understand the concept of the *losing situation:* some hands you are dealt are *losers*, and in those cases you'd be smart to do the move that simply *limits* your losses.)

What You Should Do Now

OK, now it's important that you study the charts in this chapter, practicing over and over at home until you remember every situation you will run into at the casino. Then, once you've read this book in its entirety and are ready to play at a casino, *always review your charts and notes at least an hour before you actually play*, to get your strategy down COLD. It's *your* money.

Where Do We Go From Here?

The Basic Strategy you've just learned — which beginners might use exclusively and more advanced players will use primarily as a reference point — is an Old School approach that is actually very inefficient. It's akin to using a hand grenade to open a bag of potato chips. Yeah, the bag's open, but what do you have? Crumbs. It's too blunt an instrument. You need something more intelligent, modern, discriminating, effective and profitable. (I did not create the concept of Basic Strategy; it dates back to 1953.)

I've let you keep a foot in the past to make it easier for you to transit to a new and better way to play. I believe in offering different methods on a variety of levels so players of every skill, ambition and experience level can achieve their personal best.

And yes, using my Basic Strategy, under the best conditions (at crowded single and double deck tables), along with my betting methods, will indeed make you a consistent winner. But I've created methods that are MUCH better. As you will soon see, the power of this book lies in the state-of-the-art, highly accurate methods unique to my system, which came out of years of original and innovative blackjack studies, card behavior research, shuffling studies, and computer analyses.

You are not ready to enter a casino yet.

CHART 1A:
HOW TO PLAY HARD HANDS

	2	3	4	5	6	7	8	9	10	A
4-8	H	H	H	H	H	H	H	H	H	H
9	H	D	D	D	D	D	H	H	H	H
10	D	D	D	D	D	D	D	H	H	H
11	D	D	D	D	D	D	D	D	H	H
12	H	H	S	S	S	H	H	H	H	H
13	S	S	S	S	S	H	H	H	H	H
14	S	S	S	S	S	H	H	H	H	Sur/H*
15	S	S	S	S	S	H	H	H	Sur/H*	Sur/H*
16	S	S	S	S	S	H	H	Sur/H*	Sur/H*	Sur/H*
17+	S	S	S	S	S	S	S	S	S	S
BJ	S	S	S	S	S	S	S	S	S	S

*Hit these combinations if surrender is not allowed.

50

CHART 1B:

HOW TO PLAY HARD HANDS
AFTER TAKING ONE CARD

	2	3	4	5	6	7	8	9	10	A
4-8	H	H	H	H	H	H	H	H	H	H
9	H	H	H	H	H	H	H	H	H	H
10	H	H	H	H	H	H	H	H	H	H
11	H	H	H	H	H	H	H	H	H	H
12	H	H	S	S	S	H	H	H	H	H
13	S	S	S	S	S	H	H	H	H	H
14	S	S	S	S	S	H	H	H	H	H
15	S	S	S	S	S	H	H	H	H	H
16	S	S	S	S	S	H	H	H	H	H
17+	S	S	S	S	S	S	S	S	S	S

51

CHART 2:
HOW TO PLAY SOFT HANDS
(ACE COMBINATIONS)

	2	3	4	5	6	7	8	9	10	A
Ace-2 to Ace-5	H	H	D	D	D	H	H	H	H	H
Ace-6	H	D	D	D	D	H	H	H	H	H
Ace-7	S	D	D	D	D	S	S	H	H	S
Ace-8	S	S	S	S	S	S	S	S	S	S
Ace-9	S	S	S	S	S	S	S	S	S	S
BJ	S	S	S	S	S	S	S	S	S	S
Pair of Aces	SP	SP	SP	SP	SP	SP	SP	SP	SP	SP

CHART 3A:
HOW TO PLAY PAIRS OF LIKE CARDS
(If Post-Split Doubling & Splitting Are Allowed)

	2	3	4	5	6	7	8	9	10	A
Pair of 2s	SP	SP	SP	SP	SP	SP	H	H	H	H
Pair of 3s	H	SP	SP	SP	SP	SP	H	H	H	H
Pair of 4s	H	H	H	H	H	H	H	H	H	H
Pair of 5s	D	D	D	D	D	D	D	H	H	H
Pair of 6s	H	SP	SP	SP	SP	SP	H	H	H	H
Pair of 7s	SP	SP	SP	SP	SP	SP	H	H	H	H
Pairs of 8s	SP	SP	SP	SP	SP	SP	SP	SP	SP	SP
Pair of 9s	SP	SP	SP	SP	SP	S	SP	SP	S	S
Pair of 10s	S	S	S	S	S	S	S	S	S	S
Pair of Aces	SP	SP	SP	SP	SP	SP	SP	SP	SP	SP

CHART 3B:
HOW TO PLAY PAIRS OF LIKE CARDS
(If Post-Split Doubling & Splitting Are NOT Allowed)

	2	3	4	5	6	7	8	9	10	A
Pair of 2s	H	SP	SP	SP	SP	SP	H	H	H	H
Pair of 3s	H	H	SP	SP	SP	SP	H	H	H	H
Pair of 4s	H	H	H	H	H	H	H	H	H	H
Pair of 5s	D	D	D	D	D	D	H	H	H	H
Pair of 6s	H	H	SP	SP	SP	H	H	H	H	H
Pair of 7s	H	S	SP	SP	SP	H	H	H	SUR/ H*	SUR/ H*
Pairs of 8s	S	SP	SP	SP	SP	SP	SP	SP	SUR/ SP*	SUR/ SP*
Pair of 9s	S	SP	SP	SP	SP	S	SP	SP	S	S
Pair of 10s	S	S	S	S	S	S	S	S	S	S
Pair of Aces	SP	SP	SP	SP	SP	SP	SP	SP	SP	SP

*SUR/SP means surrender if possible; otherwise, split.
SUR/H means surrender if possible; otherwise, hit.

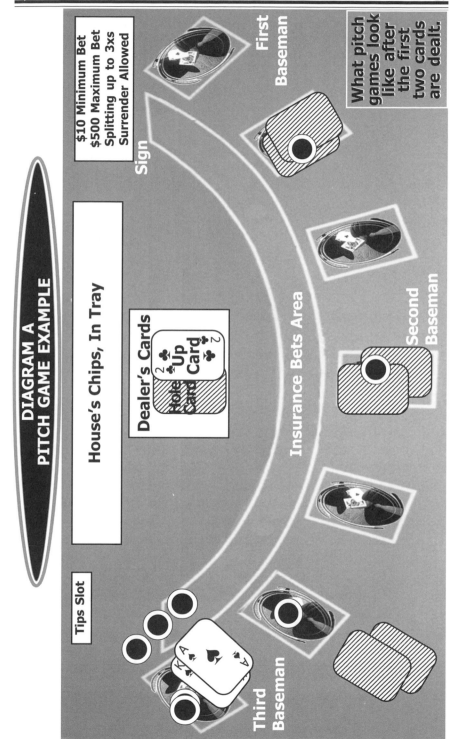

**DIAGRAM A
PITCH GAME EXAMPLE**

$10 Minimum Bet
$500 Maximum Bet
Splitting up to 3xs
Surrender Allowed

Sign

First Baseman

What pitch games look like after the first two cards are dealt.

House's Chips, In Tray

Dealer's Cards

Hole Card 2♣

Up Card 2♣

Insurance Bets Area

Second Baseman

Tips Slot

Third Baseman

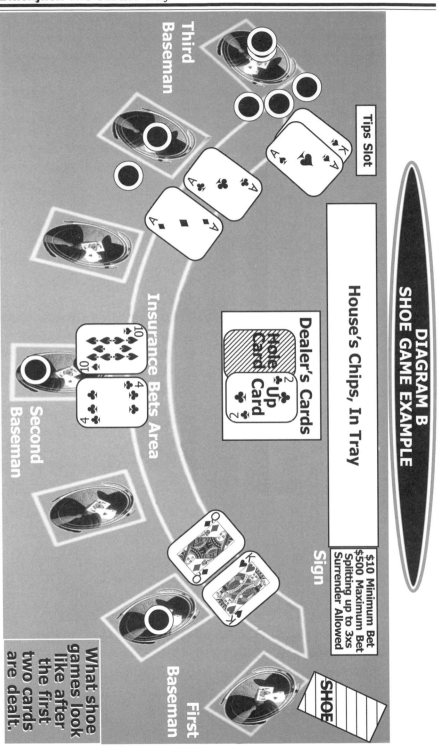

DIAGRAM B
SHOE GAME EXAMPLE

Tips Slot

House's Chips, In Tray

Dealer's Cards

Hole Card

Up Card

Insurance Bets Area

Third Baseman

Second Baseman

First Baseman

$10 Minimum Bet
$500 Maximum Bet
Splitting up to 3xs
Surrender Allowed

Sign

SHOE

What shoe games look like after the first two cards are dealt.

3 ♥

THE WORLD OF OF THE CASINO

Let me take you into the world of the casino.

The atmosphere is one of dazzling lights, shiny mirrors and gaudy colors. It is visually overwhelming.

At some casinos, the smell of stale cigarette smoke clings to every pore of the place.

At all casinos there are mazes of alleys created by cash-register-like slot machines that greedily gobble coins and bills fed to them continually by bleary-eyed slots players.

And the noise! The slot machines emit clanking sounds on their gorging cycle, and then belch out coins with cymbal-like crashes on their disgorging cycle. As if that weren't annoying enough, they occasionally let loose with the clanging of bells to signal that a slots player has scored a jackpot.

You have to walk past all of this to get to the blackjack tables. Finally, in the distance, through the dark of the casino, you see lights shining upon the welcome green of the felt-topped blackjack tables, usually situated near the craps tables – where players tend to scream and shout, adding to the cacophony.

You now notice the blackjack players, sitting in semicircles, bent over their cards, many of them obviously...*unhappy.* That's right. Most players are losers and that doesn't make anyone happy. Some even grumble how crummy the cards have been. Never mind. You don't have to let them drag you down. It does sober up the fun a bit, though, doesn't it? Let that be a reminder to you that *your money is on the line.*

It's Your Job To Pick A Good Casino

Not all casinos were created equal. Some casinos are huge, and contain many blackjack tables from which to choose, with different minimums, numbers of decks and rules (some tables, for instance, might not allow players to join the game until the shuffle). The average casino outside of Las Vegas, Reno, Tahoe and Atlantic City and one or two other stateside casino towns, however, are small to medium-sized and do NOT have many blackjack tables. The smaller the casino, the greater your limitations will be when you are looking for a good table.

Pay Attention to the Atmosphere

At some casinos, the atmosphere is cheery and friendly. You see players winning and having a good time. The dealers enjoy joking around with the players and even root for them.

Some casinos, though, have bad vibes. As soon as you enter, the negative atmosphere awakens you to tangible reasons why you should probably turn on your heels and leave.

For example, there was a casino in my home state that a lot of players avoided because the place is was dark you could barely see your cards. The place was painted black, befitting the mood of the players. Why would you want to play at a place like that, when you're looking to have some fun?

And some casinos seem to feed their dealers nasty juice. It's no fun to play when the dealer is humorless and negative, or, worse, giving you a rough time – criticizing your moves, or rushing your play. If you get bad vibes when you enter a casino, DON'T play. Walk right out. Don't be embarrassed and don't play just because you drove miles to get there. *It's your money.*

Do They Show You The Cards?

Now, this might sound like a small thing, but I prefer casinos where they bring in new cards at specific times, and then spread the cards face up so you can see the decks are legitimate – that there are no missing or extra cards. (I was at a casino once where the deck that was about to be used was missing three cards! A player complained and the cards were tossed.)

Don't Be Desperate!

Be picky about the casino you go to! The game will be far more enjoyable if you choose a place where all the factors are how you like them. Believe me, it will pay off in the end! Part of the "trick" to upping your win rate is being discriminating about where you play.

Names, Names!

Now, some players want me to mention names of casinos I recommend, but I learned long ago not to do that. I was on the Jay Casey show in Las Vegas in the late 1990s and he pressed me to give at least one name of a casino I liked. So I did. The next week, they removed the games I liked to play there. The one "good" casino whose name I'd mentioned was now "bad" and I couldn't warn Jay's listeners NOT to go there!

Good casinos can become bad and vice versa. It happens all the time. So the best gift I can give you is the ability to determine on your own how to identify which casinos are good and which ones are bad. Things change and your list of favorites will change over time.

The Cardinal Rule Upon Entering a Casino

Now if, upon entering an unfamiliar casino the atmosphere seems nice, DON'T SIT DOWN YET! *Walk around the casino and get a feel for what its advantages are and see if it has any disadvantages. Be observant.*

For example, I prefer the single and double deck games, so if a casino doesn't have either of those, I'm likely to walk right out. That's important to me. More decks at the table and it becomes a different game; less winnable.

Only two blackjack tables? You won't be able to change tables if the cards are cold. Not a very good place to play!

Many casinos have small plastic signs on the tables next to the dealer's left hand. Read those carefully. The signs list some of the game rules particular to that casino. They enumerate some of what you are allowed to do (example: "Surrender Allowed"), and any restrictions you might face (such as "Doubling Only on 10s & 11s" or "No Resplitting Aces"). If the rules are not player-friendly, leave! (In some regions, such as Las Vegas, however, it's hard to find casinos with these customary signs. So ask the dealer specifically about any possible restrictions you mightl want to avoid. Your first question should be: "Is Surrender allowed?" If it's allowed, you've likely found a good place to play - assuming everything else is player-friendly. Surrender is a powerful option to have at your disposal.

If a casino severely limits your ability to double down, don't play there – that's one of your best ways of making money. If no resplitting is allowed (that's if, let's say, you split two 8s and you get another 8, but you cannot split that new pair of 8s), you'll have to alter the way you play — see CHART 3B, page 54. You probably don't want to do that.

How To Pick A Good Casino

To summarize: One of your jobs is to shop around and find casinos where the conditions are favorable. Ones that:

- ♥ Have the game you want to play — the number of decks you prefer to play against; pitch vs. shoe games, for instance. I won't play against more than 4-decks, and prefer 1– or 2-deck games, where it's easier to keep track of the cards and the **flow of the cards** is more predictable, less prone to wild swings. Don't compromise on this issue.
- ♥ Have an ample number of blackjack tables — the more the better. You then stand a better chance of finding a good table within that casino when your table is bad and you need to change tables. (Any less than 8 tables, and you might find your only option is to leave the casino after suffering minor losses at a bad table, and that's very inconvenient and makes for a difficult time of it. In fact, it tempts you to play at a less than optimum table, and that's bad.)
- ♥ Allow doubling down on any 2-card combination. Any restrictions here severely hurt your chances of coming away a winner, or winning what you should. Plus, if there are restrictions, they usually amount to a near banning of doubling!
- ♥ Allow doubling down after splitting. Without this, you would have to change your splitting strategy and you really don't want to do that; it limits your gains. Plus, I don't recommend that you try changing your successful strategy to suit a restrictive, less-than-desirable casino.
- ♥ Allow you to split up to three times. Anything less and you'd need to rethink splitting those 8s, for example. Once again,

you don't want to have to remember several different strategies when you can win more by sticking to your guns and finding a casino that's best for you.

♥ Allow resplitting of Aces. Although a rare situation and not one of your "essentials," this lets you win more often when the opportunity arises.

♥ Allow Surrender. This is a powerful option that you should seek out. It lets you get more money on the table because you know you can always get half of it back if you are in a no-win situation with a high bet out. Plus, it spares you half your inevitable losses when you have very bad hands, sure losers.

Now, you should try to *avoid* casinos where:

♥ The dealer must hit their soft-17s. This will result in more losses to you.

♥ The dealers "burn" (place in the discard tray) more than one card after shuffling. One card burned doesn't make a huge difference to your ability to keep track of what cards have been played, but any more than that is cause to find a better casino.

♥ The dealer places the reshuffle card such that you will see less than 50% of the cards before he or she must reshuffle (this may vary from table to table however; check and see). To benefit from the predictability of the game, you need to see as many cards as possible, so find a casino that shows you at least 60% or more of the cards before the dealer must shuffle.

♥ You get too much negative scrutiny from casino employees and they subject you to countermeasures or dirty tricks. Or their heavy-handed breathing-down-your-neck style makes you feel uncomfortable.

How To Pick A Good Table

Now, *knowing how to pick a good table is a very important thing to learn.* Steer *away* from the tables where everyone's depressed and complaining. Find ones where people seem at least somewhat happy if they're not outright smiling and laughing and of good cheer. Those tend to be the best tables, where the luck of the cards has been good to great. The more crowded, the better. Think about it — no one leaves a good table!

You should watch the action for awhile at any table you're considering, before you sit down to play. If the dealer seems to be on an improbably good winning streak – winning even with his or her weakest up cards, constantly turning up high totals like 20s and 21s, not to mention an unusual number of Blackjacks – *avoid* that table at all costs! These are tables where the players are either pretty glum, or outright disgusted, saying things like "not AGAIN!" as the dealer snappily collects the player's lost bets with a strange zeal. We want to avoid these tables.

Also bypass tables where the dealer deals extremely fast or seems overly confident he or she will beat all the players, always expecting to turn up a winning card when drawing his or her own cards, not pausing a nanosecond before collecting player's bets.

Find a table where the dealer busts occasionally and loses not infrequently, at which at least two players seem to be winning. Watch at least a few hands to be sure. Look at how many chips the players have in front of them – if at least one has a large pile of chips in front of him and others have medium-sized piles, that's probably a good sign (although, granted, you never know how many chips they started off with).

You can even ask one of the players at an opportune moment, "How's this table doing?" If the answer is "Not bad," that means it's OK. If the answer instead is, "I've been losing here for six hours," move on. Once, I sat down next to an acquaintance, ready to play, and I asked him how he was doing. "This dealer always kills me!" he responded dejectedly. (Yet he then placed another bet, as I watched in amazement!) "Thanks for telling me!" I said, promptly getting up to look for a better table.

It's also wise to choose a table where there are no annoyances that would distract you from concentrating on your game – a nasty player or dealer, or someone smoking if that bothers you.

The "No Mid-Point Entry" Table

Some casinos offer tables with signs that say "NO MIDPOINT

ENTRY." Wow! I *love* those tables. While you'll have to wait until the shuffle to enter those games, it's worth it. That way you avoid what I call the "**One-Hand Harrys and Harriets**" and the "**Coupon Charlies and Charlenes.**" You also avoid the shills – the casino employees who pretend to be players (you'll learn about them in Chapter 11).

The **One-Hand Harrys and Harriets** bop from table to table, never knowing what they're doing, always seeming to come to your table in the middle of a winning streak, which they promptly mess up by interrupting the flow of the cards (in joining the game, adding a player) and by playing stupidly. They put down only enough money for one or two hands and then leave (usually after losing), having spoiled the action at your table. (This practice is sometimes called "wonging" because author Stanford Wong popularized a bop-in, bop-out style of playing.)

The **Coupon Charlies and Charlenes** are similar, except they don't bop from table to table. They're typically slot machine players who just happened to get a coupon in the mail, who interrupt action by using their "$5 Match Play!" coupon to play one or two hands, which they play poorly and lose, and they then go off to play the slots, having destroyed any winning streak you were enjoying before they came to the table. (This practice has been encouraged by a Vegas newsletter writer who I nicknamed the "Coupon King." I've heard him claim that this is the way to beat the house odds. Scarfing freebies!)

The funny thing about the NO MIDPOINT ENTRY table, by the way, is that casinos invented it thinking it would be a benefit to them, NOT the player! The theory was it would prevent card counters from watching on the sidelines, and then jumping into the action when the cards looked favorable. In actuality, it's much more of a blessing to the player. The more stable the **flow of the cards**, the better able you'll be to keep track of how the cards are likely to break for you. Plus, your winning streaks won't be jeopardized by card fluctuations. So if you can find a good NO MIDPOINT ENTRY table, RUN to it!

Should You Ever Play The Dealer One-On-One?

Another thing: NEVER, NEVER play the dealer alone. My studies have proven that this is a losing proposition. For many reasons, you're likely to go down fast:

♣ This is beyond the scope of this book, but, as you'll learn in *Cutting Edge Blackjack*, the dealer's busting rate is much lower and winning rate much higher in one-on-one situations than in other player configurations. I've discovered scientific reasons for why this occurs.

♣ You won't see many cards so your card move decisions lack a great deal of precision. Card analysis becomes more accurate the more cards you have available to factor in. (Players in one-on-one play see an average of six cards per round, for example. Players at 7-player tables see an average of 22; at 6-player tables, 19.)

♣ The play is a lot quicker and so it's easier to make mistakes.

♣ The dealer often deals you fewer cards before reshuffling, which destroys much of the predictability of the game.

Trust me. *Don't even consider this.*

The Number of Players at the Table Matters

Another important consideration: I urge you to play only at tables with at least *three* other players (or three other betting spots being played). The advantages are many:

The *pace* is more comfortable. If you're sitting in or toward the third baseman's seat as I advise (see Diagrams A and B, pages 55-56), you'll have more *time* to observe the cards and make smart card decisions.

You'll see a good amount of cards before making your decision, so you can make a more informed choice as to whether to risk taking more cards.

More important - **my studies have revealed that the dealer's busting rate goes up with each additional player at the table. This is true of players' winning rates**! (See *Cutting Edge Blackjack* for details.)

And, once again, ***crowding*** *at a table tends to be a good sign* — if it's hard to find a seat there, it might be because the players have found a good thing and don't want to leave! *No one wants to leave a good table!* Empty tables, on the other hand, are often empty because the cards have gone on a very bad streak and have driven the players away.

Avoid Tables With Horrible Players!

I have discovered, by the way, that *the best way to beat the house most often is by bringing several friends who play well.* Or, secondarily, by sitting at a table with good players. That's when you'll see your most protracted winning streaks. My card behavior studies have proven that smart player choices do tend to increase the dealer's busting rate!

Plus, a bad player will ruin a table sooner or later. The normal flow of cards is disturbed and the winning cards that would tend to come your way somehow end up being diverted. When you've played often enough, you'll find this is true.

I've demonstrated this at my seminars. We'll play a hand, and everyone sees how well playing on the right side of the percentages works. Then, we'll replay the same cards, but, this time, we'll pretend one of the players is making stupid moves. More times than not, these mistakes play into the hands of the dealer. Try it for yourself.

There is considerable debate about this subject, but, trust me, most good players have recognized the validity of this syndrome. So if you see someone splitting 10s, or standing on a hand of 5, or making other crazy moves, pick up your chips and RUN to another table!

Avoid the Blackjack Variants

Now, a word of advice: stay away from all blackjack variants, usually identified by cutesy or strange names. By the time you figure out all the rules, your money will be gone. Then, on the way home, you'll realize that the variant game had rules that made it very difficult to win.

66

Spanish 21 is the most common variant. The pips (the 10s) have been removed from the deck! Guess what happens to the dealer's busting rate under those conditions?!

"Double Exposure" exposes the dealer's hole card, but at a steep cost. Players lose when they push with the dealer. That results in 7% more losses, or more, depending on how the cards are breaking. No Basic Strategy player can beat that game.

Stick to the game you understand and know is winnable.

To "Pitch" or to "Shoe" — That's The Question

...But how many decks should you play against? Some casinos have 1- or 2-deck "pitch games" where the dealers hold the decks in their left hand, "pitching" (tossing) cards to the players facedown. The players must hold the cards in one hand as they play (see Diagram A, page 55). The idea behind having you hold your cards is to thwart card counters, but you won't get into trouble if you show others your cards or peek at the extra card you're given facedown under your chips when you double down.

There are a few disadvantages, admittedly. The card counter will find it difficult, if not impossible, to ply his trade at these tables, where players are forced to place their first two cards *facedown* under their chips, out of the view of others, when standing. For the same reason, it's harder to do an accurate job of card analysis at these tables - unless, that is, you've read my second book, *Cutting Edge Blackjack*, which reveals methods I've invented, enabling you to identify those down-turned cards! (Vegas expert Howard Schwartz hailed that method in two great reviews.)

In contrast to the pitch game tables, there are tables where there are multi-deck *shoe games* with four, six or eight decks of cards (four being almost impossible to find anymore). The cards are held in open-top plastic or wooden boxes known as "shoes," from which the dealer pulls the cards with his or her left hand, dealing them *face up* to the players (see Diagram B, page 56).

There are arguably a few advantages to playing shoe games. You'll see more cards and more rounds before the cards are reshuffled. Plus, the casinos tend to have their dealers put the reshuffle card further back into the cards, so you usually see up to 70% of the cards. And analyzing the cards is easier because all cards (except the dealer's hole card) are dealt face up.

BUT there are numerous drawbacks to shoe games and I much prefer the pitch games, whose advantages outweigh the disadvantages. And with the proliferation of casinos leading to increased competition for your dollar, pitch games can be found at many (although not all) casinos.

While finding single deck games is often difficult, double deck games seem more available than ever before. (And be careful of the single deck games. Some casinos limit you to one round of action before reshuffling at those tables, which removes their predictability, their big advantage. A double deck table where you see a substantial number of cards before the dealer reshuffles is better than a single deck table if that's the case. There's a casino near me, in fact, where this is the reality. So I bypass the single deck tables in favor of the double deck ones.) And at a few casinos in Vegas, you can even find double deck games where the players' cards are dealt face-up. Great games.

It can never be emphasized enough – with fewer cards in play, it's easier to keep track of what cards have been dealt. Playing at a table with only one or two decks is a big plus. As you will find out in Chapter 8, at a pitch game table, you will know better which cards are due and so you can make more astute decisions that will translate into bigger profits.

For example, playing at a single deck table the other day, I noticed that three Aces were dealt in the first round! Wow! That told me a LOT. Number one, it indicated that doubling with a 10 might not be a profitable move. There was only one Ace left. Number two, the dealer was then less likely to have a Blackjack in the next round, or any Ace-enhanced totals. It was time to raise my bet! Now what would that have told me if the same thing had happened at a table with *eight* decks? *Nothing*.

At a 1-deck table, there are sixteen 10-point cards in play, and four Aces. At a 2-deck table, there are thirty-two 10-point cards and eight Aces. With less of those cards in play, it's more obvious when things are askew. Because that gives you a better awareness of whether those crucial cards are either depleted or overdue, you can play a much better game. Compare that to a 6-deck game, where there are ninety-six 10-point cards and twenty-four Aces - and an 8-deck shoe game, where there are one hundred twenty-eight 10-point cards and thirty-two Aces! Can you honestly say you can keep track of that many 10s and Aces? Some of us with extraordinary memories can do a pretty good job of it. But tracking the cards is a lot easier in pitch games, no matter how you cut it.

If you're in a situation where a 10 would bust your hand, will you ever be fairly sure you're NOT going to get one, when you're playing against six or eight decks? Will you remember roughly how many 10s were dealt?

In the middle ground, there are the 4-deck shoe tables, if you can still find any. I haven't seen any for years, but perhaps you'll find them here or there, as competition makes casinos offer better games. I'm not adverse to playing at these tables if there are no 1- or 2-deck games. The action at 4-deck tables is not as extreme as it is at the 6- and 8-deck shoe tables and you can still play a good game. And there are advantages over the pitch game tables. As I mentioned before, the cards are dealt FACE UP, so card counting and **Card Observation** are easier to do (see Chapter 8). Plus, interestingly enough, splitting and doubling opportunities arise more frequently.

Shuffling machine games, no matter how many decks, are not recommended, especially the continuous shufflers and the randomizers. Why deprive yourself of the better games? Shuffling machine games destroy the predictability of the game. The good news is that some casinos, such as Foxwoods, removed them when many players informally boycotted those games.

What Minimum Bet Table Should You Play At?

Now, a word about table minimums. Table minimums are posted on a small plastic sign, usually by the dealer's right hand.

Smaller casinos typically have lower minimums – most tables

69

being in the $1, $3, $5 and $10 range, with an occasional $25 table. In the larger casinos, minimums typically fluctuate, often being raised to their maximum levels on weekend nights. In Atlantic City, it is not unusual to find that the table minimums raised to $25 or $50 on weeknights and weekends. To some, this poses no problem. I personally love the $25 and $50 tables, but most players cringe at the thought of playing there.

Lower minimum tables can still be found in other towns, though. You can still play a $5 minimum game in many locales, and even sometimes find a $3 or $1 minimum table. But too low a minimum bet and you'll never make any money and you'll never know when to quit because you'll never reach a satisfying conclusion. Too high a minimum, of course, and you're courting a scare during a down cycle. You'll need to find a happy medium, a table minimum that both fits your budget and offers enough in potential winnings to make it all worthwhile.

The $5 or $10 tables are perfect for the conservative method I'm teaching you because, while you won't make a ton of money when you win, you should make a satisfying amount of money on your winning days, and your down cycles and occasional losing days will be manageable. Plus you won't have to bring lots of cash with you. You can graduate up from these as your skills grow.

Does It Make A Difference In Which Seat You Sit?

Now although you usually have a choice of sitting at one of seven seats at any table (although, thanks to the revelations in *Cutting Edge Blackjack*, many tables, especially in Vegas, have just six seats and some just five), as I indicated before, you should try to sit in the *third baseman's seat,* the one immediately next to the dealer's right hand, or as near to it as you can get (see Diagram A, page 55). That gives you the advantage of seeing a maximum number of cards before you have to make your decision as to how to play your hand.

And by the way, always ask the players there if it's OK to join the action if you're entering the game midstream, before a fresh reshuffling of the cards. Some players resent newcomers jumping in between shuffles. If they ask you to wait for the next shuffle, decide whether you want to wait for that or not. If it's a good table, you probably would do well to cool your heels and use your waiting time constructively. Let each hand be a mental quiz as to how you would play them.

How to Join the Action

Now, about joining the action at a table: when the dealer has swept the table of cards from the last round (or reshuffled the cards if you're waiting for that), you'll gently place your money on the table in front of you, inside the Insurance circle, near the dealer, when it appears the dealer is ready for you to do that. The dealer will then grab a stack of chips to match the amount of cash you've given him or her, turn toward the pit boss (a casino boss who monitors the tables from a center section or "pit" behind the dealers) and say, "changing $100," upon which the pit boss will look over and acknowledge the transaction. The dealer will then slide your chips across the table until they're in front of you, and you're ready to play!

Oh, and if the dealer tries to give you green $25 chips at a low stakes table, politely say, "no, just red chips please." You won't be making many $25 bets. Mainly, you'll need those red $5 chips. Plus, playing the green chips can draw unwelcome casino attention at those tables.

Strategic Stacking

I'm always amazed at the haphazard piles most players have in front of them. How do they know if they're up or down, or by how much?

So listen to me carefully, now — always keep your $5 chips divided into 5-chip, $25 stacks. (Similarly, when you're ready to play the $25, $50 or $100 tables, you'll stack your $25s in piles of four and your $100 chips in stacks of five. And so on) I call this *Strategic Stacking*.

The stacking of your chips in this way gives you an instant

visual confirmation as to what you have. For betting purposes and knowing when to leave, it's essential you always know exactly how far up or down in chips you are. Strategic Stacking also alerts you to the rare instance where someone might have helped themselves to some of your chips.

Guard Your Chips!

Speaking of which, it's a good idea to keep your chips in front of you, your arms around them guarding them at all times. I always protect my chips now. I learned the hard way.

I've had chips stolen from me by sleight-of-hand artists on several occasions over the course of many years. Each time was the same. By the time I noticed my carefully-stacked piles were diminished, there was no evidence to be had as to who had taken my chips or how.

It is very unlikely the thefts were committed by players at my table. In fact, after seeing televised videotapes of casino thieves in action, I am almost certain I was most often victimized by "hit-and-run" passersby who grabbed my chips when my attention was diverted and quickly walked away. (I did catch a dealer once, stealing one of my $25 chips as he collected the cards from the prior round. So bear that in mind. What did I do? I walked out. To have made a scene would have blown my anonymity. And I wouldn't have been welcome there anymore.)

Anyway, don't be paranoid. Just be aware that this type of thing does occurs on rare occasions, so protect your chips.

Every Player's Doing Differently

By the way, you'll soon notice that unless the dealer busts, it's rare that all players win or lose at the same time. Typically, some are doing well, others not so well. It has to do with repeating patterns that affect each betting spot differently (as my studies have revealed), as well as the differing abilities of each player.

Later on, we'll discuss what this means to you in terms of strategic betting spot choices.

A Confusing Scene

Another word of warning – the casino environment can be a confusing one. Whereas, in big casino towns, such as Atlantic City and Las Vegas, dealers will sometimes help beginners by offering occasional advice (sometimes asking "Do you REALLY want to do that?" for instance), this is NOT usually true elsewhere. In fact, some casinos encourage dealers to mislead you.

At one casino, for example, a dealer tried to discourage a friend of mine from surrendering (a move that gives you a tremendous advantage when used properly). By intimidating players in such a way, some casinos successfully discourage the less confident players from using a very smart option. You have to stick to your guns and what you know to be good strategy and laugh off such bullying.

The same dealer also objected to MY surrendering one hand by saying unkindly, "Everyone lost because you surrendered!" I laughed and snapped back: "Do YOU play Blackjack? Because I'd love to see how YOU play! It was smart to surrender the hand I had!" She shut up, which is what I was hoping for, but we left the table anyway. Who needs ignorant guff like that?

Everyone's A Know-It-All

Also confusing is the advice you tend to get from other players when they notice you are a beginner, and it's often presented in a rude way. SO, LISTEN UP : DO NOT VARY YOUR METHOD BECAUSE OF SUCH ADVICE. IT IS WRONG 99% OF THE TIME.

Understand: most players at casinos are LOSERS. How else would those monuments to grandeur get bankrolled? Big shot players may sound confident with their advice, but don't listen to anyone unless you observe them winning a respectable amount of money *most of the times you've seen them play* — not just in one sitting — and bullies don't tend to be of this variety.

You will only *rarely* get good advice. But even then, don't forget that different players have different styles.   DON'T PLAY MORE THAN ONE SYSTEM AT A TIME. IT'S CONFUSING AND IT WILL LEAD TO LOSSES. STICK TO YOUR GUNS AND STAY

WITH WHAT YOU KNOW IS RIGHT FOR YOU.

Think about it: Do you really think good players would expose themselves to casino scrutiny by teaching you their secrets to beating the house, right in front of the dealer and casino bosses?? No! They'd keep their genius to themselves! Smart winners don't want to be noticed by the casino management, who might bar them from the casino or throw countermeasures at them to disrupt their game. You certainly won't catch me handing out advice at the casino right under the noses of those who could (and would) bar me and put me in the Griffin headshot software that's promulgated to casinos around the world. No thank you.

That's another reason why it should be obvious that the loud-mouths and know-it-alls are more often than not full of hot air.

Why Most People Who Go To Casinos Are Losers

The reality is: *most* blackjack players are losers. *Why?* There are many reasons:

- ♣ Many don't take the time to learn an effective strategy and hone their skills to perfection.
- ♣ Most play on hunches.
- ♣ Most don't understand how to manage their money — they'll put more money on the table when they're **losing,** hoping that their luck is due to get better; or, they'll go up and down in their bets without any semblance of a winning plan.
- ♣ Most don't know how to pick a good casino or even that it is important to learn how to do so.
- ♣ Most don't know how to pick a good table, or even that this skill is important.
- ♣ Most sit at one table and play until their money is gone. They don't think to get up and find a better table when the cards are not good. (Many, in fact, don't recognize that there are such things as good and bad card flows, so they don't know enough to look to spot evidence they're getting bad cards.)
- ♣ Most don't know WHEN TO LEAVE — either on the upside or downside — and wind up STAYING TOO LONG.
- ♣ Most are waiting for that mythical fortune to pile up. Even as

they place small bets, they're hoping to win a lottery fortune, oblivious to this simple equation: you can only win as much as you place in the betting spot. Also, if they DO win some money, they're not content to leave with it, and so they promptly throw it back.

Be Businesslike

Another thing: the temptation once you get going is to chat with other players or the dealer as you play. Resist this.

You need to concentrate! Be polite, but let people know with your body language that you don't want to be disturbed. Otherwise, you will lose track of how the cards are breaking, how you're doing and how the dealer's doing. You'll make mistakes.

Mark my words. Ignore this warning at your own peril. Your money is on the line. Shhhh!!! Think! You can talk to fellow players, if you feel the need to, while the dealer shuffles (although in general, it's best to maintain a low profile).

Oh, and part of being businesslike means you DON'T DRINK when you play. I mentioned this before, but it bears repeating: this may seem like a leisure activity, but it can also feature the sting of monetary losses if you don't respect it.

Your Relationship With The Dealer

Fitting in, with your businesslike attitude, is the way you comport yourself at the table. You'd be smart to be outwardly cordial toward the dealer (primarily in body language). No need to make any enemies. You want the dealer on your side, if possible. But keep conversation to a minimum. Remember, your goal is always to keep as low a profile as possible, to avoid casino scrutiny. If you're rather quiet and you don't get known by casino personnel because of anything you say (because you don't say much), you won't red flag yourself in any way.

DON'T Make The Dealer Your Friend

And, above all, do NOT treat the dealer as your *friend*. One of my readers (let's call him John) learned that one the hard way.

John related to me how he used to befriend all the dealers. He even tried making friends with the casino bosses.

Then, one day, bad news. The dealers John considered his friends could not allow him to play at their tables. Their bosses were concerned that they seemed too chummy. So now, John had generated unwanted scrutiny AND he was limited in the number of tables at which he could play!

But that wasn't the worst part. *Because John won more than not, the casino bosses began to suspect (wrongly) that John was cheating in cahoots with one of the dealers he had befriended.* They witnessed the unusually close relationship and suspicion raised its ugly head. I can't get into details for privacy reasons, but, suffice it to say, it got worse from there.

So don't go down this painful road!

Tipping The *SMART* Way

Now when it comes to tipping the dealer, few players seem to know how or when to do this. Many tip the dealer no matter what. Some never tip the dealer. On a rare few realize it's a strategic choice and needs to be done for good effect only.

While it's true that the dealer depends upon tips to make a living, that doesn't mean you should throw your hard-earned money the dealer's way for no reason. Would you tip a surly waitress? Please don't say yes!

And it's CRAZY to tip a dealer when you're losing. There are various things a dealer can do to make your life easier, even help you win (without cheating). But if you're foolish enough to tip them when you're losing, what incentive do they have to help you out? Tipping should be used as a tool to get certain advantages.

Along these lines, I'll never forget the dealer who, upon noticing the last shuffle had produced a very bad flow of cards for every-one at the table, promptly told us cheerfully: "I'll shuffle up after this hand!" She had not dealt out the cards down to the shuffle marker. In fact, she had only dealt two or three hands. She was just helping us out. (And she could have gotten in trouble for it!)

And then she really shuffled (beyond what the casino's standard procedures called for) clearly trying to change the mix to improve things for us. She understood what I'm trying to teach you: that each mix of cards sets up its own characteristic flow of cards, some good, some bad. She was really trying to help us out by taking the time to better rearrange the cards, in an attempt to create a better sequence.

I promptly tipped her $5 during the next round of action. That let her know: I appreciate your being nice and will reward you when you are. *The tip was not for what she'd just done. It was to give her the incentive to <u>continue</u> being nice.*

Dealers can *really* shuffle the cards, or they can give it window dressing while actually leaving a bad string of cards largely intact. Tip the ones who *really* shuffle the cards when the cards are bad. The pretenders are working against you. DON'T tip them.

Dealers also deserve tips when they see you're in the middle of a winning streak and DON'T shuffle up too soon, nor do they shuffle up every time you place a large bet. If, on the other hand, it looks like they're trying to spoil your game, and they're working hard to defeat you, to win back your winnings for the house, DON'T even THINK of tipping them! There ARE dealers who seem to be rooting for the casino to win and doing every-thing they can to beat you (and there many things they CAN do in this regard). Yet some dealers really root for you and make the game fun. Fine, tip them when you're ahead. That encour-ages them to continually do whatever they can, legally, to help your game. (But, still, don't tip them while you're losing.)

But, DO NOT tip the nasty dealers and the Quick-Ricks who throw the cards at you and speed up the game ridiculously!! You're not giving them an incentive to be nice! Would you throw a dog a bone if he had just bitten you?

How to Tip

Now there are two ways of tipping in blackjack. The simple way is to give them a $1 or $5 chip (or more if you're at a high stakes table) in between rounds. The SMART way is to place a bet on their behalf, letting the money ride on the next round's action. If you win, they win the tip plus an equal amount the tip, riding as a bet, won for them. To do this, place a separate bet in front of your betting spot, telling them, "this is for you." Smart players do it this way because then you get the dealer on your side, to root for you, and, perhaps, to even help you out somehow. (Few dealers would louse up a round on which you'd placed a bet for them. Card mechanics might, but that's a topic for Chapter 11.)

Game Changes

There have been game changes in recent years you need to know about, by the way (some of which were arguably in response to the precision my system has brought to the game). One of which is a lower Blackjack payout at some casinos (6-to-5; it's been 3-to-2 for decades). But that doesn't hurt players who use my system much. Think about it: that's the loss of $3 on a $10 bet. So what? It's regrettable, and you should seek out the casinos who still give you the 3-to-2 payouts if possible, but it's not the big deal Old School writers have made this out to be. It does hurt those who use the older methods, though. They require the extra gains from Blackjacks due to their thin gains and horrible (losing) rounds-won/rounds-lost ratio.

My shuffle tracking methods in *Cutting Edge Blackjack* helped spawn attempts to randomize the cards, through the introduction of shuffling machine games and even some computer simulated videoscreen games (like the now-defunct and God-awful Digital 21 game). Smart players simply avoid those games. And when Foxwoods removed their shuffling machines when less players showed an interest in those games, that was a very good sign.

So, not to worry.

You're still not ready to enter a casino.

4 ♠ ♠

TRICKY 2s, SILENT 7s, AND OTHER SURPRISES

Beware the Big Bad Wolf in Sheep's Clothing: *The Tricky 2*

One of the most amusing times I have ever had playing blackjack happened at a large Atlantic City casino. I sat in the second baseman's seat (smack in the middle of the table, directly opposite the dealer) at a packed table. The gentleman to my left was a tourist from a foreign country, and had many stacks of chips in front of him. He was acting like he wanted everyone to be impressed, that he was a high roller. But, although he made it clear that he felt superior to those around him (in a haughty way, he frequently criticized the moves other players had made), it was also apparent that he did not understand the nuances of the game.

The dealer had a 2 as his up card and, having watched the play of cards carefully, it was obvious to me that low cards were due. I had a 13, and elected to "hit;" that is, I asked the dealer for another card. The man immediately flew into a rage.

"No!" he shouted. "You don't hit a 13 against a 2! You don't know how to play! You should go to another table!"

He was as insulting as he was wrong. To me, it was obvious that the man's understanding of the game had not advanced beyond Basic Strategy.

I smiled, as I noticed my hit card was a 7, for a superior total of 20. Turning to the man calmly, I said in a friendly voice:

"OK, my friend. I'll tell you what! I'll make a bet with you that my way of playing is the correct way. I'll give you $5 every time I lose playing my way against the dealer's 2, if you agree to pay ME $5 every time my strategy wins. Or, make the bet $10, or, $25! I don't care, because I'm gonna win that bet."

The odds were in my favor. Figure it out for yourself: eight of 13 possible types of cards (62%), the Ace through 8, improve a hand of 13 points. Add to this equation that my system told me that *low* cards were due; NOT 9s or 10s, cards that would bust my hand. With low cards due, my move was especially correct. And that's how you play the percentages. Plus, *the DEALER's chance of getting a winning total with his 2 up card was significant*. I was aware of what I call the **Tricky 2s** and this man was not.

"No, I no do that!" he said, angrily turning down my dare. (Yet, HIS playing strategy caused him to lose that round.)

Miraculously, the dealer then seemed to come up with an inordinate amount of 2s as up cards in the next 5 minutes! I won every time, playing my way. The man next to me lost every time because of his faulty reasoning. All of a sudden, after losing against yet another 2, he went ballistic. He started shouting in a foreign language what I figure were not niceties, and then grabbed his pile of chips to leave.

"Please, sir, let me color you in," pleaded the dealer (dealers must exchange players' stacks of red $5 chips, for green $25 chips, so the table doesn't become depleted of the more commonly played red chips).

"No! I no give to you!" the man shouted in his loudest voice, everyone now turning around to look at him, wondering what set him off. Of course, I knew what had made him so angry. He'd been proven <u>wrong</u>! I couldn't help but laugh.

The man wasn't a big winner, by the way. His piles of chips didn't make him smarter than anyone else. If he were a winner then perhaps his snotty attitude might have been understandable on some level. Instead, it just ticked me off.

The points I'm making here are: *number one, watch out for the **Tricky 2s**; and, number two, stick to your own strategy and don't let a "know-it-all" bully you into playing a strategy that will cause you to lose your money.*

The truth of the matter (which you rarely read or hear about) is that – **at BEST – the dealer busts only about ONE-THIRD of the time when his or her up card is a 2**. *Many books and dealers will tell you to STAND on anything above an 11 or 12 against a dealer's 2, implying that the dealer is likely to bust. Very wrong. That 2 is practically nonexistent. The dealer can pull up to a total of 19 points (including the hole card) and win!*

Do you realize how many card combinations produce totals of 15 through 19 to make the dealer's up card of 2 a winner? Literally HUNDREDS! Especially in a multi-deck game!

In fact, what I'm telling you was hinted at in one of the many charts Julian Braun of IBM produced during his famous computer studies of the 1960s. Buried in other data, the chart clearly showed that *the dealer's 2 is <u>disadvantageous</u> to the player if the card count is moderately to very negative* (I'll teach you about counting in Chapter 8, but it basically means that *if 10s have been depleted, the dealer's 2 is strong*). And my research has shown the Tricky 2 attains high scores when the dealer doesn't bust.

Let's explore this. The 10-point cards account for only 4 of 13 cards. So, 9/13s (69%) of the time, the dealer will have cards that total LESS. If the hole card is a 9, the dealer has 11 points, with a 62% probability of drawing a 6 or greater, giving the house a winning score of 17 or more. If, instead, the hole card is an 8, the dealer now has a total of 10 and has a 62% chance of getting a 7, 8, 9, 10 or Ace, obtaining a winning total. If, instead, the dealer's hole card is a 7, and now has a total of 9, he can draw ANY card and not bust; AND 54% of the cards the dealer might get (Ace, 8, 9, 10, J, Q, K) provide a winning total. Even if the dealer's hole card IS a 10, then **9** of 13 cards would improve that score! (The popular myth that the dealer's hole and hit card will likely be 10s, busting the dealer, is right only 9.5% of the time!)

What I am suggesting is that the dealer's 2 is NOT a weak up

card. It should be played carefully. The 2 most often gives the dealer strong results. In fact, the dealer's 2 achieves the top winning score of 21 points more than 12% of the time, *more than any other up card;* roughly <u>twice</u> as often as the dealer's 7 through Ace, excepting the dealer's Weakened 10 (the 10 not considering Blackjacks, against which you don't have a turn, at most casinos); the dealer's 2 achieves <u>three times</u> as many 21s as the dealer's Weakened 10 does! (I'll share more research results in detail in *Cutting Edge Blackjack.* I don't want to over-load you with too much math here.) Given all this, you will learn in Chapter 10 that sometimes it's wise to pull a card against the dealer's 2 even if you have a stiff (that is, once you are skilled enough to know how to predict when low cards are overdue).

Just understand: *the dealer's 2 achieves winning totals most of the time, 65% of the time.* So when you *know* the dealer won't likely bust, YOU must pull to a winning total.

And that's a closely guarded secret the casinos don't want you to know. I'll talk more about the Tricky 2 in Chapter 10 on Advanced Strategy.

Take Advantage of the Dealer's "Silent 7"

Now let's talk about the myth of the dealer's 7, said to be a dealer-friendly card. Is it really? Or is it a sheep in a wolf's clothing?

Shortly after writing the First Edition of this book, I was leafing through Lawrence Revere's excellent book *Playing Blackjack as a Business*, when I stumbled across this line:

"Notice that if the deck is very negative [when, in his counting system, Aces and 10-pointers have been depleted], *the best card the dealer can have for the player is a 7.*"

(I put part of the sentence in italics and bolded it for your consideration. The bracketed explanation is mine.)

NO ONE ELSE I'VE READ HAS TAKEN NOTE OF WHAT I CALL THE **SILENT 7** BUT HERE, REFERRING TO JULIAN BRAUN'S COMPUTER STUDIES CHARTS, MR. REVERE MADE NOTE OF IT IN PASSING. He apparently did not recognize what he was onto, because *he did not integrate that insight into his strategy!*

What we want to do is not just say "That's interesting!," but instead take a closer look at the dealer's 7 and then *adjust our strategy when facing it.*

One interesting thing about Mr. Revere's chart (page 132 of his book) is that — although is based upon a far different counting method than you will learn in Chapter 8 — it reveals to us that when the count is moderately negative (when low cards are overdue), *the 7 is the **only** dealer up card aside from the 6 that provides the player with a winning advantage. In that situation, the 7 is likely to make the dealer bust or help the player win and, more to the point, **it's even more likely to cause the dealer to lose than the dealer's 6!!!***

In fact, the dealer's 7 *always* lets you to win more than you will lose. (This has been proven in dramatic detail in the data I will reveal to you in *Cutting Edge Blackjack*.)

Suffice it to say, the popular myth that the dealer's 7 is a bad card for you is absolutely WRONG.

Interestingly enough, when the count is positive — when 10s are overdue — Revere's computer studies show that the dealer's

7 is even more advantageous to the player than when the count is negative (meaning that the player will win even more against it in that situation).

I, in fact, first developed my theory about the dealer's Silent 7 years ago without the aid of a computer. It seemed painfully obvious to me. Follow my thinking:

When the dealer has a 7, what does that really mean? The dealer's hole card could be any one of the four 10-point cards, and give the dealer a total of 17 points. Or, the dealer could have an Ace in the hole, with a total of 18 points. Fine. But that's only five of 13 possible hole cards (31%). Not exactly a majority of times. (And those give the dealer low winning scores!)

Yes, it is true that three more of the 13 possible hole cards (the 2, 3, or 4) would combine with the dealer's 7 without resulting in a dangerous stiff hand total. But I believe that way of thinking is misleading. As you will see, that does NOT tell the whole story.

Because, if the dealer's hole card *is* a 2, 3, or 4, what are the odds, then, that those cards will produce a winning hand?:

If it's a 2, giving the dealer a total of 9, 7 of 13 possible hit cards (54%) would provide the house with a winning hand. However, of those cards, 2 would result in a total of 17 and 18, which are low winning totals. More to the point — only 5 of the 13 possible cards (the Ace and the 10-pointers), or 38%, would give the 7-2 combination a *strong* winning point total.

OK, now if the hole card is a 3, giving the dealer a total of 10, 8 of 13 cards (62%) would provide the house with a winning hand — but only 6 of those cards (less than 50%) would give the dealer a *strong* winning total.

And if the hole card is a 4, giving the dealer a total of 11, 8 of 13 cards (62%) would provide the house with a winning hand. But only 6 (less than 50%) would give the dealer a *strong* winning total.

So, let's see what we've shown here:

With 5 of 13 hole cards — 38% — the house has a total of between 17 and 18 points — low on the winning scale of things. If your hand, facing that 7, was higher than 18, YOU'D win those

85

hands. Well, since 18 is not amongst the three strongest winning totals — 19, 20 and 21 — you'd stand a good chance of beating it, if not tying it!

And, the 3 other hole cards we've examined (the 2, 3, or 4) would either pull to mostly weak winning scores, or put the dealer in danger of busting, more than not.

Those are the GOOD hole cards for the dealer. What about the possible hole cards we haven't looked at — the 5, 6, 7, 8 and 9? These 5 cards would combine with the up card of 7 to give the dealer *stiffs* — dangerous, bustable hard totals of 12 through 16.

Does this "picture" really give the dealer the edge with a 7 up card? I think NOT! In fact, my studies have shown the Silent 7 attains the lowest average score of any dealer up card and leads to dealer losses more than not.

So, then should you *stand* on a 13, 14, 15 or 16 against a dealer's 7? Sometimes *yes,* if, as an advanced player, you are pretty sure that the dealer's hole card is NOT a 10 or an Ace, and also that the hit card you'd get would be likely to bust you. Yes, you often should play the dealer's 7 differently than traditionally recommended!

You will really be able to take advantage of this information when you've mastered some of the more advanced concepts that I am about to teach you.

Suffice it to say, I have proven that the dealer's 7 more often than not acts like a **player's** card. I call it the Silent 7 because the 7 *silently* masquerades as something it is not. It's a sheep in wolf's clothing, and this is the first book I know of to reveal this.

So, with this understanding, let's update our list of which dealer up cards favor us.

We will now call these dealer up cards OUR CARDS, the PLAYER'S CARDS:

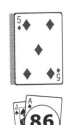

And we will now call these up cards the DEALER'S CARDS:

And No Longer Fear The Dealer's 8!

Now let me add one more surprise. <u>The dealer's 8 is also a player-friendly card</u>! My studies have revealed that you will beat it more than not (because it achieves low scores). In fact, it's more player-friendly than the dealer's 3! So meet your new friend:

So the dealer and player both have six up cards in their favor. The dealer-friendly up cards are the 9, four 10s and Ace; the player-friendly up cards are the 3 through 8.

*But what about the Tricky 2? That's a **neutral** card. A Basic Strategy player will beat it as often as he or she will lose to it, in the long run. (And if you don't play it like a <u>weak</u> card, as is traditionally taught, you can even gain an edge!)*

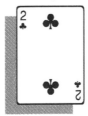

With your state-of-the-art understanding now of which cards are truly in your favor and which ones are NOT will come an ability to make smarter, more profitable moves! (More on this later.)
You are still not ready to enter a casino.

5
♣

STIFFS,
DOUBLING
&
SPLITTING

State-of-the-art blackjack is all about precision. If the Old School methods were akin to the drop-and-pray carpet bombing of World War II, we're all about laser-guided precision.

Whereas older methods were happy with looking at a lifetime of disparate rounds without discrimination and taking a one-size-fits-all tactic that produced marginal returns and opened you up to too much risk, we're looking to fine tune our moves with a flexible strategy that picks the most appropriate move of the moment to win a maximum number of rounds and max out our gains.

The Math That Busts The Myth On How To Play Stiffs

When it came to stiffs (bustable hands of 12-16 points), the Old School methods sent you down to certain defeat (without telling you) because they could not see the trees for the forest. They conveniently chose to ignore these equations:

43% wins - 57% losses = -14% (BEST case)
35% wins - 65% losses = -30% (WORST case)

For what did they tell you when the dealer was showing a low up card? "Let the dealer bust!" As if that was *inevitable!*

But what's the truth? The dealer's 4, which busts the <u>most</u>, busts just 43% of the time overall (that is, over the course of a *lifetime* of action). The dealer's 2, which busts the <u>least</u> of the low up cards, busts just 35% of the time. *So it is <u>NEVER</u> likely the dealer will bust, even with the dealer's <u>weakest</u> up cards!*

Anyone who understands probability statements understands the equations above (the top one showing your results versus the dealer's 4 and the bottom one your results versus the dealer's 2) dispute the "let the dealer bust" logic. They show you the dealer will most likely reach an acceptable score even with the most player-friendly up cards.

A smart researcher would look at this and realize his goal should be to produce a method to identify when the dealer is most likely to score. Then, you, the player would know when NOT to leave your stiffs hanging in the wind when the dealer was obviously going to beat those stiffs. This is how I approached this problem and so you now have the means to avoid unnecessary losses.

Because if you ALWAYS stand with your stiffs versus the dealer's low up cards (the Old School way), the equations above show the results. The math is clear: if you blindly stand on stiffs, you're really saying "let the dealer <u>score</u>!" Or, "let me lose!"

For if the dealer's 4 busts just 43% of the time, logic dictates the opposite is true - the dealer will achieve an acceptable score (and beat your stiffs) 57% of the time! And - worse yet - <u>you will lose 65% of the time ALWAYS standing on your stiffs of 13-16 versus the dealer's 2</u>. (Your results will fall in between those of the 4 and 2 for the rest of the low up cards.)

These are not acceptable odds. Especially since my studies reveal that <u>you will be dealt stiffs 54% of the time</u>! So these are the hands you especially need to know how to handle properly and precisely. You cannot just let them hang on a wing and a prayer. You need a modern, more accurate approach, so you can tell precisely how to play your stiffs for better results.

And there isn't one correct move that works for every such situation. The wisdom of making any particular move depends on: what cards were dealt; what the card imbalances of the moment are; what the dealer's hole card is likely to be and therefore what the dealer's likely outcome will be; what hit cards are likely to come your way and therefore what your likely outcome will be; your ability to compete against the dealer's outcome given all of this; and so on.

"Outs," "Good Outs" And "Handmakers"

In this chapter, we'll talk about handling many of the hands you get that require smart decisions. The first such category of hands we'll discuss are the stiffs. And I have some great entry-level methods even beginners can master, to handle stiffs the smart way. For instance, one learning tool that's really sets off lightbulbs in the heads of players at my seminars is a concept of "**outs**," which I borrowed from the poker world. Outs in poker are the potential cards that would make a hand competitive. In blackjack your "outs" are cards you need to turn your hand into a possible winner, or ones that at the very least won't bust you.

With stiffs, your outs would be the hit cards that would give you any one of the five acceptable "winning" totals: 17 through 21. (I put the word "winning" in quotes here because <u>a 17 point hand loses more rounds than it wins</u> and <u>an 18 point hand is below par;</u> <u>the average winning score, for the dealer and player, is 19.</u>) With hands of 11 or fewer points, your "outs" would include all cards that do not bust you. The ones that would give your hand a bustable score of 12-16 points (which I call "stiffmakers") are obviously less desirable than outs that would give you a total of 17-21 points.

That's why I distinguish between "outs" and "**good outs**" (G-Os), aka "**handmakers.**" Good outs are the ones that give you a fighting good chance of winning: the ones that give you hands of 21 or 20 points (in that order) and, of lesser merit, 19 points.

The idea is to assess the cards that have been dealt to see how likely you are to get an "out" or, better yet, a handmaker. The answer not only tells you what move to make but also how likely you are to beat the dealer. Without these cards your chances of winning are nil, so you need to know if they're available and - more important - in what proportion. Do the undealt cards contain enough G-Os to make it worthwhile to hit? Or should you stand? Surrender?

When it comes to your 16 point hard totals, for instance, your "good outs" would especially be 5s and 4s, in that order, because they'd provide you with totals of 21 and 20 points respectively. To a lesser extent, 3s might also be considered one of your "good outs." Not so much 2s, though, and certainly not Aces, because <u>a 17 point hand is a losing hand, over time</u>. You must factor that in.

With 12 point hands, your handmakers would be 9s and 8s, in that order, and to a lesser extent 7s. With 13 point hands, 8s, 7s and 6s. With 14 point hands, 7s, 6s and 5s. With 15 point hands, 6s, 5s, and 4s. And with 16 point hands, as I said, 5s, 4s and 3s. Those would give you high totals that would stand a good chance of beating the dealer - or with the lowest of the "good outs" (which give you the average score, 19 points), a good chance at least of pushing.

<u>You also need to take the dealer's likely result into consideration</u>, though. If the dealer's highly likely to bust, the subject of outs becomes moot; you'll simply stand on your stiffs. But if the dealer's not likely to bust, you need to assess the availability of your "outs" before you can tell how competitive your position is and therefore what your best move should be.

Now the good news is that even a beginner can learn to look at the cards and draw intelligent conclusions along these lines. You'll learn these skills in later chapters. But obviously, the fewer "outs" that are available, the less wise hitting becomes as an option.

Rock And Hard Place Hands

Now you need to understand that sometimes you will find yourself between a proverbial rock and hard place, with little hope of winning.

Some card situations are so bad - based upon the hand you've been dealt and the dealer's likelihood of scoring - that your chances will be almost nil or, in some circumstances, absolutely nil. I call these "**rock and hard place hands**."

This is typically where the dealer has a high likelihood of drawing to an acceptable score, you've been dealt a stiff and your hit cards are most likely to bust you. For example, this would occur when high cards are overwhelmingly overdue when the dealer's hole card is dealt in rounds where the dealer's up card is a 7 or better and you have a stiff, facing the same imbalance.

Surrender these hands if it's allowed! If it's not, whether you hit or stay depends on your read of the odds. But don't sweat it. Your chances are slim to none no matter what you do. That's OK. That's part of the game too. Get used to it.

The Law Of "Likes And Dislikes" & The Dealer's Hand

But there are plenty of rounds where you'll hold a stiff where you do have a choice and you can grab victory out of the jaws of defeat with a smart move. Sometimes that'll mean standing on your stiff when you can ascertain the dealer's likely to bust - whether with a low or high up card. Other times that'll mean taking a hit card when it might not be thought wise by those still following the antiquated Old School methods.

And I've invented an entry-level method to help you determine what move is correct. It tips you off to the dealer's likely outcome. I call it the **Law of Likes And Dislikes**.

You see, <u>when the cards that have been dealt are mostly of the same ("like") category of card as the dealer's up card - they're either both low or both high cards - the dealer statistically has a much higher likelihood of busting</u>. Why? If the dealer's up card is low (one of the 2s through 7s) and the cards dealt are mainly low, there's statistically a much higher likelihood that the dealers' hole card and hit cards will be high (one of the 8s through 10s), and these are the cards most likely to bust the dealt. And if the dealer's up card is high and the cards dealt mainly high, there's a greater likelihood the dealer's hole card will give the dealer a stiff, which makes the dealer more likely to bust.

A great way to recall this "Law of Likes" tipoff is to remember: We "like" situations when the dealt cards and the dealer's up card are "likes." The dealer's more likely to bust than normal!

Conversely, when the majority of the cards dealt and the dealer's up card are of opposite categories (they're unlike), look out. This often signals trouble. This easily spotted situation usually indicates the dealer's likely to achieve a good score.

Why? When high cards have been overwhelmingly dealt when the dealer has a low up card, the dealer's statistically most likely to get a low card in the hole and low cards as hit cards - a combination that results mainly in acceptable dealer scores. And when the cards dealt have mainly been low when the dealer shows a high up card, the dealer's mathematically more likely to have a high card in the hole, resulting in a high 2-card score.

To recall this "Likes And Dislikes" tipoff, remember: We *dislike* situations where the dealer's up card and other cards on the table are *unlike* each other! The dealer's too strong!

(FYI: To be most precise, your "cards dealt" assessments should include cards from prior rounds. What have they primarily been? High or low? You'll learn how to keep track of this later.)

Doubling The Old School Way

Now the two powerful concepts you just learned - the "outs" and the "Law of Likes and Dislikes" - also help you determine whether it's smart to double or split. But there are a few other things you need to understand about those moves to handle them successfully. Because you have to rethink these moves to throw off the old myths you undoubtedly learned before.

You see, when it came to doubling advice, the problem with the Old School methods was that they were incapable of identifying losing situations. So they told you "always" to double in certain situations, hoping you'd scrape off a few extra percent in gains over the course of a lifetime of rounds because their methods lacked the precision to guide you properly as to when doubling was smart and, conversely, when the extra monetary risk was not justified.

The end result of this indiscriminate, one-move-fits-all-situations tactic was that you wound up with a slim margin of winning rounds over losing rounds. This inflexible approach had you doubling your bet when that was tantamount to throwing good money against bad.

Because what's the drawback to doubling? You're limited to just one hit card. And so even normally good doubling opportunities - such as when you have hands of 10 or 11 points - can be highly unwise when facing bad card imbalances, ones that create the likelihood you'll receive the worst hit cards while giving the dealer winning scores. (There is an advantage to doubling, though. You don't bust!)

The good news is that even a beginner can learn to tell when the "outs" that make those moves wise are there or not. For example, what have many players have been taught about doubling with an 11 point hand? John Scarne, In *Scarne On Cards*, states: "Always double down on a count of 11 no matter what the value of the dealer's up card is." And that's typical Old School advice.

But my studies show that players who <u>always</u> double with an 11 points versus the dealer's Ace underperform those who <u>always</u> hit. ALWAYS double here and you'll win 5% more hands than you lose and your gains will be double that. Yet if you ALWAYS <u>hit</u> here, you'll win nearly 19% more rounds than you lose - giving you four times the rounds won and nearly double the gains you would get by always doubling. (This is using the Old School model, assuming flat betting - which is a false assumption. More on that in a moment.) And <u>we can do even better by doubling only when it's smart</u> (especially when you factor in how the size of your bet affects the math, as you'll see soon).

The point is, any "always" do such-and-such-a-move type strategy is destined to diminish player returns. Imagine applying that nonsense to baseball. The hitter comes up and ALWAYS swings, no matter how bad the pitch. Or he ALWAYS stands still, hoping for a walk. Would these strategies work? No, you pick your pitches. You stand still when the pitch is bad, hit the pitch when it's in the zone. That basic philosophy applies to blackjack as well.

The reason your 11 point hand is so strong is the imbalance in blackjack that favors the 10 point cards (due to the fact there are four of them - the "pips," the ones that say "10" that is, and the three face cards). This natural imbalance provides your 11 with a high percentage of hands (relatively speaking) with the top winning score, 21. And yet as you can see, doubling's drawback (the obtaining of just one hit card) is such that hitting is sometimes your best option, even with this great starting hand. For instance, when facing a bad card imbalance (in the undealt cards) where the 10s are under-represented, your advantage can disappear.

Granted, the 9s and to a lesser extent the 8s would be welcome hit cards when doubling on an 11 because <u>the dealer's Ace, sans blackjacks (when you have no turn), achieves scores of 19 or above only</u>

95

45% of the time. Even so, the most-desired hit cards when doubling on your 11 (the four 10s, the 9s and 8s) account for just 46% of the deck. And the dealer's weakened Ace (sans blackjacks) only busts 15% of the time. So doubler beware.

Yet - that being said - a state-of-the-art player should still look for opportunities to double here, because he or she has the skills to know when it's smart. Once you know how to analyze the cards (with the skills you'll learn in later chapters), it'd be smart to double here when high cards are highly likely to come next.

Now what cards don't you want in doubling on an 11? The Aces through 6s and to a lesser extent the 7s. When are these undesirable cards likely to come your way? When 8s through 10s have been over-dealt (and Aces through 7s have been under-dealt). Actually, since you most want scores of 20 or 21 points when doubling in situations where the dealer is likely to score - especially versus the dealer's Ace and 10, the two most fearsome up cards - all you'd have to track would be the 9s and 10s. And if you know you're not likely to get them, it'd be CRAZY to double. You're too likely to lose!

Are you getting it? The way to higher gains is through fine tuning your moves to suit the occasion. I won't cover all the doubling opportunities here. But let's look at one or two others, to get your brain thinking.

For instance, should you ALWAYS double on your 10 point hands versus the dealer's Ace? Some Old School books say yes, some no. (But, again, the answer should never be "always" do any one move.) Here, by ALWAYS doubling you'll suffer losses of 3%; you'll lose more rounds than you'll win. Your 10, unlike your 11, doesn't achieve so many 21 point hands, especially with the one-hit-card-only doubling drawback. You'd do better if you always hit here. You'd win 9 more rounds than you'd lose per every 100 rounds you play this situation (assuming flat betting). But we can do even better than that by doubling when it's smart and otherwise hitting.

When is it NOT smart to double here? When 2s through 8s are likely to be dealt when our turn arrives. We most want 10s and Aces to fall on our hand; 9s would also give us somewhat good odds of winning (since, as I said before, the dealer's Ace only achieves hands of 19 or greater 45% of the time). So beware situations where the 10s and Aces have been dealt in greater than normal numbers and 2s through 8s have been under-dealt. Therefore, if Aces and 10s have been overplayed before your turn, why would you risk TWICE your original bet on a situation that's a likely loser for you?

Now you were also taught to ALWAYS double on your 11 versus the dealer 10...But should you? (There's a fly in the ointment.)

A HUGE Flaw In Old School Research Invalidates It

The trouble is the Old School researchers used a flat-betting model in reaching their conclusions. They did not test for bet variations; they assumed players always made the same bet! Why should that matter?

Because the flat-betting model is just <u>wrong</u>. No one bets the same each round. And when you toss out this illogical assumption, you realize that <u>the size of your bets affects the math behind the wisdom of making card moves</u>. This factor is impossible to state in absolute terms because betting styles differ - which is why the Old School researchers chose to ignore this vital piece of reality. Here's what *The World's Greatest Book* had to say about that (and they used the computer research of Julian Braun of IBM, whose data was also relied upon by Edward Thorp and a gang of other Old School authors):

> "In practice, a player's bets would increase gradually, but this is *impractical to program* and would create *distortions* in the comparisons."

Impractical? Maybe. But that doesn't justify taking the lazy way out and ignoring this issue, especially as it impacts player losses. (This also points to the drawbacks of the Old Schoolers having done black-jack research with computer-generated data! It makes studying real-world blackjack issues "impractical.")

This exposes a glaring omission in their mathematical calculations. They're leaving out a common player trait: variations in bet size. **Therefore the Old School books set you up for far greater losses than they admitted to. Especially since they compound things by instructing players to make risky maximum bets at the wrong times! All this leads to dramatic and devastating downswings, such as the ones reported by Edward Thorp in *Beat The Dealer*.** I'm not making this up - you can read about it! (And, by the way: <u>If the Old Schoolers, by their own admission, cannot program their computers to test blackjack methods when varying bets are in the mix, how can they claim to know what strategy is the best</u>? Think about it!)

<u>Gains should be looked at NOT from a theoretical wins and losses</u>

standpoint but from the standpoint of what you actually bring home. That's the true measure of any blackjack system's effectiveness: how much money you make. I don't care what anyone says. If you come home with less money than you went with, you're a loser - even if your computer tells you that you made the "correct" moves (when considered over the course of more rounds than you'll ever play).

So here's the deal: if you ALWAYS hit your 11 versus the dealer's 10, you'll win 15 more rounds per 100 than you lose. If you ALWAYS double, you'll win 8 more rounds per 100 than you lose (you'll lose 43 out of every 100 rounds, winning 51 and pushing in 6). So you'll win fewer rounds by always doubling than by always hitting, but your gains theoretically grow by a minuscule 1% by risking twice the size of your bet in good and bad situations without discrimination.

Trouble is, in attempting to squeeze out that theoretical extra 1% you're taking on too much risk. They're not alerting you to when it's not wise to double. And if you have a huge bet on a hand where doubling's highly unwise, you'll compound your mistake by increasing the amount of money you have on a hopeless situation and with the inevitable huge monetary loss you'll suffer you'll dig a big hole for yourself. Psychologically and financially. It'll likely take several sessions to recoup those losses, a discouraging setback.

Varying Bet Sizes Only Accentuate Old School Flaws

In fact, I am going to make it painfully clear the price you'll pay in monetary terms for following Old School methods based on the false myth of flat betting, with this conservative, highly plausible example:

Let's take the Old Schoolers' dictate that you must ALWAYS hit your 16s versus the dealers' 10 (if surrender is not allowed). In doing this, they say, you'll save one percent over hitting, over the course of a lifetime of blackjack rounds.

So in our example we'll have our player ALWAYS hitting his 16s versus the dealer's 10 and we'll look at how he did in 100 rounds of doing this. Now, to keep this simple, let's say in 99 of these rounds he flat-bet; always making a $5 bet. But in one round, we'll say he placed the table maximum $500 bet. This sized bet would not be unusual for an Old School player. Most Old School books tell you to do this when Aces are overdue (which, by the way, is exactly the WRONG time to do this - if betting extremes were ever smart, which they're not). And let's say our player then loses this $500 bet, which after all is the most likely result (my studies show you'll lose 74 out of 100 rounds hitting your 16 versus the dealer's 10 and you'll win only 20 of the rounds; you'll push in the other six).

Now the Old School logic goes like this: Because players will lose 74% and win 20% of the rounds when hitting 16 point hands versus the dealer 10, overall losses would amount to: 19.57% wins - 74.44% losses = a 54.87% deficit. That's less than the 56% deficit you'd incur, they reason, by standing (where you'd win only when the dealer's 10 busted, which occurs 22% of the time, so: 22% of the rounds won when the dealer busts - 78% of the rounds lost when the dealer scores = a 56% deficit). In this way, using a flat-betting model, they concluded that by ALWAYS hitting your 16 versus the dealer's 10, you save 1% in losses in the long run.

But is this true? Let's add up the _real_ losses - in monetary terms. Because our player lost 74 out of 100 rounds, 73 of them at $5 and one at $500, he racked up real monetary losses of $865. He also won 20 rounds at $5 each, for $100 in gains. So overall, he lost $765. This means his real monetary losses amounted to roughly 90% of his total bet outlay! His _real_ overall deficit was nearly 80% (in other words, 10% in monetary gains minus 90% in monetary losses) - much more than predicted by the Old Schoolers' flat-betting model.

Given this picture, isn't it clear that the Old School one-size-fits-all approach based on flat betting sets you up for more losses than anyone had ever imagined? Think of it: The player in this example would have done far better by flat betting and standing on his 16s than by following the faulty Old School strategy.

When flat betting beats the monetary results the so-called "correct" Old School strategies produce, there's something terribly wrong! You cannot devise an inflexible card strategy - and, worse yet, one that ignores monetary factors (namely variations in the size of your bets) - and expect it to produce anything but disastrous losses.

How This Impacts Your Card Strategy

What I'm telling you is that you should quickly move beyond the Old School strategies to a more effective and modern approach; one that is more discriminating. Because the more awareness you have about the forces that make the game winnable, the less you will be willing to accept the losing ways of the past. You need a flexible strategy - one that reacts to the card realities of the moment and factors in your bet size.

Especially make sure conditions are HIGHLY right for doubling when your bet is much higher than your average bet. If they're not, your alternative to doubling as you know now, hitting, is no consolation prize; it gives you a <u>higher</u> likelihood of winning!

How does this relate to doubling on your 11 point hand versus the dealer's 10? Make sure you don't do it when you're likely to get 8s or less. The dealer's weakened 10 (sans blackjacks) achieves scores of 19 or better 55% of the time! <u>And if your bet is well above your average bet and you're not sure what to do, DON'T double! HIT.</u> That's no sacrifice, as you now know.

Another Bad Bet

Another Old School mistake, by the way, was in telling you to ALWAYS double on your 10 versus the dealer's 9 (the dealer's third strongest up card). In fact you'd win twice as many rounds and 1% more in gains by always hitting than you would by always doubling. And you'd avoid the added risk doubling brings on.

But you'd do even better by using state-of-the-art blackjack methods to tell you when doubling is smart. The dealer's 9 only achieves scores of 20 or higher 17% of the time. That's its Achilles heel. So if you know 10s and Aces are the most likely cards you'll get (as in when the other cards were over-dealt and the 10s and Aces were under-dealt), there's your window of opportunity.

One Additional Case Where Doubling Is Smart

On the flip side of things, I'm going to tell you about a situation where my research has indicated that you can safely double where others have told you not to. That is, when your total is 9 points and the dealer is showing a 7.

This is just one example of how you can take advantage of your knowledge of how weak the Silent 7 is. As you saw in Chapter 4, the dealer's 7 leads to low dealer scores. Even with the restriction of getting just one hit card when doubling, your 9 point hand will do very well. My numbers show that you will see a return of nearly 27% over time when always doubling in this situation, versus a roughly 19% benefit when you always hit your 9 versus the 7. It's a no-brainer.

And yet, even here, once you have higher skills and a more modern understanding of the game, you'll want to fine tune this move; time it to when it's smartest. That is, you can increase your gains by restricting doubling in this situation to rounds in which you know 9s, 10s and

100

Aces are your most likely hit cards.

There's No Free Lunch With Doubling

And don't think you have a free ride against even the weakest of the dealer's up cards. As you now know, the <u>highest</u> of their busting rates is just 43%. That means that the dealer USUALLY scores. And we, as state-of-the-art players, don't want to double when we're likely to lose - when we're likely to get a hand of 16 or less points when the dealer is likely to score. So always factor in the dealer's likelihood of busting and DON'T wildly double when the dealer's strong even against the dealer's 4 through 6!

In general, I like this conservative rule: <u>You should not double when the dealer is likely to score when your point total is not likely to top 19</u>, the average winning score. <u>Especially when your original bet is significantly higher than your average bet</u>. (A loss of a significantly-higher-than-average-bet can put you in a hole that may take two or more subsequent playing sessions to overcome, depending on its size, so you should be especially cautious in <u>doubling</u> bets of that nature!) So be sure to factor in your likelihood of getting a horrible low card that would produce a subpar total when deciding whether or not to double.

Bottom line: YOU ONLY WANT TO DOUBLE DOWN WHEN YOU HAVE A CLEAR WINNING EDGE ON THE DEALER! If you don't (or you're not sure), the choice of hitting instead of doubling gives you the advantage of being able to draw as many cards as you need to make your hand work, thereby increasing your odds of winning. Go for the likely win.

Doubling The SMART Way

In sum, <u>doubling is only smart if</u>:

① <u>You know the dealer's highly likely to bust (so you don't care what hit card you get - assuming you're doubling with a hand of 11 or fewer points) OR</u>

② <u>You know the one hit card you'll get will likely result in your beating the dealer's likely score</u>

...And we'll talk more about doubling in Chapter 10...

Multiple Splitting Often Leads To Multiple Losses

Now you'll also need to readjust your thinking when it comes to splitting, because if you read any Old School books, you're in for a shocker. When it came to splitting, the Old Schoolers often had you doing so (at twice or more the cost of your original bet) in losing situations - without warning you that you were in losing situations.

There's ample evidence they were aware of some splitting opportunities were likely losers but failed to tell you so - such as when they told you to "always split your pairs of 8s" even versus the dealer's 9, 10 and Ace. They also did not seem to understand that <u>multiple splitting under such losing conditions only increases your likely losses</u>. With a maximum four split hands, for example, in a losing situation (such as when splitting 8s versus the dealer's 9, 10 and Ace), you're only *quadrupling* your probable <u>losses</u>. Is that smart? (In fact, if you split 8s more than once versus the dealer's 9 and 10 and more than twice versus the dealer's Ace, your losses, even with a flat-betting model, are well above 50%! So DON'T!)

Another example - you're told to split 6s versus the dealer's 2. But my studies show that ALWAYS splitting here costs you 36% in losses - and that's based on a flat-betting model. Actual losses would be much higher. Always <u>hitting</u> costs you <u>less</u>, 26% in losses (again with a flat betting model; actual losses are much higher). One of the peculiarities of the 6 is that it has a terrible chemistry with 62% of your possible hit cards (the 6s through the 10s); they combine with your 6 to give you a stiff. Do you really want to DOUBLE in such a horribly losing situation? NOT! So simply hit if the dealer's likely to score or <u>stand</u> if you know the dealer's likely to bust when your hit cards will likely bust you.

How do you identify losing splitting situations? A good rule of thumb is: <u>If you're splitting cards whose results, as an up card, would be worse than the dealer's, you're in a losing situation</u>. For example, the dealer's 6 fares worse for the dealer than its 7. So it figures that that your 6s don't compete well, when split, against the dealer's 7! (Your losses will be 25%, with a flat-betting model.)

How To Factor In Your Bet

And by the way (you'll read it here first): <u>If you have a higher than average bet, you should multiply the projected flat-betting-model losses by the size of your bet divided by your average bet, to calculate your **true losses**</u>. *Therefore, once you're up to two times your average bet or higher, the math changes such that many splitting situations are unwise.* At double your average bet size, you should surrender your pairs of 3s versus the dealer's 9 through Ace. Splitting your pairs of 2s would save you money over hitting them as a 4 point hand at twice your average bet versus the high dealer up cards, but once your bet is 2.5 times or greater than your average bet, surrender your pairs of 2s too. *At three times your average bet you should surrender pairs of 8s versus the dealer's 9 through Ace* (if that's allowed)! If surrender's not allowed, simply hit all these hands - except the pairs of 8s, which are stiffs; here, gauge hitting against the dealer's likelihood of busting.

Aces & Preserving Your Bankroll

Can I add here, too, how <u>dumb</u> it is to ALWAYS split Aces?! What happens when low cards are overdue and the dealer is likely to score? TWO lost hands at DOUBLE the price! (Just HIT your pairs of Aces in those situations. It's a good starting hand.)

Preserving your bankroll is an essential skill if you're going to become a consistent winner, and part of that involves being smart enough to know when you're beat or when you must alter your strategy to accommodate the shifting odds created by a card imbalance or an overly large bet. The Old School idea of chasing losses with more money in order to hope to theoretically save a buck or two on losses by the end of your life is crazy. Especially since, as you now know, their math was flawed because they - admittedly - failed to do the proper research. They did not test for how bet variations affect your outcome, and this factor can lead to higher losses.

You can't become a winner if you're constantly throwing your chips to the wind and busting out. You need to stay in it to win it. Short term losers become long term losers. Conserve your chips with smart decisions so you've got the bankroll necessary to capitalize on good hands when they come your way.

And before you take the Old School books' word for it, here's something else to ponder: Another major flaw of theirs is in not designing or even testing their methods for <u>multiplayer situations</u> - the situations in which it's wisest to play, <u>the situations in which you play the most</u>! Which means they can't even begin to address the card situations you face at the casino.

Why did they fail to incorporate this essential factor into their R&D work? *The World's Greatest Blackjack Book's* offered this explanation in its description of Julian Braun's testing software:

> "*Head-on play* was chosen to make the one-to-one systems comparisons more *valid* (extra players *complicate* the comparison)." [My italics]

There are always complications in doing research. Boy do I know. But you don't <u>avoid</u> them just because they're tough to solve! And if you do avoid the "complications," your studies cannot ever hope to be valid! So much for the validity of the Old School way!

Splitting Hairs

One more word about splitting. This is a bit advanced for this book, but it needs to be understood: Yes, splitting is sometimes wise in cases where the dealer's likely to bust - even with hands you might not otherwise choose to split. But bear in mind that if the whole table splits whatever hands can be split, a favorable balance that exists before the players' turns, one that would bust the dealer, often will switch over to an unfavorable one if too many cards are taken before the dealer's turn.

Imbalances ebb and wane. So keep that in mind. An orgy of splitting when the imbalance is player-friendly is often unwise.

Splitting The SMART Way

In sum, <u>splitting is only smart if:</u>

① <u>You know the dealer's highly likely to bust (so you don't care what hit cards you get) - and you're sure that the amount of cards you take won't spoil the favorable imbalance and undo the dealer's likelihood of busting</u>

② <u>You know your most likely hit cards will result in your beating the dealer's likely score</u> (or, in winning at least one split hand, achieving a push rather than a loss)

③ You're NOT betting so much money (compared to your average bet) in a severely losing situation that the total amount of your outlay will likely result in huge losses that will take more than one session to overcome

④ It will cut losses you would have suffered by hitting

And FYI: Restrict yourself to the number of times you split certain types of pairs, in losing situations. Doing more than once or twice is often financially unwise...We'll talk more about splitting in Chapter 10. But now let's take a look at the important concept of loss-limits.

You are still not ready to enter a casino.

6 ♦

THE NEED FOR BRAKES

I debated long and hard whether or not to include this story in my book, fearing that some might misconstrue it and conclude that my strategy was to blame. Nope, my one big scare was caused by foolishly ignoring my own advice.

It happened more than two decades ago, when I was still quite young, before I had perfected my system. I was still an intermediate player testing out nascent theories and concepts. My most major blackjack research projects still lay ahead of me.

It was the night I took a friend of mine, Maggie, to her first casino. I had taught her my new method and had promised to bring her to Atlantic City. (Maggie was in her 70s at the time!)

After a four-hour drive, we arrived at the casino and found a good table. Maggie was obviously a beginner but everyone, including the dealers, took kindly to her. They helped her every chance they could. She was confused about how to give hand signals, so I occasionally had to contradict her hand signals and the dealer graciously accepted my directions. Maggie was ecstatic as saw she was winning. We had great fun.

It didn't take more than two hours before Maggie had won about $200 and she couldn't have been happier! I was up over $400 and Maggie was eager to take her winnings home with her so we stopped playing. We had been comped free dinners by the casino (I was still seeking comps back then, not yet wise to the negative aspects of casino scrutiny), and so we enjoyed one of the fine restaurants there and then took a walk on the Boardwalk.

That's when I made a greedy mistake. Knowing full well I should have left with my winnings (as I now teach you to do), I suggested to Maggie that we play on. Maggie was the smarter one. She said happily that she didn't want to play anymore. She wanted to take her winnings home. But she said she would gladly watch me play.

Oh boy. For the next three or so hours I ran into terrible hands at a string of miserable tables. I was still relatively new to the game and I made some big mistakes; disregarding my system, raising my bet dramatically, desperately hoping my *luck* would change. Big mistake! I went down over $1,000. It was a lot of money to me at the time. (Fortunately I had brought $1,500 in cash. I knew needed that kind of bankroll to stay in the game, for at most Atlantic City casinos the table minimum went up to $25 or more at most tables on a Saturday night.)

Anyway, here I was, with an elderly friend, four hours from home at midnight on a Saturday night, down a lot of money and mentally fatigued not only from normal play but also from the emotions that had been gripping me for the past three hours.

I decided that if Maggie agreed to stay, I would not stray from my system and I would make one final *levelheaded* attempt to make up my losses. Maggie, who'd been having a great time watching everyone play, graciously agreed.

We were at one of those casino behemoths with lots of tables; a blackjack player's dream! I was confident I'd find a good table eventually. So I moved from table to table, going down even further initially. I was down to about $300 when, at about 2 a.m., I found a table where the players seemed happy and celebratory even, one fellow having a huge stack of green chips in front of him. He was clearly getting great cards. Then something interesting happened. Someone to his left walked away from the table and I sat down to his right. I was now essentially in the seat order he'd been in before and I intuitively surmised I might be dealt the same good flow of cards he'd previously been enjoying. (In *Cutting Edge Blackjack* you'll find that I later proved that each betting spot does tend to get a repeating cycle of many of the same cards! I was essentially stealing his winning cards!)

The next two hours were unbelievable. I exhausted my wits keeping track of the cards, this time betting strictly according to my system, and I quickly began to recoup my losses. Hundreds of dollars in chips began to come my way and by night's end I came out ahead by about $50. Of course if I had been smart, I would have brought home *nine times* that amount and gotten home at a more reasonable hour.

I learned a lot of lessons that night, which led to important innovations and changes in the early development of my system.

I learned you need to quit while you're ahead. That you shouldn't chase losses with bigger bets. That you can lose a lot of money if you play stupidly. And that the higher the minimum bet you play, the higher your losses can become if your system doesn't have an intelligent "braking" system.

Now high rollers might wonder why I was upset over a $1,200 down cycle that, at the $25 minimum bet tables I played at, was equivalent to 48 Units (a Unit is equal to your minimum bet as you will learn soon). It's because the momentary downswing was caused by a stupid mistake; one that, if repeated, could quickly become a costly bad habit. I foolishly abandoned my more conservative playing approach partly due to my playing inexperience at the time. If you let one-day losses become higher than your average one-day gain, you are looking for trouble. Losses add up just as surely as gains do. Forty-eight Units is too high a loss. These days, I keep my losses on my very occasional losing days down to roughly 6 to 10 Units. This is how you become a winner. (FYI: It's interesting to note that had I started the night by playing at the table I last played at, I would have walked away with more than $1,200 in winnings.)

That night turned out to be a pivotal watershed event, a necessary experience in the evolution of my system. I realized that I needed to formulate a smart system of "brake-points," to determine when it made sense to stop playing, whether I was winning or losing. So I did more research and created fail-safe measures to eliminate the possibility of wild downside swings; reduce overall risk; ensure that winnings were brought home and were not ever thrown back; and make my system smarter and more conservative. You will find these innovations scattered throughout this book; they are now an integral part of my system, which has come a long, long way since that fateful night.

Incidentally, Maggie, God rest her soul, never returned to Atlantic City. She unfortunately lost her mobility shortly afterward. But to the day she passed on, she proudly bragged to everyone how she once won $200 playing blackjack in Atlantic City. Such are the joys of (smart) blackjack.

MONEY MANAGEMENT & MODERN BETTING TECHNIQUES

If you saw the movie "Casino," you might remember the scene where Robert de Niro, a casino boss, notes how commonplace it is to see kids playing in a Las Vegas kiddie place while their Moms and Dads "drop their house payment in the casino."

It's no joke. One of the most common mistakes players make is in not knowing when to stop. In fact, de Niro's character also comments that his job as a casino boss is "to keep the players playing. The more they play, the more they lose." If casinos understand that equation why don't most players get it?

Money management in blackjack involves numerous factors. Betting is just one of them. All play a part in your likelihood of winning or not. So in this chapter we'll talk not just about smart betting but also about limiting the time you play; protecting your winnings; limiting your losses; and knowing when to leave.

But let's start with betting. Now can you guess what I call "the average players' biggest disadvantage in placing bets?"

They have no clue as to what their money is riding on when placing a bet. They cannot tell if the cards in the next round will be good or bad. So they don't know how much to bet.

Blackjack was *designed* with this inherent challenge. Its inventors built in that mystery when they made you bet before seeing what cards you and your opponent (the dealer) would get.

I'm sure they didn't think anyone would ever unravel that mystery. But, guess what?! Happily, after years of research and development, I solved that centuries-old riddle! In the First Edition of *Cutting Edge Blackjack*, I introduced my Auxiliary Betting Indicators method, which worked very well at identifying your odds of winning in the next round. And now, after years of refinement, I've improved upon that with my Precision Betting Method, introduced in the Third Edition of *Cutting Edge Blackjack*. So now you can predict with great accuracy your correct odds of winning in the next round based upon what was dealt before.

But you're probably not yet ready to tackle a state-of-the-art method of that skill level and sophistication yet. No problem!

I am about to introduce you to a new entry level method, revealed in this Edition for the first time, so even newcomers to modern blackjack methods can profit from the discoveries that have come from my many years of research. I will teach you to *time* your bets wisely so you will have a better likelihood of betting higher when it's smart and lower when you need to cut your losses to reduce your downside risk.

The Failures Of The Old School Systems

First some history. You need to understand why the ways of the past should be discarded.

Card counting was invented more than a half century ago in an effort to time players' bet increases to when it was wise. But it was highly ineffective. The Hi-Lo method created by Harvey Dubner in 1963 and used by the famed MIT blackjack teams of the early 1990s, for instance, provided a puny 2% advantage. That's basically a break-even system. MIT player Jeffrey Ma, in fact, complained that those meager returns forced the teams to bring huge amounts of cash to the table ($150,000 each) and make risky bets in order to hope to profit from it.

Truth is, few players are Old School card counters anymore. Most grew disillusioned with the paltry returns they got with that faulty, tedious and antiquated betting approach. (Even Old School stalwart Arnold Snyder admitted that in his last book.) Modern blackjack players want to do better than that.

And there's a reason why the Old School methods born of the 1950s (and still being hawked today) are so ineffective. They are based upon computer *simulations. Phony blackjack, as data. Produced by a computer's random number generator.*

This brings to mind the time an Old Schooler approached me after a book event at which I emphasized how it important it was that I did my research with real card data.

"The only thing you'd miss by using computer simulations is shuffle tracking, right?" he whispered nervously, hoping no one would hear how little confidence he now had in his computer simulations as a means of doing valid blackjack studies.

"No," I explained. "Your data, with simulations, is hopelessly just...wrong! You cannot use it to detect or profit from what we

111

now know about card behavior. You cannot know anything about repeating phenomena or profit from them. You cannot know anything about or profit from winning and losing cycles caused by the nonrandom nature of the cards. You cannot figure out how to predict your likelihood of winning in the next round. And so on."

"Oh," he said dejectedly and walked away. He was obviously an author or web site owner taking the lazy way out as so many had before him, using his computer to simulate data. (Can you imagine NASA doing research that way? Here's how that would go: They wouldn't send probes to Mars. They'd just program their computers to <u>guess</u> what Mars was like! Yeah, right!)

It's no wonder the Old Schoolers deny the very existence of winning cycles. Computer simulations cannot reveal the truth about those because they are <u>randomly</u> produced. Nonrandom patterns such as card-driven winning cycles would not appear in computer-simulated data.

I've also noticed that they confuse consecutive wins (often called winning streaks) with winning cycles. A string of consecutive wins only lasts so long (although I've discovered that <u>70% of all player wins occur within such streaks</u>!). Winning cycles, though, carry on through many shuffles (see the chart on the next page) and usually encompass many consecutive winning streaks.

It's true that we cannot predict when consecutive wins will occur. We can, however, identify when we're in winning cycles and we can profit from that knowledge through smarter betting.

My intensive card studies (and a shuffling study done by a major university in the early 1970s) have proven that casino-style shuffling does not randomize the cards. I've also proven that the cards do not play out randomly in casino blackjack. And it is precisely the information I've gained about one nonrandom phenomena, winning cycles, that enabled me to create state-of-the-art betting strategies.

The chart on the next page represents just one of innumerable winning cycles I documented in my research. Here's visual proof they exist. <u>What you're observing is a repeating pattern of good cards being delivered to one betting spot, through many shuffles</u>!

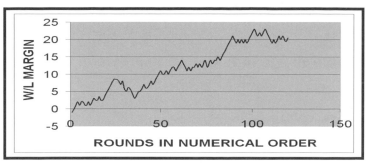

My last major card studies proved that winning cycles are produced by groups of cards that mostly repeat together in the same round from shuffle to shuffle. And the <u>predictable</u> nature of most of them (based upon the indicators I've discovered) allows us to ride these waves of success. I've literally spent years investigating winning cycles and my discoveries on the root causes will benefit you whether you use the entry-level methods here or move on later to my more precise innovations.

The Unseen Forces That Create Winners And Losers

Let's begin with a little introduction to card behavior, as it affects your betting spot and your betting approach. My studies have shown that at most tables some betting spots are winners and some losers. It's rare that any table's spots are all losers or winners. If you're at a table where all spots are losing, run!

Although more sophisticated methods and a more in-depth look at the repeating phenomena I discovered are best left to those who are ready to tackle my second book, *Cutting Edge Blackjack*, what you need to understand right now is that <u>it's no accident that some betting spots seem to get the best cards and others get the worst</u>. It's not voodoo. <u>There are good and bad betting spots</u>. Repeating phenomena create them. And you can learn to identify them.

The Five Betting Spot Classifications

In fact, I've identified five classifications of betting spots, by the quality of cards they tend to get. We'll use these classifications later to fine tune your bets:

❶ **Great:** (during play, you're winning a great majority of hands and you're going way up in chips rapidly)

❷ **Good:** (you're moving ahead but not quickly)

❸ **Neutral:** (you're in a period where you're up a bit but it's not conclusive yet whether you're eventually going to end up or down)

❹ **Bad:** (you're going down in chips slowly)

❺ **Horrible:** (your chip stack is diminishing rapidly)

When you first arrive at a table (or new cards are brought in), play the cards as if they're "neutral" until the **personality of the cards** reveals itself. It sometimes takes many rounds for the card quality to become known. More on this in a moment.

Choosing The Most Profitable Games

Now it'll be easiest for you to get a handle on these things at single and double deck games (aka "pitch games"). There, even a beginner can learn to notice patterns and keep track of the cards. Plus, the quality of the betting spot becomes apparent faster than at multi-deck tables since the cycle is shorter between shuffles. There are less cards to keep track of, so you get a feel for what kind of cards are coming your way faster. Translation: they're more predictable so you have a higher winning potential.

And there are other reasons to seek out the better games, the pitch games. For one thing, while repeating phenomena operate in every blackjack game, multideck games require greater skills and a better memory to beat. Plus, it's kind of like sex; once you've had great sex, just any partner will not do. Similarly, once you've played blackjack's best games, you'll see that the less winnable multideck games become less attractive.

What it boils down to is that any good blackjack method is most effective against the pitch games. That's reason alone to seek them out.

Job One In Knowing How To Bet

Knowing what I've just told you about winning cycles and betting spot behavior, it's not hard to figure out what job one is.

Your first job when sitting down to play is to determine whether you've got a winner or loser.

Are the repeating phenomena in play feeding your betting spot cards you can work with, to win, or instead giving you a steady diet of losing hands? Can you identify which of the five classifications of betting spots you're at?

A smart betting system only works if you're raising your bets when the cards are good and keeping them at their minimum when the cards are bad. Here are several ways to gauge things:

The Simple Chip Count

The easiest way of telling if your betting spot is good is by keeping track of your chip count. And by keeping your bet to the minimum at the outset, you can get a very accurate answer early on *because the number of chips you have will tell you how far up or down you are* - that is, how many more wins than losses you've had or vice versa.

Say for example you're at a $5 minimum bet table and you started with $50 in chips (10 times your minimum bet). If you find you've got four more chips than you started out with, it means you've won four more rounds than you lost. That's a good sign. If instead you're down four chips, it means you've lost four more rounds than you won. That's a bad sign.

That's actually a more telling indicator than you probably realize. And if your chip stack is steadily going down, your betting issue then becomes a <u>leaving</u> issue. Should you leave the table? (Probably.) If your chip stack instead is steadily increasing, it would likely be time to start placing conservatively higher bets. (As a beginner, you should never raise your bet dramatically, however. Do it gradually. That reduces your downside risk.)

Now, once you start raising your bets, your chip count becomes a less accurate means of determining your winning rate. Your chip total no longer has a one-to-one correlation with wins and losses. So you'll need a more sophisticated method than this once you're beyond the early going. Or, you could learn to restack your chips as you raise your bet so you can continue to track your relative number of wins and losses on a round-to-round basis. That might be difficult for you, though, unless you're a more experienced player, ready for a higher level of play.

What Simple Observation Tells You

A second method of telling how good your betting spot is through simple observation. It yields a lot of clues (empirical evidence) just as it does in research. In other words, you should pay close attention to the <u>types</u> of hands and point totals you're getting (with your first two cards). Is there a pattern?

Are you getting stiffs mostly (hands of 12-16 points)? That often indicates a bad flow of cards; your betting spot is likely either "bad" or "horrible." That repeating phenomena is not uncommon at downward spiraling betting spots. You'd definitely not want to raise your bet if that's what you're seeing.

Or are you getting primarily 9s, 10s and Aces, creating hands of 19 through 21 points, with some Blackjacks, along with promising starting hands of 10 and 11 points? That's likely a sign you have a "good" or "great" betting spot where it's appropriate to raise your bet; that is IF you're beating the dealer more than not. <u>That's a consideration you have to factor in, too: how your hands are faring against the dealer's.</u> That reveals what the repeating phenomena are truly producing in the way of betting spot results. It's not good enough to get hands of 20 points if the dealer is constantly beating you with Blackjacks or hands of 21 points.

Keeping Track Of Your <u>Winning Margin</u>

A third way of evaluating your betting spot is to keep track of how your wins stack up against your losses. I call this your **Winning Margin**. (This is the most skill intensive way, but it is the most state-of-the-art and precise.)

For example, if you've won three rounds and lost one, your Winning Margin would be +2, because you've won two more rounds than you've lost. If instead you lost three rounds and won one, your Winning Margin would be -2, because you've lost two more rounds than you've won. (Pushes can be ignored.)

You can keep a rough estimate of your Winning Margin if you're not able to do better, but I'd suggest you try to be as accurate as you can. Here are some suggestions:

As each round goes by, count each win as +1. Count each loss as -1. Just remember the sum. We don't care about the exact number of wins or losses you've had. It's the sum or Margin that tells you what you want to know.

In this way, as each round goes by, you'll know precisely how you're doing. For example, if your count is up to +3, you'll know instantly you're doing well; you've won three more hands than you've lost. If your total is -4, you'll know instantly you're doing badly; you've lost four more rounds than you've won.

You might be able to keep a running tally with the use of chips or other devices to make this more simple. But don't let the dealer see what you're doing or he or she will suspect you're a system player and you'd risk getting barred. So if you use chips, move them in place when the dealer's not looking your way, when the dealer's distracted (such as when the dealing starts).

How about playing with a small number of chips like a poker player does?! You know, shuffle them in your hand as if you have a nervous tick. If you're winning, have your right hand play with the number of chips indicating how far you're up. If you're losing, use your left hand and play with the number of chips indicating far you're *down!* Or you could simply <u>hold</u> the number of chips in your right hand that indicates your Winning Margin; or the number of chips in your left hand that indicates your Losing Margin.

Or you could use your fingers, or feet, or a rotating dial of a watch. Fold your arms and count off your winning margin on the now-hidden fingers of your right hand; or your losing margin on the hidden fingers of your left. Or you could subtly count off the winning margin with your right hand in your lap, or the losing margin with your left hand in your lap. Because you're not keeping track of your total number of wins and losses but just one number that goes up or down by one point each round to indicate your margin of success or failure, this is not really hard.

Keeping track of your Winning or Losing Margin gives you a very accurate picture of what's going on at your betting spot! It's a highly valid indicator of things to come. The higher the number, in general, the more likely you are to do well (in fact, once your total climbs to +5, my studies show you're statistically more likely to continue upward in a winning cycle).

But I won't ask you to tie the Winning Margin to your betting level. That's best left to when you're at a higher skill level. The most important things to know right now is: negative Winning Margins mean you should place the table minimum bet only and get ready to leave (possibly to find a better betting spot); positive numbers mean you should typically be making higher bets.

Thinking In Units

Now before you can adopt modern betting techniques you've got to learn to think in terms of **Units**. What's a Unit? It's the lowest bet you want to place at any given time. For argument's sake (because it's such a popular low stakes minimum for most players), we'll use the $5 chip as our 1 Unit bet in this chapter.

I speak in terms of Units for several reasons. For one thing, it makes it easier for me to teach players of all levels and betting inclinations; whether you play the $5 tables or the $500 tables, $5,000 tables or whatever, you'll be able to relate to what I'm about to teach you. Also, thinking in terms of Units makes things easier for you to remember if you choose to play at a wide variety of betting minimum tables or vary your minimum bet within any playing session. Plus, you don't want to think in terms of money when betting, because then your emotions take over and you'll make mistakes by becoming overly cautious.

Thinking of our bets in terms of Units will also make it easier for you to keep track of where you're at in the system, visually. If, for instance, you momentarily lose track of how many hands you've won, you can simply look at your bet, see how many Units there are, and you can probably think your way back to where you were in your betting system. Along these lines, you can make things easier on yourself at this point in your playing career by making 1 Unit equal to 1 chip. In other words, choose a comfortable playing level where you can represent 1 Unit as one chip. Since there are $5 chips, $25 chips, $100 chips and so on, choose a game initially where one of these chips will represent your 1 Unit bet. (Once you're ready for a bit more sophistication, I'd like you to move up to a minimum bet that involves two chips. That will fine tune your betting further, increasing profits and decreasing your risk factor, as you will see in a minute.)

OK, so, for our purposes, we'll define *1 Unit* as being *the lowest Basic (minimum) Bet you'll ever place. At a $5 table, it's very simple — 1 Unit will equal one red $5 chip.*

 = 1 <u>Unit</u> (your minimum bet)

Now a Unit differs from what I call a "Basic Bet."

The Concept Of The "Basic Bet"

A **BASIC BET** is *variable. It's the lowest minimum bet you will make on whatever betting LEVEL you're on in my newly fine-tuned 3-Level, Notch-Up, Notch-Down Bet Management System.* That System's great because it's conservative (greatly minimizing your downside risk) yet it maximizes your potential gains. Plus, it's very easy to apply and it's been tested and proven highly successful.

As the name implies, your **Basic Bet** (whatever minimum bet you're placing at the moment) will be of three different sizes, depending on what **LEVEL** you're on: **Levels 0, 1, 2, or 3** (your Basic Bet is the same at Levels 0 and 1). You want more money on the table only when good cards are coming your way. So you will steadily go up in the Betting Levels I've proscribed at good or great betting spots, increasing your **Basic Bet** to catch the wave of a winning cycle; or lowering it at bad betting spots, to avoid the brunt of a losing cycle.

Levels 1-3 are only for times when evidence points to the detection of a winning cycle affecting your betting spot. And on each of these Levels, you will "notch up" your bet by one Step increase when appropriate, to further fine tune your betting.

Level 0 correlates with the "bad" cards classification - when you're losing more rounds than winning. Level 1 is your "neutral" cards level. Your wins slightly outnumber your losses. Your bets should be on Level 2 once you've identified the cards as being in the "good" cards classification. And Level 3 is your "great" cards betting level. We'll talk about how to move up and down the Levels in a moment. (FYI: There's no "Level" for "horrible" betting spots. It's simply time to get up and leave the table. Or more to a different seat, if you think that might help.)

When first coming to a table, it's difficult for someone without more sophisticated skills to know what Level to start at in betting. So the safest thing is to assume you're on Level 1 and follow the instructions for that, which follow shortly. But be aware that this is one time where you're not really sure what Level you should really be on. And it sometimes take a number of rounds for the cards to "shake out" in your betting spot, reveal themselves as to their quality. So you'll especially want to be alert at this time for evidence that warrants betting on a different Level, especially if the cards quickly reveal they're bad, when you should cut your losses.

As you will see in a minute, one reason this entry-level system works so incredibly well is that, by the time you start to raise your bet, you're using house money! You're playing only with money you've won!

It's also great because it's timed to take advantage of times when you have a higher likelihood of winning than losing. It's a very flexible method, designed to respond to the changing **personality of the cards** over time during any one playing session. And it masks what you're doing; most casino employees won't notice you're using a system. Your increases are gradual.

Always Start At 1 Unit

OK. Now if you've just arrived at a new table your **Basic Bet** should start at 1 Unit. You'll assume, at least at first, that you're on Level 1. And 1 UNIT will be your "home base." You will return to this level, which we'll call **Basic Bet**, LEVEL 1, when things are not going your way and as recommended on the top of the following page.

<u>ALWAYS RETURN TO A 1 UNIT BET WHEN</u>:

- ♣ <u>New cards are brought in</u>. The quality is unknown.
- ♣ <u>The cards are bad</u>. You need to cut your losses.
- ♣ <u>A player joins the table.</u> The flow of cards will change, altering your probability of winning; you can't yet tell how good the new flow of cards will be.
- ♣ <u>A player leaves the table</u>. This changes the flow of cards.
- ♣ <u>A player sits out a hand</u> simulating the loss of a player. This changes the flow of cards.
- ♣ <u>A player takes an extra betting spot</u> simulating the arrival of an extra player. This changes the flow of cards.

The 3-Level, Notch-Up, Notch-Down Betting System

To raise and lower your bets and coordinate them with the classification system on page 114, you'll use my **3-Level, Notch-Up, Notch-Down Bet Management System.** The beauty of this method is that it brings your bet down to a much lower level during so-so and bad times than it will be during good times, therefore weighing the odds much more in your favor.

Blackjack pundits often get confused when they weigh the odds of anyone coming away a winner at blackjack. They concentrate solely on the number of hands they are likely to win. They forget how important an influence the bet management system you use has on your outcome.

If it gets your bet up to a high level (relative to your minimum bet) when the cards are good for you, and reduces your bet severely when the cards are bad for you, you will then come away a winner even if you win only 50% of the hands! This is one reason even beginners (whose rounds won versus rounds-lost ratio is at its lowest) can become winners with my system.

When Should You Raise Your Bet?

So how do you accomplish this? It's simple. Your Basic Bet – your starting point on any Level – is based on what Level you're on. The higher the Level, the higher the Basic Bet. The better the cards, the higher the Level you're going to want to be at.

Now, within each Level, you will raise your bet in increments, too, to take advantage of a good flow of cards.

Within each Level, you're going to raise your bet by one Step once you've concluded based upon the evidence on the table in terms of wins versus losses that you're on an upswing. For newcomers to this system, that Step up will translate into a bet increase of 1 Unit.

Now, in the past, I've given newcomers some discretion in moving up to higher Levels, based upon detecting a steady flow of good cards or a good winning percentage. But ideally, as you become more sophisticated, you should be accurately following the action (and your Winning Margin) to more precisely guide you in moving up or down Levels. And in this new Fourth (Gold) Edition, I'm actually removing much of the discretionary license I gave before, because that can lead to lazy play and that's not a good habit to get into.

Basic Bets On Each Level

Here are your **Basic Bets** (BBs) and **Step increases** for each **Level**:

Level 0: 1 Unit at all times
Level 1: 1 Unit BB + 1 Unit Step increase (when appropriate)
Level 2: 2 Units BB + 1 Unit Step increase (when appropriate)
Level 3: 3 Units BB + 1 Unit Step increase (when appropriate)

That is, that's the method best followed by beginners. As you become more adept at identifying what Level you belong on, you can use this slightly more aggressive Basic Bet approach:

Level 0: 1 Unit at all times
Level 1: 1 Unit BB + 1 Unit Step increase (when appropriate)
Level 2: 3 Units BB + 1 Unit Step increase (when appropriate)
Level 3: 5 Units BB + 1 Unit Step increase (when appropriate)

Now a creative way to further reduce your risk, cutting your losses while increasing your profits over time, would be to choose a personal minimum bet that's *higher* than the table minimum - if your budget and skill level allows. Then, your Level 0 Basic (and only) Bet would be a HALF Unit (or less if possible), keeping losses from losing periods (which you can easily identify with this method) to a bare minimum.

For instance, if you make your personal minimum bet (under good conditions) $10 at a $5 minimum table, then upon realizing you're in a Level 0 card flow situation, you can reduce your losses by going down to the table minimum, half of what your lowest bet had normally been. Or if your personal minimum bet is $15 at a $5 table, you can further reduce your risk by going down to the table minimum, $5, on Level 0. Now you're only losing a THIRD of a Unit when times are tough (when you're considering leaving anyway). This is a fabulous loss-limit tactic.

A Clever Way To Further Reduce Risk

Now I'm going to complicate things a bit here, but it shouldn't be hard to understand. Most of you will play at tables where your 1 Unit bet will naturally equal one chip. At a $5 minimum table, your 1 Unit bet will be one $5 (red) chip. At a $25 minimum table, your 1 Unit bet will be one $25 chip. The realities of casino chip denominations and the games most players tend to play are partly responsible for why I chose this approach.

But if it doesn't overwhelm you, we can further fine tune your betting system by moving you to tables whose minimum bets don't correlate with a casino chip denomination. There, I'd suggest you make Step increases of LESS than 1 Unit.

Why? This more closely reflects your increasing likelihood of winning. And it's more conservative, which suits this stage in your career. In doing so, you're pruning off more of your gains, stashing them away as profits, and increasing your likelihood of winding up a winner at the end of the session. And newcomers to modern blackjack need every edge they can get.

This kind of thing is a luxury at tables where the minimum bet doesn't correlate with a casino chip, one that other tables often don't offer. Think of it. If you want to increase your bet at a $5 table <u>you have to double your bet</u>. And yet your increase won't likely correlate with a doubling in your probability of winning. (More sophisticated players using the methods in *Cutting Edge Blackjack*

123

will time their bets precisely with their odds of winning in the next round, which is your ideal.) I mean, I guess you could ask for white ($1) chips at $5 tables to use in bumping up your bet more gradually. But no one does this typically and you'd stick out like a sore thumb if you did it. We want to stay anonymous to avoid getting pegged as system players who can get barred.

So, if you feel comfortable playing at the tables where the minimum is different than a casino chip denomination, so much the better. Or (if your budget allows) just place a higher minimum bet (once you feel confident in your skills that is), which also lets you raise your bet more gradually! At a $10 table, your Step increase on each Level with this approach then would be a HALF Unit; one ($5) chip. At a $15 table, your Step increase would be TWO THIRDS of a Unit; two ($5) chips. A $50 table would operate like a $10 table because your "Unit" is two $25 chips. Step increases would be by HALF Units; one ($25) chip.

Now some tables are kind of hybrids. I mean, at $25 tables, you could use $5 chips to raise your bets more gradually. And that would be ideal. In that case, your Step increases should be by 60% increments; three ($5) chips. But I urge caution in doing this. Gauge how the casino reacts to your doing this. This might be a bit too provocative. If you notice the dealer giving you strange glances or making a comments about it, stop this practice immediately and use $25 chips only as most players do. ALWAYS avoid this practice, for instance, at casinos where dealers continually swap out players' red chips for green!

It's the threat of getting barred by certain practices that makes the lesser bet increases easier to make at tables where the minimum does not correlate with a casino chip denomination. At $10 and $15 tables, for instance, you're already using $5 chips so increasing bets with them won't raise anyone's eyebrows.

How The 3-Level System Works

OK. Now when first arriving at a table, make your minimum bet. Also make note of your stash (and stack it Strategically, so you can tell visually, immediately, what you have). Unless and until you go up by three Units (meaning you won three more

124

rounds than you lost), keep your bet the same. If you go down six Units, however, leave the table; and if the same thing happens to you in short order at another table, leave the casino.

As you move up in chips, you'll eventually move up in Levels. After witnessing your stash going up three Units from the start (in other words, you're now playing with the house's money, money you won), you'll move up a Step (increasing your bet by 1 Unit). On Level 1, that means you're at a 2 Unit Bet. Keep your bet at that size unless you find you: 1) have lost 4 Units from that point (which means you went down two points in your Winning Margin) - then go back to your **Level 1 Basic Bet**; or 2) have won 4 Units from that point (which means you went up two points in your Winning Margin) - then go up to your **Level 2 Basic Bet**.

Once moving up a Level, place the Basic Bet at that Level until and unless: 1) you lose the equivalent of two Basic Bets (which means you went down two points in your Winning Margin) - then move down to the next lowest level's Basic Bet; or 2) have won the equivalent of three Basic Bets (which means you went up three points in your Winning Margin) - then make a Step increase. Once making the Step increase, keep your bet at that size until: 1) you lose the equivalent of two Basic Bets with the Step increase (which means you went down two points in your Winning Margin) - then go back to your Basic Bet on that Level; or 2) you win the equivalent of two Basic Bets with the Step increase (which means you went up two points in your Winning Margin) - then move up to the next Level. (See the graphic demonstration on the next page and the 4-color chart following page 22.) Increases are discretionary at the top end, but I suggest you max it out at 5 Units and stay there until you detect the winning cycle is over. After you've made the Step increase on Level 3, the issue becomes when you should leave. Winning streaks last only so long. I'll give you some advice on that in a moment.

Beware choppy action (you know, win one, lose one, win two, lose two), especially at Level 1. It can lead to losses, especially if its pattern catches you in between bet increases. The chart on top of page 127 demonstrates what a choppy period looks like, and how long it can last. (This one lasts from about the 45th

The (Conservative/Beginner's) 3-Level System:

Level 0: 1 Unit always.
(Or less if your personal minimum is higher than the table's)

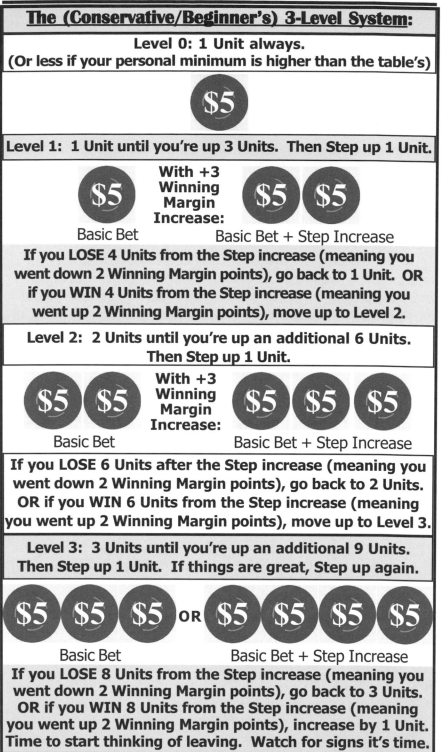

Level 1: 1 Unit until you're up 3 Units. Then Step up 1 Unit.

With +3
Winning
Margin
Increase:

Basic Bet

Basic Bet + Step Increase

If you LOSE 4 Units from the Step increase (meaning you went down 2 Winning Margin points), go back to 1 Unit. OR if you WIN 4 Units from the Step increase (meaning you went up 2 Winning Margin points), move up to Level 2.

Level 2: 2 Units until you're up an additional 6 Units. Then Step up 1 Unit.

With +3
Winning
Margin
Increase:

Basic Bet

Basic Bet + Step Increase

If you LOSE 6 Units after the Step increase (meaning you went down 2 Winning Margin points), go back to 2 Units. OR if you WIN 6 Units from the Step increase (meaning you went up 2 Winning Margin points), move up to Level 3.

Level 3: 3 Units until you're up an additional 9 Units. Then Step up 1 Unit. If things are great, Step up again.

Basic Bet   OR   Basic Bet + Step Increase

If you LOSE 8 Units from the Step increase (meaning you went down 2 Winning Margin points), go back to 3 Units. OR if you WIN 8 Units from the Step increase (meaning you went up 2 Winning Margin points), increase by 1 Unit. Time to start thinking of leaving. Watch for signs it's time.

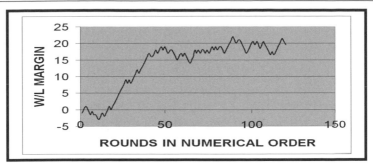

round to the 120th round!) Here, the player would have done best to have left after the 50th round!

Up/down turbulence means it's either time find a better betting spot or leave. Or go down to Level 1 until the static pattern breaks out, up or down.

Money Management Begins With Your Bankroll

Of course, this is a chapter on money management and, as you might have surmised, betting is just one aspect of that. There are other factors that also contribute to your likelihood of winning (causing some players to be losers, for ignoring them).

First, you have to make sure you have enough cash with you when you go to the casino. *I always suggest that you take 40 times the minimum bet you're going to make.*

Now when I tell students that "your bankroll should bring 40 times your minimum bet, to stay in the game," they often respond, "that's a lot of money to lose!" To which I respond, "I don't go to the casino to lose. I expect to win most of the time, which I do." Plus – there are brakes in my system, as you will learn, that will prevent you from losing very much on an occasional losing day.

The reason for the guideline of bringing roughly 40 times your minimum bet is that there are down cycles you will encounter. And, during one of those down cycles, you might have a great hand, where you'll want to split your hand of two like cards, split again, and then again, and then later want to double upon several of those new hands.

If you don't bring enough money, you might find that you've run out of chips and can't make those desirable moves. You might then leave a loser, when you might have scored a big gain had you brought enough cash to stay in the game.

Another reason to bring an amount of cash equal to 40 times your minimum bet is that — if you don't — you might then get into the dangerous habit of running to a money machine for more cash, which I hope you NEVER do. That would cause you to get confused about how much money you've played and lost, and get into a syndrome of throwing money away on days where you might do better to cut your losses and leave.

The lowest I've generally gotten in a down cycle in recent years has been 16 Units. And most times, I bounce back up. So bear that in mind, as a guideline, and also to reassure you that down cycles of that nature are not necessarily insurmountable.

But don't ever allow yourself to lose more than 20 Units. You MUST have a way in which to cut losses on bad days, so that, by year's end, you will come out way ahead. More on this soon.

Incidentally, don't give the dealer all the money at once. Place five $20 bills on the table when you first arrive at a $5 table, for instance (never give them a $100 bill at a low stakes table; you'll draw too much attention). The great majority of times, that will be sufficient. I want you to have to reach into your pocket for the rest of your cash if needed, because that will serve as a reminder to you to take a moment and think about whether you should continue playing much longer.

When You Should LEAVE a Casino

At some point, you need to put on the brakes and leave the casino. Here are the primary reasons you should stop playing and head for the door:

- ♣ You've won a good deal of chips (at least 20 times your minimum, 1-Unit bet), and the card flow has changed for the worse. You've lost three hands in a row, or three out of the last 4 hands.
- ♣ You're up more than 10 Units, but after two hours of

choppy play (not on a winning cycle), you're tired.

♣ You've finally returned to neutral after a long struggle back from a down cycle.

♣ **You've lost 6 Units within a dozen or less hands of sitting at a table**. This is my **6-Unit Cheat-Proof Rule. Your losing percentage is way too high.**

♣ You've lost roughly 20 Units, you've been at the casino for an hour or two, winning streaks are hard to come by and it isn't likely things will change for the better. This is my **20-Unit Down-And-OUT-Rule**.

♣ After a winning streak, a pit boss suddenly takes an "interest" in you and directs the dealer to use counter-measures against you. *Especially pay attention to this!!!*

The point is, ***winning cycles don't grow on trees***. You're only likely to see one or two major winning cycles during an average playing session (if you limit the time you spend there as I advise). If you've surpassed gains of 10 times your minimum bet, don't leave without taking home your winnings. Remember the **First Principle of Winning at Blackjack**: be happy with your gains, no matter how meager they might be.

Your one winning cycle of the day might be one long steady climb that suddenly changes, turning into a steady loss of hands, at which point you should leave.

Or, suddenly – in no time (perhaps within 15 minutes of entering the casino) — you've got a winning stack of chips anywhere from 20 times your minimum bet, to, perhaps, 40 times or even more on an extraordinary occasion. *Then* you run into several losses within 4 or 5 hands. THAT's when you leave.

Or, you've been unable to go on any protracted winning streak, you're even, or a bit down after two hours of play, and the cards just won't break in your favor. You leave.

You get the idea. *Knowing when to leave is the most important thing I will teach you*. It will greatly contribute to making you a winner. (And watch how surprised everyone is when you walk out a winner!)

How To Know When to Take Your Winnings Home

The hardest thing to do is to leave when you're ahead. You keep thinking you're going to win even more. That's when greed starts to kick in and you're about to make some costly mistakes.

One night 20 years ago, going up more than $100 after only 15 minutes at a $5 table, I knew it was time to go, and I forced myself to walk away. But part of me wanted to keep playing. I love the game, and HAVING to leave after only 15 minutes of fun seemed almost unfair. A new dealer had come in, I'd lost the first three hands, and the small casino didn't have another pitch game table open, where I prefer to play. I left.

You must get used to that fact – the winnings sometimes come right away. If you don't know enough to leave, you'll throw your winnings back and get very depressed as your chips go into a swoon and you realize how stupidly you've been playing. A smart player refuses to play foolishly.

Stack Your Chips My Way!!!

In always stacking your chips with the **Strategic Stacking** method – in 5-chip, $25 piles at $5 tables, for instance – as I have advised you to do, you will always know what you have. You will set aside your gains in 5-chip stacks in an area to your left that symbolically indicates that these chips are "saved." As you win more and more, add stacks of chips to the area reserved for "saved" winnings. Tell yourself, "if I start to go down, this is what I will bring home – I will <u>leave</u> before I get down to these chips!"

You should start doing this when you reach 10 UNITS of winnings ($50 at our $5 table). You go up to $65, let's say, but come back down to that winnings level of $50 — LEAVE.

If you surpass 15 UNITS in winnings ($75), raise your mental marker to that level, and make sure you go home with at LEAST that amount in winnings. Keep raising your mental marker every 5 to 10 additional UNITS in winnings and you'll have a system of checks and balances going for you so you'll always leave a winner.

Don't forget – this is not a game that will make you rich at the $5 minimum bet level. So don't get greedy like most players and expect to make a lottery-sized fortune at any one sitting. *Ten to 40 UNITS will be your most likely "take" on any winning occasion.*

Conversely, don't let your LOSSES ever exceed your typical one-day "take." That way, your winning days will outnumber your losing days, and your losses will not overtake your winnings.

While in testing this book more than 10 years ago I did on one occasion fall to $125 (25 times my 1-unit bet), that was on an occasion I discovered that the dealer was cheating and I promptly left the casino, never to return there. Losing when the dealer is cheating is a foregone conclusion. (I will help you spot and avoid these rare rogue dealers in Chapter 11.)

Leaving if your losses mount to roughly 20 units is a good rule to use to keep a losing day to a minimum. Some days you might want to leave BEFORE you get that low, if you've played a couple of hours, and your losses, whatever they are, seem insurmountable. Or as I said above, you will want to leave if you've gone down 6 units within a dozen or less hands upon arriving at the casino and you're not sure if you can win there – I don't call that my **6-Unit <u>Cheat-Proof</u> Rule** *for no reason!*

I once went to a small casino I'd been to only once before. On my prior visit I'd gotten the impression that no one could win there. But since I had some time to kill, and since I had become pretty good at spotting dirty tricks, I thought I might as well conduct a research project for this book.

I took out only $30 (normally I'd give the dealer $100 at a $5 table, but I was wary of this casino), and I sat down at the only table that had an empty seat. (There were only two tables in use!) There was just one other player, whom I am now convinced was a casino employee pretending to be a player – a *shill*. (In hindsight, one tipoff was that the dealer and the overly-well dressed guy at the table were chatting away, without any apparent interest in playing the game.) The dealer, though, sprang to attention, ready to deal the cards as soon as I got to her table.

In sitting down, I disobeyed two of my rules. I didn't wait and watch how the cards were breaking. And I sat at a table with too few players (you shouldn't play at a table unless there are at *least*

three other players there, to maximize the favorable break of the cards). I could have saved myself some money. I will never make those mistakes again!

I don't remember exactly how many hands were played. No more than a dozen or so. This dealer got TWO Blackjacks within the first FOUR hands, and, miraculously, kept pulling scores of 20 and 21. I noticed there seemed to be a torrent of 10s, mixed with an occasional lower card, and then a torrent of low cards began. I only had one or two good hands (two 10s each time), but I won only one of those hands! In fact, I think I won only 2 hands the entire (brief) time. *The dealer never busted.*

In hindsight, because the dealer frequently won by just one point, and the cards seemed to follow a pattern of having been set up beforehand (they "smelled"), I believe what I was facing was a **cooler deck**. That's a set of cards prearranged by the dealer to beat a certain arrangement of players (in this case, it was an apparent trap for the straggling lone player who might walk into this dead casino).

I'm at the point where I can smell when something's wrong. So I got up after losing five chips in less than five minutes, as I have advised you to do. After I brought my sixth chip to the cashier (who seemed surprised and annoyed that I did not BET my last chip) I walked out and I will never play at that casino again. I was very pleased at how well my **6-Unit Cheat-Proof Rule** had worked. If you can keep your losses way down on a bad day, like I had done, you're going to do great.

On the flip side, I once encountered an attractive young woman who moved to a table where I was playing. I asked her how she was doing. "I'm down $2,000," she said dejectedly.

I didn't know what to say at that point. She didn't seem like the sort of person who could afford to lose that kind of money. That's what happens when you don't learn to play properly.

Don't Panic and Act Out of Desperation

It's the low cycles that cause the most problems for players and lead many to dig a hole too deep for themselves. They don't have a good system and they play from desperation when the losses mount. They panic when they're down and they start throwing extraordinarily large bets on the table, thinking "next bet, my luck will change!"

The Dangerous Small Martingale System

That's akin to what's called the Small Martingale System, where players try to recover their losses by putting down bets that exceed the amount that they've lost. Let's do the math on this one so you never attempt to do this:

OK, you lose a $5 bet. So, thinking you're very smart, you put down $10 on the next bet. You think, "my luck's gonna change, and by increasing my bet to $10, I'll make up my $5 loss and win $5 more!" But, you wind up losing that hand. So, with the same philosophy in mind, you put down a $20 bet. Oops! You lose that bet, too.

But then you think: "my luck's really due to change now!" and you put down a $40 bet, which, upon losing, leads to an $80 bet. Your heart starts to pound. That's a lot of dough to you. That hand, you draw two 8s and want to split. Now you have $160 on one bet, and you draw another 8. Split again? Most players do. You're thinking, "a 16 is no good," and you believe that splitting 8s is a good move. Now you have $240 on the table, and you draw a 3 on the first 8. Double? You think that's the right move so you feel you almost *have to!* Now you have $320 on the table. Lose this, and you might run up against a $500 maximum bet limit, on your next hand. (Maximum bets were instituted to thwart this tactic.) CAN'T HAPPEN? I've SEEN it happen!

You get the idea. *You get into dangerous territory very fast with this method and, believe me, the losses can mount very, very rapidly.* DON'T EVER TRY THIS. Especially in today's modern casino environment.

NEVER bet more money than the minimum table bet when the table is horrible. *NEVER play out of desperation, or allow losses to grow so large they frighten you.* Sometimes the cards just refuse to break well for you no matter what table you sit at and you have to call it quits.

One of the purposes of this book is to teach you how to avoid such pitfalls and play a safe, conservative game that minimizes your exposure to losses.

The Myth of The High Roller

Now some people think high rollers are immune to this kind of thing. But that's not true. Because while many people assume high rollers can afford to risk the bets they're making, that's not necessarily the case. And the mystique surrounding high rollers, that they're the best players, isn't always true. Matter fact, I've found it's rarely true. Most of them play poorly. Plus, it doesn't take long to throw away a fortune.

I was in Las Vegas when I saw a high roller using the Small-Martingale scheme at a posh Strip casino. He was at a $100 minimum table, playing the dealer one-on-one (bad idea!). He placed a $200 bet, and the dealer drew a face card as his up card. The dealer won the round, and the player upped his bet to $300. He was probably thinking: "I'm due for a win. I'll win back the $200 I lost and make $100 on top of that by winning the next hand!" But the dealer's up card was again a face card and the man lost that hand too. His next bet was $1,000. He must have been thinking: "OK, now I'm REALLY due to win. I'll win back the $500 I lost and wind up $500!" But the dealer's next up card was an Ace. You guessed it. The man lost this round too.

After this guy lost the $1,000 bet, he looked as if someone had knocked the wind out of him. The dealer stopped dealing for a second, making small talk to calm the guy down. He clearly felt sorry for the guy. This player was playing blackjack like it was a game of roulette, a game of chance, instead of a game of probabilities. The lessons are clear:

A smart player never relies upon luck to win. And if your betting approach is overly aggressive and based on hunches rather than sound thinking, it doesn't matter what card strategy you use – you're going to wind up a big loser. Especially if you don't know enough to leave when the cards are bad.

Don't repeat this man's mistakes!

You are still not ready to enter a casino.

CARD
COUNTING
&
CARD
OBSERVATION

135

To card count or not to card count? That is the question.
And, if you *do* card count, what does it tell you? Can you really
base your betting and card decisions on what it indicates?

I'll answer these questions shortly, but, first, let me make it
clear that you do not *need* card counting to be become a winner.
In fact, I have created methods that far surpass card counting in
accuracy and effectiveness in making card and betting decisions.

That being said, the card counting system I invented several
decades ago before moving on to create more state-of-the-art
methods can be useful for intermediates and those who play the
tougher multideck games. If you don't have the necessary
memory skills for advanced card methods, then my All-Inclusive
Card Counting System might very well be the answer for you.

Keeping Track Of The Cards

As you learned in Chapter 1, one of the three primary factors
that make blackjack a winnable game is its predictability. It's very
similar in that regard to the game of Bridge, where by keeping
track of every visible card played, players try to predict what their
partners and their opponents have.

If you're playing a 1-deck game, for example, and you've seen
three Aces in one round, you know there's just one Ace left. Or,
perhaps you've seen ten 10s in one round. Then, only 6 remain.
That's powerful information.

Blackjack's easier than Bridge, however, in that you don't have
to keep track of the cards by suit. You're more interested in
determining what the card imbalances of the moment tell you
about your chances of beating the dealer.

But one way or another, you need to become skilled at keeping
track of the cards. And if card counting is not for you, I will give
you an alternative (even better) way of accomplishing the same
task, later in this chapter. That's my **Card Observation**
method. It's an entry-level state-of-the-art card analysis method
that provides even more precise answers to the card questions
you face.

The important thing at this point in your career is to get thinking about the cards. First, you must train yourself to observe what's going on, what the cards that have been dealt tell you. (I see the cards as a kind of language. They talk to you if you know what you're looking for.) Then you must learn to draw intelligent conclusions from what you've observed, as to how the cards that have been dealt affect your odds of winning.

The Limitations Of Card Counting

Now, to answer the question at the start of this chapter, we'll use card counting only to help you make smarter card strategy decisions. My studies have proven, however, that card counting, an antiquated system dating back to 1963, is not good either at predicting your odds of winning in the next round or at guiding your bets intelligently.

In fact, I'd like to debunk the myth of card counting as "god," in this day and age of multideck games and casino countermeasures. To me, it's not even in the top eight most important tools that make you a winner, which are:

❶   My method of picking a good casino. If you're in a bad casino, card counting can't undo the damage.

❷   The *Blackjack The SMART Way* method of picking a good table. If you're at a bad table, card counting can't make you a winner.

❸   My rules with regard to knowing when to leave both a table and a casino. The card count doesn't speak to this at all.

❹   The **X Factor** (explained in the following chapter).

❺   **Card Observation**, which you will soon learn. The card count will often mislead you — for example, it can be "neutral" in situations where the important 10-point cards are actually depleted; **Card Observation** won't let you miss that fact. **Card Observation** also helps you predict what the crucial dealer hole card is; card counting cannot do that with any kind of accuracy (and others' counting systems were not created to do this, either).

❻   *Blackjack The SMART Way's* perspective on which up cards are in your favor. If you play the up cards wrong, it doesn't matter what the card count is.

❼ **The 3-Level, Notch-Up, Notch-Down** betting system, along with its companion money management method (Chapter 7). This is much better than card counting at timing your bets wisely and determining your odds of winning.

❽ A complete understanding of the mathematical foundation underlying the game, and of repetitive card behavior. (We'll discuss some of the repeating phenomena I discovered through years of card studies, in a later chapter.)

In my second book, *Cutting Edge Blackjack*, we'll add other concepts that are also more important than card counting, such as **The Circle of 13** (also found, in part, on my audio book *Richard Harvey's Blackjack PowerPrep Session*), my **Precision Betting Method**, and much more. But that's for when you're ready to deal with more state-of-the-art concepts and methods.

My card counting method can still be a useful tool to the intermediate (and we'll use in *Cutting Edge Blackjack* to identify players' facedown cards in pitch games), but it should not be the only tool you rely upon to manage your card strategies.

Card Counting Can Actually Spoil Your Game

Another warning — be careful before you attempt card counting at the casino. It can be confusing and misleading, not to mention distracting, for beginners or even intermediate players. This practice is really only for advanced players.

If you try to card count before you're ready to, you will undoubtedly find that while you might be able to keep a good count, you are no longer able to keep track of the game as well, which I believe is more important! Considerations such as how the dealer's doing and how you're doing are much more important to how you play the game (that'll be covered in the next chapter, about the **X Factor**).

Like everything else in this book, you must practice card counting at home until it's second nature to you. You'll know when you feel capable of pulling it off at the casino. It's especially important that you get to the point that you can do this seamlessly, without tipping off the casino that you're doing it – they don't like card counters!

That Being Said...

In spite of all this, card counting can be the icing on the cake – helping you with an occasional hand. So, once your skills are honed and you are verging on becoming an advanced player, you will then be ready to tackle this practice.

I certainly don't mean to throw out this aid. I just want you to put it in its proper perspective.

The Basic Premise of Card Counting

Now, here's how my card counting method works. Those who are uninitiated are often unduly afraid of attempting to learn this, because they think it involves memorizing every card that was played — their point values and suits. No. This is an approximate way to predict whether high or low cards are likely to come next. (We deal with *groups* of cards with card counting. That's one reason it's less precise than my more modern methods.) You're trying to determine whether you will get a high card or an Ace when you need one (or DON'T want one), or a low card when you need one (or DON'T want one)?

One reason my system is more accurate than others is that we include all the cards in the count (although we count Aces separately because Aces can either be high or low cards). The six "high" cards – the 8, 9 and four 10-pointers – balance out the six "low" cards (as I define them) — the 2, 3, 4, 5, 6 and 7.

What we can do with this kind of method is to keep a finger on the pulse of whatever card imbalances are in play, in an approximate way - according to two big groups of cards. If the count shows us one group has been dealt more frequently than the other, the one dealt less is more likely to be in the hole and be in the hit cards that come our way.

Here's an example of how this works. Let's pretend for a moment that we have just 10 cards in our game. Here's what they are:

= +1 point each

= -1 point each

As you can see, 2s through 6s comprise our five low cards, and the 9s and the face cards are our five high cards. We will assign each of our low cards a value of **+1**. To balance these out, we will assign each of the high cards an opposite equal value: **−1**.

Since you have five low and five high cards, they balance each other out in *number* AND in arbitrarily assigned *points*. (The points assigned to the five low cards total **+5**, using our counting system. The points assigned to the five high cards total **-5**.)

Let's start our game, which will follow the rules of casino blackjack. You're playing alone against the dealer and this was dealt:

DEALER

YOU

Four cards were dealt. All were high cards, carry a **−1** point value. So the card count is:

4 times −1 = −4

What does this tell you? The high negative count tells you that *low cards are most likely to be coming* because a disproportionate number of high cards were dealt. You can be especially certain here because our little game contains only 10 cards. With 52 or more cards, the same principles apply with regard to your ability to predict what's coming next *but your certainty level will be lower.*

In the good old days, when blackjack was played with one deck and the cards were dealt to the bottom, card counting's certainty level got especially good toward the end of the deck and smart players made a killing off this factor. But, in the 1960s, changes were made to end this player advantage. Dealers were required to reshuffle well before all cards are dealt, and multideck games were introduced. It's still a worthwhile tool, however, even with the lower accuracy level caused by the casino game changes.

Another example. Let's say these were dealt in the first round:

DEALER

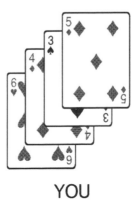

YOU

Here, your hand consists of four low cards, for a total of **+4**, and the dealer's hand has two high cards, for a total of **−2**, making the count:

$$+4 \text{ plus } -2 = +2$$

That tells you it's more likely that high cards are due to come next. The "**+**" indicates that more LOW cards were dealt than high cards so far, and the number, "**2**" tells you by how much. So the cards remaining are richer in high cards. Inspecting the cards we have left, you will find this is true: one Jack and two 9s remain, as well as the 2 – three high cards to one low.

However, it's still a mystery as to *when* that *low* card will be dealt or the torrent of high cards. You only know that, if you draw a card right now it would most *LIKELY* be a high card (from a *probability* standpoint). (And with only 10 cards in play, we can express this probability exactly: you have a 3 to 1 likelihood of getting a high card; or a 75% probability.)

And *that's* how card counting works. It's approximate, but it's useful in making certain types of card strategy decisions. High cards, for example, are often desired when doubling, so this kind of approach can tell you if it's wise to double down. Low cards are desired when you need a hit card, but it has to be low or you'll bust, so my card counting system will help you decide whether your most likely hit card with help or hurt you.

But What Makes Low Cards +1?

One reason why low cards are assigned a positive point value is that card counters consider it a good thing when low cards are played out, making the remaining undealt cards richer in high cards. It's a positive situation, because high cards are what the player wants – especially 10s. They combine to form hands that add up to great scores, and they are often needed as hit cards when doubling or splitting. It's also a positive situation when low cards are played out because low cards especially benefit the dealer. The dealer will bust far less when their hit cards are of smaller point values.

High cards are assigned a *negative* point value, because card counters consider it a negative thing when high cards are depleted. In that case, it becomes harder to successfully double or split in certain situations, limiting your money-making opportunities. It's also a negative situation because, with less high cards, the dealer will bust less.

Once again, *card counting gets more reliable the deeper you get into the cards.* Keep that in mind. Another reminder: you should assume the count to be neutral (zero) when cards are first dealt after a shuffle. *If and when the card count reverts to zero, we'll assume the cards are again neutral, and that's when you'd follow Basic Strategy.*

The All-Inclusive Counting System

My **All-Inclusive Counting System** gives you a lot more information than most other systems, which leave out one or more cards. And it breaks the low and high cards into halves that make more sense when you're considering whether to double, split or hit your hand. Here's how it works:

You assign a point value of **+1** or **−1** to all of the cards *except* the Aces, as they're dealt. You count the Aces separately. You should know at any time how many you've seen, and how many remain unplayed. For example, with a 2-deck pitch game, if four Aces have been played, you know there are four left. (We'll talk about Aces more in a moment.)

You'll *add* a **+1** to the count if one of the 2s through 7s are dealt. You'll *subtract* a point from the count if one of the 8s through 10s are dealt.

*You will then take whatever **total** you arrive at and use it to assess, based upon how high its numerical value is: 1) how well you can predict whether low or high cards are coming (the higher the number, the greater the imbalance between the high and low cards, so the more accurate your card count becomes as a predictor); and, 2) how, therefore, you want to play your cards.* You'll see how this works in Chapter 10.

(FYI – The card count total you arrive at through the method I've described above is known as a *running count*. In the First Edition of *Blackjack The SMART Way*, I had you dividing the running count by the number of decks that remained, to use that number, which is known as *the true count*. However, players reported getting confused – after dividing the running count properly to get the true count, they started counting using the true count, instead of reverting back to the running count. So, I am no longer recommending that you use the true count. And, in fact, it's not necessary. You have to remember, though, in keeping a running count, that, the greater the number of cards dealt, the more accurate an indicator it becomes. A +6 running count will not mean as much at the start of a 4-deck game as it does once you get toward the last round or two. Then, the percentage of high cards among the undealt cards will be higher and your count will be that much more reliable.)

Now here's how the *Blackjack The SMART Way* **All-Inclusive Counting System** divides the cards, with their valuations:

= +1 point each

= -1 point each

Notice how the six lower cards are balanced out by the six higher cards. Because the Aces can behave as either high or low cards (therefore fitting in neither category), you will be counting those separately. They're important to keep track of, however, because of their near-equal importance to both the dealer's hand and yours.

Why Divide The Cards In This Way?

I like my **All-Inclusive Counting System** most, of all the plus-minus systems, because it separates the cards into what I believe are very logical camps. It puts cards that tend to behave similarly together.

If you need a high card, a 7 won't probably help you. Nor will the 7 be a very strong card for the dealer as a hole card, in combination with most up cards. It acts like a weak card, and so it makes sense to group the 7 with the low, weak scoring cards.

Plus – this division makes the count that much more useful. If you want to double down, any of the cards I've put into the "high cards" category will help you in most doubling situations. Conversely, if 7s or lower value cards are due, you would know it is probably NOT a good time to double down.

If you want to split your cards, you often need to know if the dealer is likely to bust. Well, any two of the cards amongst my set of high cards would bust the dealer's 5 or 6 (except for the unlikely appearance of two 8s – one as the hole card, one as the hit card). Plus, since these high cards are rich in 10s (66% of them are 10s), this grouping is also likely to cause the dealer's 2s through 4s to bust. Conversely, if the low cards (as I've defined them) are due, you will know it's probably NOT a good time to split some of your pairs of like cards, because the dealer will probably not bust with those dealer-friendly cards.

If you must decide whether or not to draw an extra card to your hand, this grouping of the low and high cards will be especially helpful when your hand totals 14 or less. You'd know you could safely hit your hand if the low cards, as I define them, are due; you could NOT safely hit your hand if high cards are due.

Admittedly, this division of the cards won't help you as much when you have a hands that total 15 or 16. But, no grouping will solve all problems all of the time. And you're still getting an acceptable level of accuracy.

With your 15 point hands, only one of my designated low cards would bust you — the 7. So, my system would still be a good guide, with a good deal of accuracy. It would tell you that if the high cards are depleted, you'd have an 83% chance of getting a good card, within the group of low cards that are due. That's a pretty strong indicator. And, if you know Aces are also overdue, you'd have an 86% chance of making the right move with your 15 point hands with my **All-Inclusive System**.

And with your 16 point hands, only two of the low cards would hurt you, so you'd still have a 67% probability of getting a good card from amongst that bunch if you knew that low cards (as I define them) were due. And, if your independent count of the Aces showed you the Aces might start to appear as well, then the **All-Inclusive Counting System** low cards would give you a 71% probability of drawing to a winning score. That's not bad in the way of accuracy, especially for an entry-level method.

My System Is Also Revealing About The Dealer's Hand

Now let's say the count is strongly positive *when the dealer gets his or her hole card* - meaning high cards are overdue. Here's what that would mean, with the various different types of dealer up cards:

With the dealer's strongest up cards (the 9 through Ace), you'd be in trouble. Any one of the high cards in the **All-Inclusive Counting System** will combine with those up cards to give the dealer a winning score. The dealer will likely have a winning score of 17 on up.

With the dealer's 7 and 8, that's another matter. Then, with a high positive count at the time the hole card was dealt, you'd know that the dealer at BEST will have a 17 or 18, but possibly less (unless Aces are also overdue). The high positive count in this case will tell you that you have a shot at winning.

With the dealer's weakest up cards (the 2 through 6), the strong positive count would be great news. This is when the dealer is most likely to bust.

What About Counting The Aces?

Aces have no assigned point value. As I suggested above, you should count them – "1 Ace, 2 Aces, 3 Aces," etc. — separately. Now, Aces amount to just one of the 13 "flavors" of cards, or less than 8% of the bunch. At any one time, that's not a likely card to get.

However, there are reasons why you should get a handle on the relative depletion or surplus of Aces in the remaining cards, and for two diametrically opposed purposes. Since the Ace is an especially powerful card for the dealer, you want to keep track of the likelihood of the dealer getting one. Unlike others, my studies have proven that it is in your favor when Aces are depleted. The dealer's Blackjack is equivalent to a dealer trump card — most everyone loses in that situation. Plus, the Ace, as the dealer's up card, is so strong that it is in the player's interest to see it LESS!

On the other hand, there are times when you might want to know if an Ace is coming your way. Aces can be great hit cards – say if you're doubling down on a 9 or 10 – and that's why you keep a separate count of how many are left (and when you saw the last one), to give you an idea of the probability of getting one.

So, BEFORE a round begins, you should be encouraged if Aces are depleted. When it's your turn, however, knowing if there's a surplus of Aces might lead you to double where you otherwise would not.

The dual nature of the Ace, therefore, poses a conundrum of sorts, but I feel I've placed it in its proper perspective. Aces are kind of off in their own category. While the high cards as I've designated them benefit the player (especially in doubling and splitting) and the low cards as I've defined them benefit the dealer (in drawing to a winning total and in avoiding busting), the Aces provide a benefit to BOTH the player and the dealer. That's because of their dual nature (from the standpoint of their point value), their potential for forming all-powerful Blackjacks, etc.

The Ace is, however, (unlike the 10s) just one of 13 cards. No card counting method can isolate one card, and tell you with certainty when that particular card will come with the next hit card. But, you can "guesstimate" the probability of getting one, based on how many Aces were played, and how long it's been since you've seen an Ace.

The Neutral Count

By the way, there's another, subsidiary reason why counting

Aces separately makes good sense. I believe that a card counting system works best when the cards on both sides are equal in number, thus balancing out to a neutral total count of zero. Our system has six cards in each logical "camp," and so this achieves that goal.

This way, when the count is zero, you then know there are an equal number of high and low cards left. That's important information. A zero or "neutral" count tells you three things:

❶ That you can't predict necessarily which type of card, high or low, will come next. While it appears the cards are balanced, that's not likely the case. This is just a grey area, in all card counting systems; one of this method's drawbacks.

❷ That you should play according to Basic Strategy, unless **Card Observation** tells you that the 10-point cards are either depleted or overdue (since there are other cards grouped with the 10s in the "high cards" category, this situation is possible).

❸ How the dealer up cards are likely to behave (you'll learn about this in the chapter on Advanced Strategy); in a neutral count, with the cards divided as they are with the *Blackjack The SMART Way* **All-Inclusive Counting System**, you will know that some of the up cards will be more "player friendly," for instance than they might be, for instance, with a strong positive count.

What Your Count Tells You

Let's look a little more at how card counting works:

If the point total is positive, it means that more LOW CARDS have been played than HIGH CARDS; therefore, it's more likely that HIGH CARDS will be dealt next. If the point total is negative, if means that more HIGH CARDS have been played than LOW CARDS; therefore, it's more likely that LOW CARDS will be dealt next.

The count will NOT tell you very much when it totals **+1** or **−1** level, or even **+2** or **−2**. That's not enough of an imbalance to produce a strong probability statement. But the higher the count gets, the more valid it is in predicting what cards are due to come.

That is not to say that if the count is very positive, stray low cards will not appear in the bunch to come. They will. The reverse is true, too. If the total is very negative, stray high cards will appear in the flood of low cards to come. When we say a count indicates that something is *most likely* to occur, we understand that there will never be 100% certainty. We're playing the percentages. If we made decisions based on the majority likelihood, we'll win more than we'll lose.

And that's basically what card counting tells you, in a nutshell — the *relative* likelihood of what's to come.

Why You'd Be Smart To Play The Pitch Tables

Of course, the count is more valid right off the bat with 1- or 2-deck games than with the (rare) 4-, 5- (shuffle machine), 6- and 8-deck tables. It goes back to our example earlier, which contained only 8 cards. The fewer the number of cards in the game, the more the count tells you about the undealt cards.

The problem at 1- and 2- deck tables, though, is that the cards are dealt facedown, then held in players' hands or slipped under players' chips facedown, so you can't see many of them when your turn arrives. So how do you count there? When you are ready for more advanced concepts, read *Cutting Edge Blackjack* to learn my new, breakthrough method on how to count cards at pitch game tables! (Until then, you'll have to count the cards as they are picked up after a round, using a number that's unfortunately not very valid by the time the dealer's hole card is dealt, or your hit card.)

The Drawbacks Of The Hi-Lo Method

In contrast with my **All-Inclusive Counting System**, Harvey Dubner's Hi-Lo card counting system from 1963 and Edward Thorp's very similar "Simple Point-Count Method" (presented in his 1966 revision to *Beat The Dealer*) have you counting 2s through 6s as "**+1**" and 10s and Aces as "**-1**." That leaves out the 7s,

8s and 9s. That does not give you a complete enough picture. If you're trying to decide whether to hit a 14 against a dealer's 2, for example, an 8 or 9 would bust you just as quickly as a 10. Plus – a 7 would help you, but it's not being tracked. It is easier for beginners to master but it's severely handicapped - especially since my studies have shown that the 7s through 9s are crucial cards to track; their relative proportions tell you much about your likelihood of winning in the next round, for instance (see *Cutting Edge Blackjack* for my Precision Betting System, which clues you in on such matters). The 7s through 9s are also instrumental in busting the dealer. And the 7s and 8s, as you now know, are among your player-friendly dealer up cards. So you want to know how many of these cards are left proportionally at any given time.

In my humble opinion, I also disagree with the Hi-Lo's inclusion of the Aces in the count, because their impact and desirability is very different from the 10s and other high cards. For example, a 10 could provide a winning score when splitting Aces. Drawing an Ace after splitting Aces, though, will often guarantee a certain loss because it would add just one point to your total (and many casinos won't let you re-split those Aces). The same problem exists if you have a total of 11, and that's the hard total with which you double the most. The Ace is not the universal good card you want when you're considering double down or splitting that the high cards, with fixed point totals, tend to be. (In fact, an Ace, as a hit card - for you or the dealer - is most often unwanted.) No – it's better to count the Aces separately.

The Spark For My System

Interestingly enough, on page 84 of *Beat the Dealer*, Dr. Thorp says, when testing his Point-Count system at a casino he suddenly VARIED it. You'd really have to be paying close attention to notice this change in thought. He doesn't explain it, nor does he go back and alter what he recommends YOU do with that information. He mentions it in just one sentence:

"I was using the *variation of the point count* where 2, 3, 4, 5, 6, **7** are +1, 8 is 0, and **9**, 10, A are −1, when they fall." (I added the Italics and bolded characters above.)

150

In essence, he was *abandoning* the system he had recommended earlier, in favor of something he felt gave him more useful information. Here, he includes the 7 and 9, as I suggest you do. But he leaves out the 8, which puzzles me. Why?

In practice, Thorp's system is much more complicated than I've indicated. He would have you keeping track of exactly how many cards have been played and then have you divide the count by the number of cards left. You would then use the resulting <u>fractions</u> as your point counts, and, boy, God bless you if you can do that!   I know I can't. That's the case of someone devising a system only a rare genius can follow - maybe the Rainman (Kim Peek).

Another of Many Alternatives

And there are many other card counting systems. The thing is: do they give you the information you want to know? The only other one I will tell you about was the one I used when I first started card counting – a variation of Dr. Thorp's plus-minus system contained in Edwin Silberstang's book, *The Winners Guide To Casino Gambling*.

In that system you count 3s through 6s as +1 and 10s as −1. Although easier to use, I just didn't find it provided an accurate enough picture of what the card imbalances were. So it was hard to make intelligent card moves off the count.

If You Play A Shoe Game, Be Brilliant

Here's one great way to apply what you've just learned:

There will be times, I know, when you will wind up playing a 4- or 6-deck shoe game (but please try NOT to play 8-deck shoe games; 4-deck games, granted, might be hard to find anymore). If you do "go shoe," try using your skills cleverly:

1) Get the card count at the moment the dealer's hole card is dealt!

2) Then use it to identify the dealer's hole card.

To me, the count at the moment the dealer deals his or her hole card is even more important than what the count is when your turn comes up! If you think of it, this is the best way to use card counting!

For example, let's say it's the fourth round following the shuffle, and the count is +8 when the hole card is dealt. Don't you think it's most likely the hole card will be a high card? *Pay careful attention to this!!!*

Now, the count at your turn will give you even more information about how to play your cards now that you know so much about the dealer's. For instance, if the dealer's up card is an 8 (meaning the dealer most likely has a hand of 17-19) and the count is still strongly positive at your turn, shouldn't you think twice about hitting your 14s-16s (because your likely hit cards will bust you)? That's what I call a rock-and-a-hard-place situation. The only good move would be to surrender, if it's allowed.

Multi-Deck Headaches

A word of caution: your card count at multideck tables will not be very valid or accurate until at least two decks of cards has gone by (and it will continue to grow more accurate as more decks are spent). Think about it in terms of keeping a true count, where you've got to divide your point total by the number of decks that remain unplayed. What would a running count of **+4** mean at 6- or 8-deck tables? At a 1-deck table, the running count would be the same as the true count, and +4 might encourage me to double down on 10s and 11s even in some marginal situations. At an 8-deck table, a count of +4 would be equivalent to a true count of +1/2! What's that? Nothing. In other words, the creators of the concept of card counting were telling you, by suggesting you use a "true" count, that this method really was not very useful in the early going at multideck games.

This is another reason to seek out the better pitch games (single and double deck games), where the count offers you a good deal of predictability from the get-go. (The 2-deck face-up games, though rare, are great from this standpoint!)

Why NOT To Tie Bets To Count

As I pointed out earlier, some pundits will tell you that, when the count is at least moderately positive – high cards are, in theory, due to come – you should make a significantly bigger bet on the next round. Some will even encourage you to wager the MAXI-MUM BET ALLOWED BY THE CASINO. I'm here to argue that this is very foolish indeed.

Number one, if high cards are due, isn't the dealer just as likely to get those cards as you and get a high, winning score? To my mind, that is NOT the time you want more money down!

Number two, the count that you obtain AFTER a round is done does NOT pertain to your next hand. If you were sitting in the first baseman's seat, it might be fairly good at telling you what your *first* card might be (although card counters warn you not to sit there) but, depending on the number of players at the table, not your second. It would also say something very general about what the other players and the dealer might get as their first cards. Beyond that, I think you'll agree, the post-round count those pundits want you to use to make your bet would get a bit "old" and inaccurate. I don't know of a count that continues to be terribly relevant eight or more cards down the road, do you?

Early in my blackjack playing days I followed these schemes, raising my bet when the count was moderately to very positive, only to lose when the dealer pulled a strong combination. The added risk was not justified by the results. The implication of the card count seemed like flawed reasoning to me and it led to higher losses than I would have had normally, that I then had to make up later. At the very least, it was NOT a conservative way to play.

So, what do we learn from all of this? Should we instead re-verse what we were taught by the pundits and increase our bet when the count is *negative*, when we know that *low cards* are due (with the hope that the dealer will then have a weak up card)? The problem with *that* is, if you double down when low cards are coming, you're less likely to get the 10 or other high cards that might "make" your hand. And, the dealer will be less likely to

153

bust.

It should be pretty clear now that you'd do best to divorce your card count from your betting strategy. Card counting is much more useful as a predictor of what's to come, in the way of the dealer's hole card, or in fine tuning your choice of possible moves, than it is in predicting whether you're going to win the next round or not.

In *Cutting Edge Blackjack*, which more advanced players will want to study, I provide the research data to back up my assertions above. Suffice it to say, the evidence is overwhelming.

And There Are Other Reasons...

I hasten to add that in the years when I was starting out, I found that, of the many books on blackjack that were out there, there were a few interesting books from which there was something to learn, however outdated they were. *But the cult of the card-counting-based bet management strategy* always puzzled me. Why did the older methods unfailingly suggest placing huge bets – hundreds, if not thousands of dollars – on one hand?

Number one, the average player cannot afford to bet on this scale. So I feel it's especially irresponsible to urge beginners and intermediates to play that way. It leads them to believe there's a great deal of certainty in pursuing what is, in my opinion, a reckless course. Number two, I believe that it's foolish to risk a fortune on <u>one</u> turn of the cards, when the odds are never close to 100% that you will win that one hand.

I mean, is that really wise? Especially since, with the average favorable hand, your odds of winning will only be in the range of 50–60%, if that! (If you hold an 11 point hand versus the dealer's 10 for instance - a good starting hand - you will only win approximately 48% of the time.) So, when you make an extremely large bet, ask yourself: 1) can you afford to lose this bet?; and 2) how long would it take you to make up that loss, given the average bet you normally place? The answers to those questions will tell you if that large bet is wise or not.

And, finally, increasing your bet significantly when you think you have an edge will only alert the casino bosses that you're a card counter. It's the quickest path to getting barred. The days when you could do that and get away with it are long since gone.

Leave The Big Bets To High Rollers

One more point: don't forget that if you are foolish enough to place what for you might be a huge bet on one hand, you might often find that you'll actually need to put much more on the table before your turn is through! You might get a pair of like cards that might make sense to split into two hands. Then you might get another like card on one or both of those new hands so you might want to split those, resulting in your now playing FOUR hands. You now have FOUR TIMES your huge bet on the table. And then perhaps you might want to double down on at least one of your hands, if not ALL of them! You would then have EIGHT TIMES your huge bet on the table. And remember: you made that large bet based on the count from end of the prior round, a very ineffective indicator of your likelihood of winning in the next round. It's not unlikely, based upon my research data, that you will find you were misled by it.

Some authors talk of winning these risky kinds of bets. Yet even the first of the card-counting-driven bestsellers, 1962's Beat The Dealer, admitted to large downswings in fortune. I wonder how many readers paid attention to those confessions.

Read Between The Lines

It's also interesting to note that that book's author, Edward Thorp, admitted he did not put HIS money on the line when he tested out his theories at various casinos. He went to Vegas with Manny Kimmel, a millionaire, who bankrolled his game! That way, he could survive the losses his system was incurring, and could then afford to return to play another day. As TV's Breaking Vegas reported it, HE COULDN'T AFFORD TO PLAY HIS OWN SYSTEM!

Few of us have the luxury of having a millionaire fund us - and dig us out of costly betting mistakes (which Kimmel did).

Whereas Thorp tossed off losses of about $10,000 with a shrug, you are unlikely to do the same. And so, while Thorp was a brilliant mathematician and Wall Street investor, I argue that his betting schemes for blackjack were borderline irresponsible. And, according to my research findings, his recommendations on when you should make large bets were not timed properly.

Let's not lose our heads – blackjack, for most players, is *not* a way to get rich. Sure, if a $1,000 bet means nothing to you, then you can make $10,000 to $40,000 or more in one sitting – using the *Blackjack The SMART Way* system. That's doable.

But, understand — blackjack's typical "yield" is only large if your bets are large. You make what you put on the table. It's a simple equation.

Please, leave the big bets to the players with money to burn. Don't mortgage the house to get blackjack money. Play only with surplus cash, and make bets that are reasonable for you. You will have some losing days, and you must be able to survive them.

Card Counting Is NOT A Precise Predictor

Again: card counting is an APPROXIMATION of what's to come — especially in this day and age of multiple decks and partially distributed decks. Why do some pundits pretend it's a science? And you need to see a fair amount of cards before the statistical probabilities really start to become usable.

No player can tell you with certainty *exactly* what card is coming next under today's casino practices, especially when you're lumping great numbers of dissimilar cards together in just two groups from which you cannot hope to have any kind of precision. Nor can the older methods predict what your next hand will be before it's dealt. Nor can they predict what the *dealer's* next hand will be – which might be even more important! And yet, isn't that what's being implied, when you're being urged to bet the mortgage on the next hand based upon the count at the end of the last round?

The truth is: no matter what the count of the cards is at any

time at any table, some players will be doing well, others not so well; so what is it REALLY telling us? How well we might do – the probability of our winning the next hand – is NOT, in my humble opinion, what the last round's final card count total tells us.

So, if that's true, do you really want to take the bulk of your "stash" and put it all on one hand? C'mon! That's the best way to LOSE a lot of money FAST, become depressed and then get desperate.

At the very least, those risky betting systems are not for the average player. Blackjack, in my opinion, should be kept a form of entertainment for the typical player, and be played conservatively.

An Easy (And BETTER) Alternative To Counting: Introducing...Card Observation!

If all of this is too much for you, the good news is that you will likely do just as well or better using my entry-level state-of-the-art card analysis method, which I call **Card Observation**. You can get just as much information from this method as you would from the more strenuous exercise of counting, and arguably more. It's really amazing what it tells you about the dealer's hole card and your hit cards. Plus – unlike card counting – you can even use it to good effect when joining a table between shuffles.

Here's an example: Let's say you have an 11 against the dealer's 8. You want to double down but you notice that, of the five players who drew extra cards ahead of your turn, four were dealt 10s and one got a 9. Once you've mastered **Card Observation**, it would tell you in this situation that it's not unlikely you'll get the cards you'd need the most to come up with a successful result in doubling - a 9 or 10. Therefore, it would tell you to HIT your 11 instead. Here, it guided you to an intelligent decision based upon the hit cards that immediately came before your turn, and a higher understanding of what makes for successful doubling. (A state-of-the-art player doesn't do this blindly.) I'll explain the nuts and bolts of this method in a moment.

You'll find that **Card Observation** gives you more information

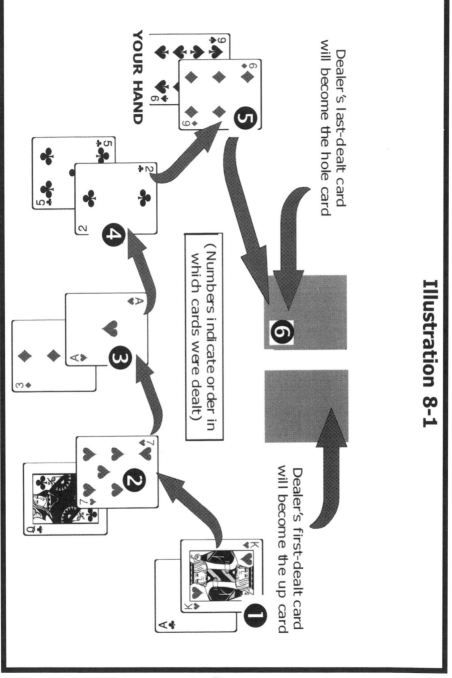

Illustration 8-1

Dealer's last-dealt card will become the hole card

Dealer's first-dealt card will become the up card

YOUR HAND

(Numbers indicate order in which cards were dealt)

than card counting, so your moves will be more accurate and intelligent. It has as its basis the laws of probability, which enable you to get a handle on the cards' predictability. And, whereas card counting has you seeing the forest, Card Observation shows you the trees - in other words, you see things in greater detail.

Here's How To Do It

OK – here's how to make **Card Observation** work for you. It's a two-part process.

The first thing you'll want to do is guesstimate what the dealer's hole card might be (it is admittedly guesstimation, but so is card counting). For this, you have an often-revealing set of indicators – the second set of cards the players are dealt! These cards lead directly up to the dealer's hole card! (See **Illustration 8-1**, on the previous page.)

Now, if you've done as I've advised and are sitting in the third baseman's seat or close to it, you will also have as hole-card indicators any hit cards that the players sitting to your right have taken. Those cards have come directly AFTER the dealer's hole card was dealt. So, you'll study these cards for what they might tell you.

The second thing you'll want to attempt to predict, if you need to take an extra card to improve your hand, is what hit card you will get. That necessitates studying the 10 or so cards that were dealt immediately before your turn arrives.

(If you're at a table where there are only two other players playing, and they don't take hit cards, there might be fewer than 10 cards exposed for your analysis. You can still learn important information from those cards, but, obviously, the more cards, the better. That's another reason to consider playing at a table with more than 2 other players.)

Believe it or not, if you observe carefully and ask the right questions, you will often be able to ferret out the answers you need to know in order to make your best move. Let's see how this works.

Card Observation Involves Asking The Right Questions

OK – you now know what cards you need to analyze to figure out what the dealer's hole card might be, as well as your hit card. What does that tell you? A *lot*, if you know what questions to ask:

1. ***How many of the cards that you are observing are 10s? (Plus — what is the total number of cards?) So...in what proportion have they appeared?*** You'll need the numbers in the first two of these three questions to figure out roughly the percentage of 10s that comprise the cards on the table. Because 4 of the 13 cards in each suit are 10-pointers, comprising 31% of each deck, probability dictates that these cards should show up during the course of play in roughly this proportion. If there were 13 cards on the table that you were analyzing for hole or hit card information, you'd therefore expect approximately four of them to be 10s. If, instead, there are only 10 cards on the table, you would now know that there should be approximately three 10s (because you know that the 10s would then comprise 30% of the cards you're considering, which is roughly what their proportions should be). OK, so, if the cards you're analyzing contain less 10s than you'd expect, then the card whose value you're trying to predict (the dealer's hole card or your hit card) might very well be a 10. If the 10s, however, are present in their proper proportion, or in greater than normal proportions, then it's likely the card whose value you're trying to predict will NOT be a 10.

2. ***How many of the cards are Aces? (And how long has it been since you've seen an Ace?)*** If an Ace is due, factor it in with the information you have on the 10s. If both are overdue when the hole card was dealt, and if both would combine with the dealer's up card to make a winning total, you must adjust your strategy to assume the dealer indeed has a strong hand. Keep in mind that the normal proportion of Aces amongst the cards is 1 in 13: $1/13 = 7.69\%$, less than 8%. That's not much. So, if there is an Ace amongst the cards dealt in the current round, it's highly unlikely the hole

card, or your hit card would be another Ace.

3. ***How many of the cards you're analyzing are not 10s or Aces? In what proportions have they appeared?*** The 2s, 3s, 4s, 5s, 6s, 7s, 8s and 9s – like the 10s and Aces – should also appear in their normal proportions. Like the Aces, each of these cards has less than an 8% probability of appearing. That is: if you see two or more of one these cards amongst the 10 or so cards you're analyzing, then it's unlikely the card you're wondering about is one of those cards. However, if any one of these cards does NOT appear in the 10 or so cards you're studying, then you know that you have to consider those cards as possibilities when guesstimating the value of the card you're investigating.

4. ***What is the relative proportion of low cards to high cards?*** Sometimes, instead of looking at individual cards, it is more telling to reflect on generalities. Just as with card counting – it's the same principle – if a lot of low cards precede a card you are investigating, then that card is likely to be the opposite, a HIGH card, because high cards would then be overdue. And vice versa. If an overabundance of high cards precedes the card you're interested in figuring out, then that card is likely to be the opposite, a low card, because low cards are overdue.

5. ***What does the Flow of the Cards tell you?*** The **Flow of the Cards** is my term for the order in which the cards you're analyzing were dealt. That is often a good indicator. For example, if you see four 10s in a row leading up to the hole card, it's unlikely that card is a 10. However, if the four 10s in a row were the *first* cards dealt to the 7 players at your table, and the cards following those consisted of low cards, an Ace and a 9, well, then the hole card might very well be a 10.

Here's One Area Where A Shoe Game Is Better

Of course, determining what strategic cards might be, through **Card Observation**, is easier with a shoe game. That's because the players' second dealt cards, which lead to the dealer's hole card, are dealt *face up*, unlike in pitch games, where they're dealt face down. Plus, any hit cards taken by players ahead of you (which are important indicators because they immediately follow the dealer's hole card), are also dealt face up – unlike some of the players' cards in pitch games (such as the extra cards dealers place face down under players' chips when they double down). This is one advantage to playing shoe games.

As with card counting, however, you'd do best to use **Card Observation** at tables with no more than 4 decks of cards. With 6 or 8 decks, the cards go through radical fluctuations and become very unpredictable.

(**Card Observation**, by the way, can be done at 1- & 2-deck pitch game tables — it's just not quite as precise. First, you should try to see all of the cards that were played in the prior round. Then, you should try to glimpse as many player cards as possible during the current round. You can do this by subtly peeking at the cards being held by neighboring players, or by politely asking your fellow players to show you what they have. Many times they won't mind doing so, if you extend the same favor to them. You might not be able to tell which of the players' two cards were the second-dealt cards that led up to the dealer hole card, but you will often find useful information. For example, if you're holding a 13 at third base against the dealer's 2 and you have seen NO 10s, or 9s for that matter, amongst players' cards by the time it's your turn, you'd probably be smart to stand. When you're ready to tackle a skill that's on a more advanced level, once again, I will give you my breakthrough method of accounting for the facedown cards at pitch game tables, in *Cutting Edge Blackjack*.)

Determining The Hole Card

OK, let's go to some examples of actual hands played out in one of my research projects. First, look at **Illustration 8-2**, on the following page, and see for yourself how the second cards dealt to the players (numbered 1 through 5) lead up to the dealer's hole card (numbered 6). Also, examine the cards and see what you notice, before I tell you how to apply **Card Observation** here. Take a moment right now to do so.

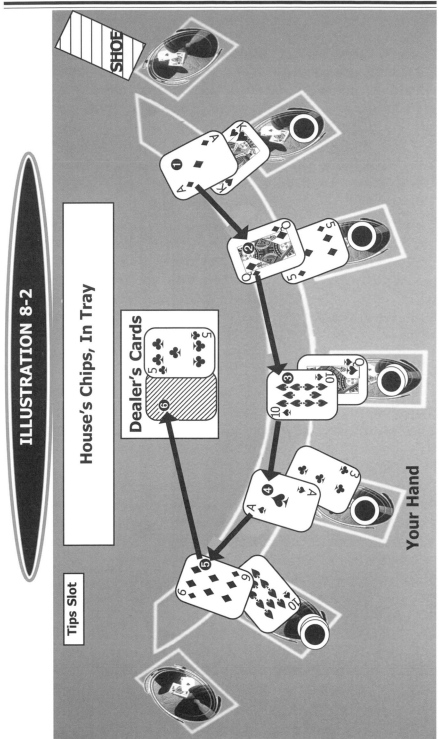

ILLUSTRATION 8-2

Five Players Makes For A Good Number

Now, with five players, you always have 12 cards on the table after everyone's initial two cards were dealt. That's a pretty easy number to work with. We know, for example, therefore, that there should be no more than four 10s amongst those cards, because 10s account for a little less than 31% of the deck. (And even that would be high, because if four 10s indeed do appear, they would account for 33% of the cards on the table being 4 of 12 cards present.) All of the rest of the cards should appear just once, because they each make up one of the possible 13 cards in each suit.

Fine. Let's go through the **Card Observation Questions**, and see what you can learn. Let's start with **Question 1**:

How many 10s are there, and in what proportion? Five out of the 11 cards whose values are visible to you! That's nearly 50% of the cards you can see, and two more than the laws of probability would say you should expect (you should expect 11 x 4/13 = 3 10-pointers)! You know now that it's unlikely – not impossible, but unlikely – therefore, that the hole card is a 10.

Question 2: Are there any Aces? Yes! Two! That's one more than you'd expect. You can write Aces off the list in guessing what the hole card might be! It's very unlikely – not impossible, but highly improbable – that you'd find a third Ace on the table, according to the laws of probability.

Question 3: What about the rest of the cards? There are TWO 5s – they are overrepresented (you'd expect just one per 13). There are NO 2s, 4s, 7s, 8s, or 9s; they are under-represented. So, the hole card is unlikely to be a 5. However, it might be any one of the cards NOT accounted for on the table.

What can you gather from **Card Observation Question 4** about the generalities you observe? Well, there is one more of the high cards than there are low cards (remember: you don't count the Aces in either camp). So, according to that standard, which mirrors the thinking that goes into card counting, the odds lean a little in favor of the hole card being a low one.

And, finally, **Card Observation Question 5** asks you: what does the **Flow of the Cards** tell you? Remarkable. *You've seen TWO Aces and two 10s amongst the five cards that were dealt immediately before the hole card!* It doesn't appear the hole card would be a 10 or an Ace!

Well, as it turns out, you're right! The hole card in this particular card trial was in fact...a 3. Since your main concern is predicting whether the hole card will be a 10 first and foremost, and then, whether it is going to be a high or a low card, I think you'd agree that **Card Observation** served you pretty well here.

Your questions on the relative proportion of 10s and Aces produced especially useful and revealing answers. You were able to ascertain that the hole card was unlikely to be a 10 or an Ace. Your question on generalities was also correct in predicting the hole card was a low one. And the **Flow of the Cards** question was likewise very telling.

*The one question that was NOT immensely revealing was **Card Observation Question 3** – the one regarding the non-10s and non-Aces. That was inconclusive. So, remember: that question will often be the least important or helpful one of the five **Card Observation Questions**. You'd do best to rely most heavily on the others. Use Question 3 as the "icing on the cake," but don't expect it to give you too precise an answer. You're covering too many cards with that question.*

Now, let's get back to the example in **Illustration 8-2**, on page 163. You have already figured out what the hole card would be, but let's not get ahead of ourselves.

Let's say you are the player sitting just to the left of second base, with the Ace-3, and it's your turn. Let's pretend you haven't yet seen the hole card and the players to your right took no hit cards. What would you do, given what **Card Observation** This particular example is a bit tricky. As you will see in Chapter 10, on Advanced Strategy – when low cards are due (which is equivalent in card counting to saying "when there is a negative count"), you have to be a bit more careful against the dealer's weak cards. However, in this case, the balance of low to high cards is not off by very much. So, we're not in dangerous territory.

Careful, now – the only card that's under-represented which would give you a winning score if you double now would be the 7. But, then again, the dealer's 5 is one of the very best up cards for the player, and so you would still be smart to double in this situation.

Well, as it turns out, that player's extra card, after doubling down, was indeed a 7! Not unexpected, given what **Card Observation** told you about the relative probabilities of what cards might come after the third baseman's 6.

Impressed yet? You should be!

Good job! Let's see what you make of the next example.

Insurance?

Another way **Card Observation** can be very useful is when you must decide whether or not to take Insurance, when facing the dealer's Ace. As an advanced player, there will be times you would want to take that option, whether you have a Blackjack or not. And one reason to take Insurance is if **Card Observation** tells you the hole card is likely to be a 10.

Let's look at **Illustration 8-3** on the following page, and see how this works. This is another example taken directly from the thousands and thousands of hands I've run in research trials.

The dealer has an Ace as the up card, and she asks the question all the players dread hearing: "Insurance?" It tends to make you nervous – no matter how many years you've been playing blackjack. It's a warning that the dealer might have a Blackjack, and anyone who doesn't take Insurance anxiously awaits the results of the dealer's checking the hole card, even though advanced players know that taking Insurance is NOT usually a smart move – since 10s account for less than 31% of the cards, you will LOSE your Insurance bet about 69% of the time!

OK, in this case, let's examine whether you should take the

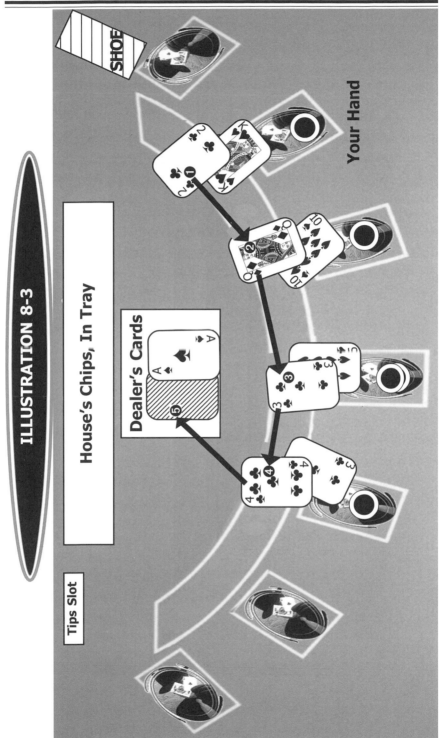

ILLUSTRATION 8-3

dealer up on her offer of "Insurance?" Once again, **Card Observation** begins with asking yourself the five **Card Observation Questions** as you look over the cards on the table.

Look closely at the table as represented in **Illustration 8-3**. In this example, you're playing with three other players, so there are 10 cards on the table, one the hole card, out of sight, after the first two cards are dealt to everyone.

Question 1: What about the 10s? There are three 10-point cards, which is in line with what you would expect. Remember, the 10s make up 31% of the cards, so 3/10 = 30%, which is exactly right. So, your first **Card Observation Question's** answer seems to tell you the hole card is probably not a 10.

Question 2: What about Aces? Since the dealer's up card is an Ace, it's very unlikely the hole card would be one, too. Plus, according to the laws of probability, only one Ace usually appears in 13 cards, and here there is one Ace in 9 cards – a higher concentration than normal. No, the hole card is not an Ace, in all probability.

Question 3: What about the other cards? There's one 2, two 3s, one 4 and one 9. With 3s being overrepresented, it's unlikely the hole card is a 3. Nor is it probable that it's a 2, 4 or 9. Perhaps it's a card that hasn't shown itself – a 5, 6, 7, or 8, most of which are low cards.

The answers you've gotten so far are good for you! The hole card is unlikely to be a 9 or 10, so the dealer's score will probably not be 20, nor will the dealer likely have a Blackjack. No need for Insurance.

Question 4: What about generalities – the proportion of low to high cards? They're roughly balanced. Nothing learned here.

Question 5: What about the **Flow of the Cards**? The higher cards seem to have come to an end with the 10 of clubs. There appears to be an imbalance in the flow here than benefits you – the low cards seem to be starting to come in a flood. Of the last five cards dealt, 4 were low cards. By itself, that news might be worrisome, but you know that the high cards have already ap-

peared in greater numbers than would be expected (they accounted for 4 of 9 visible cards – nearly 50%!), and so it makes
sense that low cards might be due.

No, you would not want to take Insurance here. You'd only be
throwing that bet away.

And, once again the educated guesses we made through **Card
Observation** were correct. In this card run, the hole card
turned out to be a 5.

Card Observation For The Hit Card

One more thing. Let's say you're the first baseman. Let's use
Card Observation to answer one more question: should you be
afraid to bust here, with your hand of 12?

Based upon what **Card Observation** tells me, I don't think so.
Why?

Your hit card would be the 11th card this round. As you saw,
four of the nine visible cards were high cards. Question 3
showed you that two of the three cards that have not yet turned
up on the table are low cards (the 6s and 7s) and might soon
appear.

It's unlikely you would get the only card that would bust your
hand – another 10.

In fact, the hit card that the first baseman was dealt in this
card run was...a 6, one of the cards that Question 3 indicated
was on its way!

Interestingly enough, the next card to be dealt, the third
player's hit card, turned out to be an 8! That was another one of
the cards that Question 3 told you was likely to show up soon.

So, **Card Observation** once again proved its merit, and pretty
impressively, I might add!

Another Effective Way To Use It

I often speak of the **personality of the cards**, and the **Flow
of the Cards**. This is one area where **Card Observation**
excels, which card counting doesn't begin to address. At the

heart of it, **Card Observation** is an analysis of the cards, to detect revealing clues.

At my blackjack seminars, I bring players up to a simulated blackjack table, and show them, among other things, how powerful **Card Observation** is, how it works.

At my most recent seminar, the seminar-goers were amazed to see how I used **Card Observation** to pick out important patterns and trends within the cards, that lasted from shuffle to shuffle – the **personality of the cards**, as demonstrated in the **Flow of the Cards** – that led to a certain predictability.

For example, I pointed out that three Aces appeared in close succession. I then predicted that they would remain that way for quite some time, through several shuffles, at least. And they did. Knowing when Aces will appear is powerful information, indeed.

The same pertained to four 3s during the same demonstration.

And more important – there was a sizeable group of 10-pointers that appeared in a flood from shuffle to shuffle. You should have seen the looks on the faces of those watching these patterns unfold, and repeat again, as revealed through **Card Observation**.

A Fly In The Ointment: Flunky Cards

Granted, **Card Observation** is not a 100% exact science. But it is a much more accurate means of choosing the correct moves than the ways of the past. In fact, it's been tested and proven highly accurate. No system can provide 100% certainty. And this goes beyond a comparison of how effective a system is.

There will be a minority of times where your predictions will not follow the laws of probabilities and that has to do with what I call "flunky" or "minority" cards. I'll give you an extreme example that drives this point home. Let's say you're doubling on an 11 versus the dealer's 9 and you know the dealer's likely got a 10 in the hole. So you need a score above 19 to beat the dealer. And let's say there are nineteen 10s left and just one other card, a 3. Well, your odds of winning by doubling are extremely high here -

higher than they would normally ever be. You have a 95% likelihood of winning. But, hey, guess what?! You will be dealt that 3 and lose 5% of the time. Some players, upon getting that 3, would grumble and say my methods don't work. But they do. We're playing the law of percentages and there will never be a situation where the undealt cards contain 100% good cards.

This is very important for you to understand. Hence the limitation on our ability to get 100% precise. But my studies show we can get into the 80-percentile range with my methods, which is MUCH better than was ever imagined possible by the Old Schoolers.

Card counting is MUCH less precise and I don't see players rejecting that practice because of its limitations. (The MIT teams of the early 1990s complained about the low 2% "advantage" the Hi-Lo card counting method provided them.)

Card Observation is a viable skill you can develop, that will lead to big payoffs at the blackjack table. It is better than card counting in deciding how to handle card situations where an advanced player has to choose between two or three possible ways to go. It is not to be confused with the hunches upon which many players base their decisions. The **Card Observation Questions** speak directly to the underlying mathematical principles that make the game of blackjack winnable.

A Word to the Wise

Now, DON'T attempt card counting or **Card Observation** at the casino until you've practiced this at home to the point where you can pull these off with ease. If you try tracking the cards at the casino before you are really ready for it, your brain is going to overload, your game will suffer, you will probably look visibly agitated AND you might tip off the dealer or casino bosses that you're a card counter or a player with a system and you might get barred. *I want to emphasize that this takes practice, like anything worthwhile, to pull off smoothly. It is, however, well worth your investment of time.*

You are still not ready to enter a casino.

THE
X
FACTOR

I'll never forget the time I took a girlfriend to Las Vegas and, saying, "it's MY time to play," she sat down at a large Strip casino and proceeded to lose all her chips...er, my chips, the chips I gave her. I was powerless to help her because she was head-strong and was in one of her "don't tell me what to do" moods. Yet, unbeknownst to her (and everyone else at the table), the table was being decimated, so to speak, by one of the worst mixes of cards you could possibly face. I knew from the get-go that she and everyone else would be wiped out, and fast.

Well, everyone did go broke. In 15 minutes. Fortunately, my girlfriend somehow managed to have a good time. But she would have had a better time (with more profitable results) had she let me help her. I wanted her to leave that table after the first few rounds. There was no beating this devastatingly bad mix of cards, no matter what approach you used.

The dealer had done a very poor job of shuffling new cards that had been brought in just before my girlfriend sat down to play. The result was a mix of cards in which all the cards of one suit and half of another were dealt each round, mostly in con-secutive order! (I was the only one who seemed to notice this. No one even seemed aware that every player was losing. Hello!)

Long story short: if the players had known what I'm about to teach you, they'd all have gotten up from that table within three rounds at the most. And it is just this kind of thing for which I invented the concept of the **X Factor.**

You see, few players understand that choosing a good mix of cards is very important. Even fewer understand that the quality of the mix of cards in play has a great deal to do with how well your betting spot will do; especially if you are a beginner. Even fewer understand how to spot bad mixes of cards and respond appropriately (that is, by either lowering their bets to the table minimum, moving to a different seat at the table, or by leaving altogether). Nor, for that matter, do they know how to spot good mixes of cards and respond properly (that is, by raising their bets to a level appropriate to precisely how good the cards are).

And aside from giving you this kind of essential and modern

awareness (of a typically ignored aspect of the game) that few players now have, I have another goal in this chapter: to get you to realize what is normal in blackjack, so you recognize either when something is wrong or bad. Now, before I go any further, I need to explain: I'm not trying to make you paranoid. I don't want you to be paranoid. I just want you to learn what my girlfriend in Vegas didn't, so you don't get trashed by a bad set of cards.

I don't want you to become one of those bitter yet uninformed players who, without proper training or knowledge, accuses every casino of cheating them. The fact is these players, the Bitter Billys, undoubtedly were NOT cheated, but ran up against a bad mix (which most often occurs naturally, through no fault of the dealer) and didn't have the skills to recognize it or respond properly. Cheating is rare (but it does exist, and that's what Chapter 11's all about); but bad mixes of cards are, unfortunately, not.

So one of your jobs as a player is to find a good mix of cards, as evidenced by a good flow of cards to your betting spot. And the X Factor will help you ferret all this out.

It is my years of research into card behavior, shuffling and blackjack, which uncovered the existence of repeating phenomena among other things, that enables us to use the X Factor, because we know, scientifically, the cards have a repeating personality. The X Factor is an entry-level way to profit from this knowledge.

My studies have proven that a personality is given to a set of cards with its initial shuffling (after its first introduction, as new cards). And that personality persists through numerous shuffles giving that set of cards a predictability from which even beginners, once made aware of it, can profit.

The mix of cards, by the way, is an issue that you'll never read about in the Old School books. It's yet another factor they cannot talk about intelligently because they do not recognize is as an issue or even a phenomenon. That's because: a) most of them are not true players (players intuitively understand that some cards are bad, even if they lack the expertise to spot what's wrong); and b) with their random-number-generated computer simulations, they can't possibly spot this nonrandom card phenomenon. Computer simulations do not repeat, so can have researchers who use that kind of data discover how shuffling creates repeating patterns?! There's no way!

Yet, at my seminars, I demonstrate with cards how certain types of mixes can hurt players, causing most to lose. This issue is not theoretical. It's <u>demonstrable</u>.

And if you read Bill Zender's excellent book, *How To Detect Casino Cheating At Blackjack*, you'll realize that the few rogue casinos who cheat understand this issue well, for some of them purposely create bad mixes of cards to cause players to lose. This alone is proof that the card mix is an issue players must understand; it's a factor that, if ignored, creates losers.

You might think of the X Factor as being akin to the guidelines that help a wine lover assess a vintage: is it good or do you toss it? You're about to become betting spot connoisseurs.

Being Observant: A Priceless Skill

Now I talked earlier in this book about your powers of observation, a most underrated skill. Sadly, it's a very under-utilized skill. Because much can be gained by simply observing what's going on.

A friend of mine who was like a father to me taught me to be observant when I was a child. It was actually done as a friendly scolding.

"Richie, you've got to learn to look at the world around you. Really look. And not just look. *See.*"

He was always full of interesting observations about the world around us. Great lesson. That eye-opening lesson made me a great journalist and it made me a great blackjack player and researcher.

Most people look but do not see. They do not notice anything. And they do not draw conclusions or learn anything from what their eyes transmit to their brains. Their brains are asleep.

176

It's amazing what you will learn if your mind is open and you really take in what you see. Actually, it starts with an active decision to look around and focus on what's in front of you. And it requires thinking and a natural curiosity.

Indeed, when I was trained in proper scientific research procedures at the University of Chicago, we were taught a researcher must develop and possess the power to <u>observe</u> and <u>draw conclusions from</u> whatever you were studying. The skills of observation are essential to the scientific process. So we're not talking about voodoo - notwithstanding the minor anonymous and cowardly Internet carping I get from competing authors who want you to close your eyes and check your brains at the door (otherwise, how could you accept their systems' shortcomings?!).

In fact, I developed many of the theories I later proved true in my years of blackjack research simply by observing the break of the cards at the casino. If you have eyes to see, much becomes apparent.

But you don't have to be a scientist to be a great blackjack player. It doesn't hurt if can learn to think like one, though.

Especially when it comes to the X Factor. Because the X Factor is all about being <u>observant</u>. And no one can become a great card player, no matter what the game, without working this skill to perfection. The beauty part is that the X Factor gets you thinking along these lines even if you haven't been an overly observant person. To do this, we'll start with a set of questions you should subliminally always be asking of the cards.

I'll also give you a set of median "norms" you can use to compare with what you're experiencing at any spot so you can tell when the flow of cards to you and/or the dealer is bad or something's wrong. You can use these concrete guidelines to assess whether you're at the right betting spot and, if you are, how you should bet.

The beautiful thing is that, with the X Factor, you don't have to be a whiz at identifying types of bad mixes. All you need to do is detect the symptoms. It's like being a good patient: you don't have to know what illness you have; all you have to know is when

177

it's time to see a doctor.

The X Factor gives you a constant measure of how good the table is for YOU in particular. And it factors in how well the DEALER is doing versus you.

I mean, who cares if the point count is upwards +10 if the dealer beats you every hand? That can and does happen! That's one of the reasons why I've jettisoned card counting in making major decisions. (I offer my own take on it in the Advanced Strategy chapter, but I've morphed it into an intermediate-level state-of-the-art approach.)

Plus — who cares if the dealer is busting a lot, if *you* bust before the dealer? Who cares if everyone at the table is doing great, if YOU are doing poorly?

The **X Factor** keeps you focused on **indicators** that matter most to your game. The **X Factor,** mostly important, informs you as to *how well you are doing versus the dealer.* You'll come to recognize when the cards' personality is: in your favor; mildly against you; or, a terrible buzzsaw (when you'd want to leave that table). You will also get a feel for when the cards are "breaking funny" – when something is amiss. (Along these lines, it is also handy in quickly getting you away from the occasional crooked dealers so you will never again fall victim to them. It will alert you to a problem you otherwise would have missed and will get you away from the table, *rapido.*)

In addition, you will come to notice the repeating patterns peculiar to the cards at your table; the cards that stay in close association with one another, for example, no matter how many shuffles go by. Eventually, this will help you make smarter decisions. (FYI: This comment on a repeating phenomenon is based on original research and is not an endorsement of the card clumping school of thought, as I will explain later. I do NOT agree with that theory.)

How The X Factor Works

On the next page, you'll find the **X Factor Questions** I

referred to before, which will awaken you to what's going on and make you more observant. Don't drive yourself crazy asking all of these questions all of the time, though. Familiarize yourself with the concepts behind them so simple observation will trigger one or more of these questions in your mind as you're playing:

- ♣ **How many hands have you won** (approximately what percent)? 70%? 50%? 5%? The answer is very telling! (I gave you ways to go about this in Chapter 7.) Basic Strategy players, whose winning rate is the lowest among those who've learned any system, can expect to win a little less than half the rounds they play, over time. No matter what your skill level, however, you should never be happy with a winning percentage *below* that.

- ♣ Have you had any **winning cycles or streaks**? If so, how long did they last on average (how many hands)? As my studies show, 70% of all player wins occur within streaks of two or more consecutive wins. So if you've had NO consecutive wins, that's a red flag indicator to leave your spot. That's an extreme example.

- ♣ Have you had any **losing cycles or streaks**? If so, how long did they last (how many hands)? You can't afford to ignore these. They can go on for the length of time a set of cards is in play. No amount of "luck" will turn losing cycles around. In other words, don't have patience when it comes to these.

- ♣ **How often have you busted**? Over time, the Basic Strategy player should expect to bust about 15% of the time (with standing on stiffs taken into account and optional surrendering of some stiffs) *when surrender is allowed*; about 20% of the time when it's not. Busting is often a function of how many stiffs you're getting; if you're getting stiffs well more than 20% of the time, that's a red flag, especially if those stiffs lead to your busting more than not. Leave the table.

- ♣ **How often have you drawn *great scores*** (totals of 19, 20, 21)? (Including Blackjacks, this should be roughly 40% of the time. This reflects player choices not taken by the

179

dealer - such as the standing on stiffs.)

♣ How are you doing with regard to **your chips**? Up? Down? Neutral? We discussed this factor in Chapter 7.

♣ How often have you gotten a **Blackjack**? They should come your way approximately 5% of the time, over time.

♣ **How often have you split, or doubled down unsuccessfully – gotten very poor hit cards and totals and then *lost*?**

♣ How long was **the dealer's longest winning streak**? (Any dealer winning streak is a red flag; protracted ones tell you to leave the table, especially if everyone's losing.)

♣ How long was **the dealer's longest *losing streak***? (Frequent dealer losing streaks are signals to bet higher.)

♣ **How often does the dealer *bust*?** (With weak *and* strong up cards. Overall, the dealer should bust roughly 30% of the time, depending on the number of betting spots in play; the dealer's busting rate should be higher than yours because the dealer must pull to 17 or better.)

♣ *If the dealer busts, how often is it that you have already busted too?* (This might reveal you have a higher-than-normal busting rate, if it occurs too often.)

♣ **How often does the dealer score a great total with the weakest up cards** (the 4 through 6)? The dealer should score roughly 58% with these cards and achieve hands of 19 to 21 points 31-34% of the time.

♣ **How often does the dealer get a Blackjack?** And, how often does the dealer get a Blackjack with an up card of *10? Like you, the dealer should get Blackjacks roughly 5% of the time. Less than 10% of the dealer's 10s should pull a Blackjack, over time.*

♣ **How often is the dealer's up card an Ace?** This should occur only about 8% of the time, over time.

♣ **How often does the dealer get great scores of 20 and 21?** This should occur no more than 30% of the time, over time, factoring in all dealer up cards (the rate varies per up card however; see *Cutting Edge Blackjack* for details). If it's much more frequent, that's a warning sign you're facing bad cards.

♣ *How often does the dealer get the weakest up cards* (4s, 5, and 6s)? This should occur a little more than 20% of the time. If it's much less frequent, that's likely a bad sign, unless the dealer's strong cards are busting a lot.

♣ **How often does the dealer get the most player-unfriendly up cards — 10s and Aces?** This should occur less than 40% of the time. If it occurs much more, that's a red flag - IF the dealer is simultaneously beating you more than not with those cards. Leave the table.

♣ Have you detected any **clumps of low or high cards**? This is a phenomenon that can plague multideck games. Clumps of low cards result in low dealer busting rates. Leave the table upon seeing these. (A clump is a long string of primarily low cards that carries over from shuffle to shuffle.)

♣ How many players seem to be doing well? Is everyone doing well? Are you the only one doing well? Is no one doing well? If EVERYONE'S losing, run! If EVERYONE'S winning, it's time go to Level 3 in the 3-Level system.

What The Answers Tell Us

Why do we want to know the answers to these **X Factor Questions**, and what do they add up to? For one thing, you can use the X Factor as an adjunct to your 3-Level Bet Management System (in Chapter 7). Once you start recognizing the **personality of the cards**, you'll see that the **X Factor** is a very good indicator, especially with regard to how to manage your bets, and knowing when to leave a table.

For instance, perhaps you've grown confident that the cards are player-friendly. Then, you'll be playing at Level 2 or 3 in your **3-Level Notch-Up, Notch-Down Bet Management System** (see Chapter 7). Or X Factor indicators might tell you that something is wrong! All the dealer's up cards are 10s and Aces, and the dealer always winds up with 20 or 21 points! Run!

Measuring How YOU Are Doing

*The approximate percentage of times you win is the most important number of all the numbers you must ascertain during any stay at a blackjack table. We will call this your **table winning percentage**. This X Factor issue also ties in with your 3-Level system.*

At a neutral table, your **table winning percentage** should be in the general range of 50% of the number of hands played, or more (not counting pushes) - if you're a Basic Strategy player.

Good to great tables, however, will give you significantly more wins. If you detect this is the case, go to Levels 2 or 3 in your 3-Level system.

If, however, you're down around 10-20% or LESS, something is terribly wrong! Leave the table, or the casino! If it's 25-30%, this is a cause for concern. Go to another table! If it's 40%, you're under the average of what the computed odds are for you to win but it might just be a temporary down cycle.

You'd be surprised at how many players stay rooted to one table, even when they're losing much more than they should! If they were simply aware of this concept – the **table winning percentage** — there would be a lot less losers.

Winning And Losing Cycles

How many winning cycles or streaks (consecutive wins) you have had, and how long they've lasted is another important **X Factor Indicator**. At some tables, it's hard to find a winning cycle. That's a sign of a neutral or bad betting spot. At difficult spot, it often seems that, if you raise your bet, you get clobbered. *You want a table that provides you with a healthy winning cycle.*

Losing streaks (consecutive losses) are very good things to keep track of because they will keep you focused on how BAD a table is. Two or three consecutive losses should wake you up. Four or five and you should be in gear, moving elsewhere. Don't wait until all your chips are gone!!!

182

Bust Not, Want Not

How often you bust is another good **X Factor Indicator**. It shouldn't happen a LOT. If you're busting 40% of the time or more, it indicates you're getting a lot of "stiffs" (hard totals of 12 to 16) that you have to hit to improve. It's a good indicator something is wrong. Use this to put your feet in gear. If you find yourself saying "NOT again!" — that's when you leave.

Seen Any 20s and 21s Lately?

How often you draw great scores is also a very telling **X Factor Indicator**. Great scores — good betting spot. Crummy scores — bad betting spot. Something might be wrong. Leave.

With nearly 31% of the cards being 10s, you should have 2-card hands of 20 points nearly 10% of the time; overall, you should get 20 point hands about 15% of the time. Collectively, you should get 20 and 21 point hands more than 20% of the time. If you factor in Blackjacks, you should get these top hands nearly 30% of the time. If you NEVER seem to get 20 or 21 point hands, LEAVE THE TABLE.

When The Chips Are Down

How your chips are doing is another important **X Factor Indicator**, and one of the more obvious ones. In fact, we talked about how to handle this factor in Chapter 7.

However, you can layer the X Factor on top of what you learned in that chapter. If you're down, a light bulb should go off in your head, alerting you to use the **X Factor** to tell you if the table might turn around for you, or if it's hopeless. Ask yourself: is there a persistent down pattern or personality to the cards that seems to repeat itself, shuffle after shuffle? Repetitive, bad patterns are a sure sign something is wrong.

Sometimes down cycles will turn around. But not at tables where you have been unable to put together a good number of wins. And not when you rarely if ever get great point totals. Pay attention to these **X Factor Indicators**.

If, however, you are up in chips, and the **X Factor Indicators**

are all go, then you can afford to make more risky moves and increase your **Basic Bet** to Level 2 or 3.

Your Blackjacks

How often you get Blackjacks is only of use in telling you how GOOD the table is, not how bad. I've been at tables where I'm not doing well and yet I might get two or three Blackjacks! They won't outweigh the effect of the majority of hands if they are bad. Plus, at bad tables, you're typically betting the table minimum so your extra Blackjack gains won't be much.

So this is the least important of all our **X Factor Questions**. I mention this because some players are convinced that this is an important indicator of how good a table is. NOT.

Splitting And Doubling Indicators

How often you've split or doubled down and gotten horrible hit cards and lost can be significant. Three times or more and you should be on your guard. If it happens a fourth time, LEAVE.

Especially Watch How "Lucky" The Dealer's Been

How the dealer is doing is an extremely revealing X Factor Indicator. Does the dealer go on long winning streaks (winning many hands in a row)? Or many short winning streaks, punctuated by one win for you? That would be a sign of a bad or terrible table. Dealer winning streaks are a sure warning sign and you should immediately consider leaving the table.

If, however, you win one or two, the dealer wins one or two, back and forth, you're at a neutral or choppy table.

Or, does the dealer go on moderately long losing streaks? That's an obvious sign of a good to great table. Get more money down.

If the dealer often busts, this can be a significant positive indicator – IF you're not busting first. If you're always busting when the dealer busts, beware!! A card flow where everyone's busting more often than normal might be a tip off of cards that were "arranged" to break that way. (You'll learn more about that

184

in Chapter 11.)

And *if the dealer often wins and doesn't bust with up cards of 3 through 6*, this is very revealing. You might be in big trouble. This could be a sign of a clump of low cards, or too many low cards. Leave the table! (Once again, Chapter 11 might hold the answer to what's going on.)

Beware The Dealer's Blackjacks

If the DEALER gets three Blackjacks in short order, LEAVE that table!! Beware especially if the dealer gets two or more Black-jacks in close succession with up cards of 10! Beware, too, if the dealer gets a Blackjack immediately after each shuffle – if you see this happen twice, shame on you if you stay at that table! Especially if the dealer's repeating Blackjack consists of the SAME CARDS!!! It may be a coincidence, by DON'T STAY AT THAT TABLE, just in case it's NOT!

How often the dealer gets Aces as up cards is also useful **X Factor** information. Too often and you should be "outta there." Remember – Aces only account for 7.7% of the cards!

Beware The Dealer's 20s And 21s

Pay attention to how often the dealer gets great scores of 20 and 21, especially if it seems constant. That's the pattern you'll run into at tables where the cards are rigged or the dealer is something of a "magician" (see Chapter 11). Now, it might also be a coincidence, but, just in case, LEAVE!

Two-card hands that total 20 points should occur less than 11% of the time! If the dealer is "bucking the odds" and getting those hands much more often, don't stick around!

How Strong Is The Dealer?

How often the dealers get weak or strong up cards is also very telling. If they get their share of 3s through 6s, and then bust at least 30% of the time, fine. Stay. *If, however, the dealer gets more than his or her share of 10s and Aces in a dozen rounds, that's a wake up call*.

185

Another **X Factor** red flag is the "grouping" of cards - where high and low cards travel around separately. Clumps of low cards lead to minimal dealer busting. LEAVE the table.

How other players are doing is usually insignificant to us. It's only *when ALL the players are doing poorly* that it really matters. That's an **X Factor** tip-off that it's time to leave. At a 7-player table, the dealer will normally beat all the players 9% of the time. That should happen twice in a row only .8% of the time. ***It is highly improbable that this would ever naturally happen three times in a row***. These are the guidelines; if it happens more frequently than this, you leave.

Applying the X Factor to Money Management

Now the **X Factor** can help guide you as to what Level you should be on in your 3-Level betting system. Ask yourself:

- ♣ Are things kind of neutral? You haven't won anything but you haven't lost anything...Stay at Level 1.
- ♣ Are you winning a good percentage of hands...The dealer is busting on weak cards...Your chips are up... The dealer is getting a good number of weak up cards and not too many strong cards...You've gotten Blackjacks and the dealer hasn't...Go to Level 2.
- ♣ Are you on a long winning cycle...The dealer is busting a LOT and right and never seems to get good cards... Your chips are piling up...In fact, everyone at the table is doing well...Go to Level 3.
- ♣ Does the table seem totally cold? You never seem to win and neither does anyone else...The dealer just had two Blackjacks and now has a total of 21 after having a weak up card? Leave. Bad cards don't grow warm.

I've given you a lot to think about. And on many levels, I think you'll find the X Factor is a great entry-level way to profit from state-of-the-art blackjack concepts. Please return to this chapter later on and fully absorb the many ideas I've presented here.

You are still not ready to enter a casino.

ADVANCED CARD STRATEGY

187

OK, now you are ready to put everything you've learned together, to work toward becoming an advanced player.

We will synthesize all of your newfound knowledge and use it to arrive at a higher skill level. The great thing about what you are about to master is that it brings with it a higher win rate, and all the profits that go along with that.

We'll layer *Blackjack The SMART Way* Basic Strategy and concepts with what you now know about:

♥ The **personalities of the dealer up cards**.
♥ The mathematical probabilities underlying the game.
♥ The perils of handling stiffs, doubling and splitting.
♥ Money management.
♥ The **3-Level, Notch-Up, Notch-Down Bet Management System**.
♥ Keeping track of the cards (either by card counting or by **Card Observation**).
♥ The **X Factor**.

Your goal here will be to achieve flexibility. You will want to draw upon your understanding of the *Blackjack The SMART Way* concepts and methods you have discovered here to make smarter decisions *on the fly at the blackjack table* based on the card action you observe unfolding before you. Your thinking now should be moving beyond the charts toward a higher conscious-ness. This is the hallmark of the *Blackjack The SMART Way* advanced player.

In my second book, *Cutting Edge Blackjack* – which will open up new worlds to you when you are ready to go further — you'll have much more information at your fingertips, to make even more precise decisions, on the spot. You will learn to divorce yourself from the traditional chart-driven mentality and do a lot more independent thinking based upon the underlying mathemati-cal realities uncovered in *Blackjack The SMART Way* and the results of my most recent research projects.

But, let's not get ahead of ourselves. First, there's a lot of information for you to digest right here and use to your great advantage before you will be ready for that more advanced book. Let's take it one step at a time.

For now, you will still need to study charts reflecting the guidelines that will lead you toward becoming a great player. Please take time now to review your Advanced Strategy Charts (they appear at the end of the chapter, on pages 207-210).

Looking at these charts, you'll see that your options are greater than they were in the Basic Strategy charts. Now, you can push the envelope and make educated choices in grey areas that you weren't wise enough to make before.

These extra options will give you the potential to win even more money than you would by following Basic Strategy.

How To Play Hard Hands for the Advanced Player

If you take a look at CHART 4 (page 207) you will see that, unlike the corresponding Basic Strategy chart (CHART 1A on page 50), there are now boxes that contain TWO or even THREE possible moves. These fall in what I call grey areas where sometimes **the flow of the cards** makes an unconventional move smarter. The move listed first, often marked with a question mark, is usually the move you were taught in Basic Strategy. But *now it is only to be done in instances where the card count and/or Card Observation indicate it can be done successfully*. If your card analysis skills tell you that the move listed first is likely to cost you the hand, then do the second (or third) recommended move instead.

By the way, sometimes the new choice offered to you (one that was not suggested in Basic Strategy) is the more *conservative* way to go! For now that you know something about keeping track of the cards, why not use that added knowledge in sometimes playing it *safer* than you did with Basic Strategy, if you are in a situation that points to dangers in following a more standard approach?! Knowledge is power.

Your goal as an advanced player, therefore, is not to become more reckless or risky – far from it! Your goal is to make the smartest moves based upon sound logic. That will often mean taking the path of AVOIDING risk, to conserve your money and prevent losses! Like an experienced sailor, you will be a bit more cautious at times; unlike the younger, less experienced sailor, you might elect to steer your boat toward port when proverbial storm clouds appear.

The Advanced Player Must Understand Nuances

With added room for discretion, of course, comes the price of having to *think* more. But, to me, this what makes the game so thrilling – the challenge of out-thinking the cards and the house, and the rewards that come with doing so.

Please note: we won't be looking at any of the moves in the Advanced Strategy Charts that coincide with the Basic Strategy Charts. You should know those by now, by heart.

Let us, instead, talk about the areas in the Advanced Strategy Charts where you will now have choices to make, where you'll have to exercise your judgment to adjust to **the flow of the cards,** based upon what you now know about the mathematical forces that rule the game.

You Mean I Can Double On A 7 or 8 Point Hand?

First, you'll notice that you now have doubling down opportunities even with hands of meager totals of 7 and 8, in four limited cases – if your 8 is against the dealer's 4, 5 or 6, or if your 7 is against the dealer's 5 (which often causes the dealer to bust more than the 4 or 6 when the count is positive) and you believe the dealer will bust. THESE MOVES, HOWEVER, DEPEND UPON THE COUNT AND/OR WHAT **CARD OBSERVATION** TELLS YOU. Making extra money is nice, but *exercise caution.*

Do these ONLY if you are *certain* that high cards and Aces are due (in the case of the 7, you should have a good idea that 10s and Aces, specifically, are overdue). For card counters, you should have a relatively high All-Inclusive Counting System positive count, at least in the range of **+5** or so to double on the 8; it should be **+7** or more to double on the 7, give or take.

But, use your judgment. Otherwise, HIT these totals, as you did before. You have nothing to lose by hitting your 7 or 8. Don't forget, in avoiding doubling you will gain the ability to hit your cards again if you are dealt an unhelpful low hit card. Doubling on a 7 or 8 is definitely on the riskier side of things.

Plus, if you're being watched closely by casino management, NEVER do these provocative moves. You'll give yourself away as a system player.

However, if you have the opportunity, and it seems wise, hey, why not make some extra money?

Doubling on totals of 7 and 8 are moves that are definitely "on the edge." It's important that you understand: 1) that they will raise eyebrows; and, 2) you should proceed with caution.

Playing Against the Tricky 2

Ah! As an advanced player, you can really take advantage of the knowledge presented in Chapter 4 regarding the **Tricky 2s**.

Interestingly enough, although the dealer's 2 is a hazardous card, I've added a doubling down opportunity against it, when your total is 9. Only do this, though, when you know higher cards and Aces are due to arrive, which would give you a strong winning total. When LOW cards are due (in a negative count), you'll simply HIT your 9 versus the dealer's 2. You don't want to wind up with a stiff, a sure loser, with *twice* your bet on the line!

OK. Now, I'm placing two former doubling down suggestions into the grey area pile. I'm recommending that you HIT your totals of 10 or 11 against the dealer's 2 if you know that high cards have been depleted (and the Aces too, with your 10) and that low cards are likely to fall upon your cards. This would be in moderately to strongly negative counts. (In 1- or 2-deck pitch games, I'm talking about counts of **-4** or worse. In 4- or 6-deck games, I mean when the count has dropped to **-8** or lower. In

8-deck games: -12 and beyond.)

With regard to stiffs: if you have 13 or 14 points versus the **Tricky 2**, you should HIT if the count is negative, or if **Card Observation** tells you that low cards are due. (Even with the 14 the odds are in your favor — you have a 54% chance – with 7 out of 13 cards — of bettering your score without busting.) If you chose instead to STAND with those stiffs, you'll have a greater than 54% chance of LOSING versus the dealer's 2, so your preferred choice is obvious – you HIT. However, if the count is positive, or when **Card Observation** says that high cards are due (or 10s, especially with your 12), STAND on all stiffs.

If you have totals of 15 or 16, you'll want to HIT when it's likely the dealer's 2 will achieve a good score. But only do so when the count is very negative (**–8** or more at a 1- or 2-deck table; **-12** or more at 4- or 6-deck tables; and **-16** or more at 8-deck tables) or when **Card Observation** tells you low cards are way overdue. *This is a very risky move, so remember: hit totals of 15 or 16 with extreme caution*.

More Caution Against The Dealer's 3

In positive territory, the 3 is our friend. Not so in moderately to strongly negative counts however.

The dealer's 3 is a better card for the player than the 2 but as the count sinks to moderately negative territory, it begins to act like a dealer-friendly card, drawing to winning totals. As a result, you'll want to HIT your 13s and 14s in that situation. Your chances of improving those hands WITHOUT busting will then outweigh the risk.

On the flip side of that coin, you should STAND if you have totals of 12 or 13 and the count is moderately *positive*, and/or **Card Observation** suggests that your hit card will likely bust you (specifically, when it is probable that your hit card will be a 10, or a 9 in the case of your 13). That's a more cautious approach than I suggested in CHART 1A. But, as an advanced player, you can make more informed decisions.

I'm now also suggesting more caution when you have scores of 9, 10 or 11 against the dealer's 3. You will NOT want to double as suggested in Basic Strategy if the count is in a dangerous moderately negative zone, or when **Card Observation** tells you that the high cards that would make your hand have been depleted. With the 9 and 10, you should also get more cautious if Aces are unlikely to be dealt to you. Simply HIT your cards in those situations.

When The Dealer's 4, 5 and 6 Are NOT Your Friends

Now, many players incorrectly assume that the dealer's 4, 5 and 6 are always great cards for them. Not always. You really have to be careful here.

Like the 2 and the 3, the 4, 5 and 6 are sensitive to card imbalances. These cards actually become strong dealer cards when low cards are overdue, reaching high winning scores more than usual. They become turncoats and broadside your stiffs when you were thinking the dealer was likely to bust. Your signal that this is going to occur is when the count is moderately to strongly negative, or when **Card Observation** makes it obvious that high cards have been depleted and low cards are ready to come in a flood.

That's why I suggest that you NOT double down on traditionally great doubling totals – your 9, 10 or 11 – against the dealer's 4, 5 and 6 when the count is **−4** or lower. (Also be more cautious with your 9 and 10 in particular if Aces are also in short supply).

Again, when you HIT your cards rather than double, you have NOT given up any edge in your attempt to win. In fact, you are gaining an edge, because you are not limited to taking just one hit card. What you are doing is protecting your money in case the odds turn against you in a risky card count. You don't want to jeopardize TWICE as much money by doubling down when your chances of beating the dealer are iffy.

In fact, once the count is moderately negative (**−4** or lower), you'll want to treat the dealer's weakest up cards very much like the Tricky 2 - or worse, depending on how negative the count becomes. Their bust rates drop below the 2's during these periods, hitting bottom at around 30% or lower! So HIT your 12 point and possibly even your 13 point hands at **-4**. And when the count is **-8** or lower you would be smart to hit ALL your stiffs.

These moves will make some of your fellow players question your sanity but when no one else can hear you, just tell them to read this book. They might eventually see the light, but don't expect too many miracles. The average player cannot understand anything that goes beyond their limited understanding of Basic Strategy. So, you will have to expect your share of groans when making brilliant moves. How ironic, isn't it?!

Standing Against The Silent 7

Remember Chapter 4 regarding the **Silent 7s**? As an advanced player you are now in a position to take advantage of that information. For example, when you have a hand of 15 or 16 points against the dealer's 7, you might now wisely choose to STAND in certain situations.

This option is a bit tricky, though. You'll want to be pretty certain the dealer's got a stiff, based on having, preferably a 7, 8 or 9 in the hole.

Conversely, you'll want to be sure the dealer's hole card is NOT likely to be a 10 or an Ace. If your **Card Observation** skills and the card count strongly suggest there's a 10 or Ace in the hole, then your decision is easy – you have to hit your 15 or 16. If you've determined that the dealer is UNLIKELY to have a 10 or an Ace in the hole, then you should definitely STAND - UNLESS you're very, very sure you're likely to get a hit card that will help you. In the case of your 15, you'd need a 6 or less; in the case of your 16, you'd need a 5 or less. The other times you'd be wise to hit your 15s and 16s would be when you're sure the dealer's likely to have a 2, 3 or 4 in the hole, which would give the dealer a very strong starting hand.

Your likelihood of busting with a score of 15 if the count is neutral is about 54%; with the 16, it's nearly 62%. That's a difficult place to be. If the count is **+4** or more, your chances of busting go much higher.

You, as an advanced player, should think this one through and remain flexible. This is one of the more difficult decisions you will have to make.

At a shoe table (and the rare face-up pitch game tables you'll find occasionally in Vegas especially), you have the added advantage, in doing card analyses, of being able to watch what cards players before you got as their *second* cards – *those are the ones that came directly before the dealer's hole card*. These cards as you know, give you a huge clue as to what the hole card is. Also, you can see what *hit* cards players to your right drew — *those cards came directly <u>after</u> the dealer's hole card!* They can help reveal situations where the dealer has a weak hole card and YOU'RE likely to be dealt a bust card.

For example – if players' second cards were 2, 3, K, 10, Q, and 5, and players' hit cards to your right were 4, 10, 6, J, 4, 3 and Ace, that would be a prime time to STAND with ALL stiffs versus the dealer's 7. The hole card is most likely to be a 7, 8 or 9 (because these cards were not dealt amongst this mix), so the dealer is highly likely to bust; and you are likely to bust especially with your 15s and 16s if you take a hit card.

Situations like that happen all the time and if you exercise the skills I've taught you, you'll squeeze more gains out of winning situations others cannot hope to identify.

Taking Advantage of the Silent 7 With Your 9

This move was introduced to you in Chapter 5, but it bears repeating and a word of caution. We now know the dealer's 7 is a player's card. *And given the weakness of the 7 (which reaches an average score of 18 - the lowest average score of any up card), it often will be wise to double down on your 9 against it.*

With a 9, you'd benefit from getting an Ace, 8, 9 or any of the four 10-pointers as your extra card. So 7 of 13 cards, or

54%, would be great as your one hit cards in doubling, against this weak up card. Don't forget, too, that, when you double here, you won't bust, and so that's one advantage over hitting; the dealer, however, will bust about 26% of the time overall and you will win every time that occurs (if you hit your 9 instead, you'd bust occasionally, and some of those losses would occur when the dealer busted as well, so you would not benefit from every dealer busting event when hitting your cards).

Do NOT consider this if the count is **-3** or lower however, or, if by using **Card Observation**, you're pretty certain you'll get a low hit card that will give you a stiff total.

More Caution At Times Against The Dealer's 7

That being said, my research shows that the 7's busting rate goes way down when 5s through 9s are unlikely to be in the hole. And, actually, its busting rate (over time) is lower than the dealer's 10 if there are no 8s or 9s in the hole! So in these situations I'm now telling you NOT to double down on your 10-point hand UNLESS you're certain you'll draw a score of 18 or higher.

If you're going to get a 7 or less as your hit card, be conservative and HIT that hand. You can then take more than one hit card if you indeed pull a low one.

New Doubling Possibilities With The 8, 9, 10 & Ace

In Basic Strategy CHART 1A, I eliminated three traditionally recommended doubling moves at times when you have totals of 10 or 11 – that is, against the dealer's 9 in the case of your 10, and against the dealer's 10 and Ace in the case of your 11. I feel strongly that doubling in those cases without the benefit of knowing how to card count or use **Card Observation** is foolish against such strong dealer cards.

As an advanced player, you can understand why doubling against those formidable up cards in a negative count (when low cards are overdue) is an overly greedy move. Your hit card is likely to be one of the overdue low cards and the dealer is likely to arrive at a high winning score. Once again, choosing to HIT your 10 or 11 instead of doubling doesn't limit your opportunity to win; it INCREASES your chances. (Refer back to Chapter 5 for more details.)

That being said, you, as an advanced player, would now be WISE to double down on your 10 and 11 in the situations listed above in *limited* cases — that is, IF the count is moderately to strongly positive. Using **Card Observation**, that means you should double down when you know that high cards are overdue (and Aces, in the case of your 10) that would give you hands of 20 or 21 points.

On the other hand, you will always want to hit your totals of 10s and 11s versus dealer 8s or above, when you're certain, using **Card Observation**, that low cards are overdue, which would give you stiff totals with doubling. (Or if the count is **-4** or lower.)

A Fresh Look At Surrender

A word about Surrendering. Now that you're an advanced player, DON'T Surrender your stiffs if the count is negative, or if **Card Observation** tells you that low cards are overdue. To be more specific: HIT your totals of 14 to 16 against the dealer's Ace, your 15s and 16s against the dealer's 10, and your 16s against the dealer's 9 in those situations. In this situation, you're more likely to get the cards you need and less likely to lose.

On Insurance

Insurance is not listed in the Advanced Charts because, when it's wise, it's an across-the-board kind of thing. *You might want to take Insurance with any hand you're dealt.* It would clog up the charts if I put "Insurance?" in every box, wouldn't it? So, let's discuss right now when, if ever, you might want to avail yourself of this sometimes very useful option.

197

It's most often a losing bet, after all. Don't forget – in neutral counts, the dealer has less than a 31% chance of having a 10 under the Ace up card. This does not mean, however, that you won't want to use this option on rare occasions, *no matter what your hand is.*

If the card count is very positive when the dealer deals the hole card, and/or if **Card Observation** tells you that the hole card is super likely to be a 10, you should take Insurance *even if you do not have a Blackjack.* This is one thing players do not seem to understand. I'll never forget the time a player questioned me for taking Insurance when I did not have a blackjack, as if I was crazy. He did not get it. You're not Insuring your hand; you're Insuring your money. You're protecting your money in a situation where you're a sure loser. So who CARES what hand you have?! (FYI: If you have a Blackjack and you are sure the dealer has a Blackjack, I would suggest that you simply ask for Even Money. You're paid off right away - without the typical Blackjack bonus, of course. It's simpler, it prevents any confusion later on and the results are the same.)

This is another move that other players might question, but, once again, stick to your guns. 'Better to laugh at the know-it-alls than to get into distracting arguments, or, worse yet, allow them to ruin your game by letting them bully you into making the wrong move.

So don't forget: Insurance is a separate bet and is on occasion a smart move. Use it correctly and it will spare you unnecessary losses. For card counters — consider doing this perhaps when the count is **+6** or more when the hole card is dealt. If you're confused about when to do this DON'T ever take Insurance. It's a move for a seasoned player.

Additional Soft Hand Opportunities

You'll notice that the Advanced Players' CHART 5 for soft hands (page 208) differs in only 14 boxes from CHART 2, and we already discussed one of the boxes, regarding Insurance (that is,

198

you should STAND on a Blackjack UNLESS the count is very positive when the hole card is dealt because you want to get the extra bonus (whether it's 3-to-2 or 6-to-5) when a dealer Black-jack is not a serious possibility).

Here are the other items in CHART 5 that are new (you'll probably not see the following in any other book):

For one thing, we're taking advantage of what we know about the dealer's **Silent 7** – that it is really a player's card. *(It draws to a 17 or busts 66% of the time!)* So when it's your turn, if **Card Observation** tells you that any of the cards that might help you are way overdue, then you might consider doubling on your Ace-4, Ace-5, Ace-6 and Ace-7.

The Ace-4 draws to winning totals with the 2, 3, 4, 5, and 6; the Ace-5, with the Ace, 2, 3, 4, and 5. Your Ace-6 and Ace-7 draw to winning totals with 8 of 13 possible cards – the Ace-6, with an Ace, 2, 3, 4, and the 10s; the Ace-7, with an Ace, 2, 3, 9 and the 10s. Not bad! (Doubling on the Ace-4 and Ace-5, admittedly, is a bit trickier and requires more certainty that you'll get the cards you'll need, since fewer cards benefit these hands.)

With the Ace-8 combination, you can now DOUBLE DOWN against the dealer's 4, 5 and 6 PROVIDED that high cards are moderately to strongly overdue — that is, the count is **+4** or more, especially if your independent tracking of Aces tells you that Aces are also likely to start appearing soon. If the count is less than **+4**, or **Card Observation** cannot confirm the conditions spelled out above, STAND as you did before.

The Lower Ace Combinations

Another difference in this Advanced Chart is that you will sometimes be *more cautious* when you have the lower soft hands — the Ace-2 through the Ace-5 — versus the dealer's 4, 5 or 6. Double ONLY if the count is roughly neutral or in positive territory. Otherwise, HIT them. The dealer's 4 through 6 are much more likely to score winning totals in negative territory and these small Ace combinations have a smaller than even chance to score winning totals if restricted to the one hit card you'd get with doubling down.

However, you have two NEW doubling opportunities here, with the Ace-4 and Ace-5, against the dealer's 3 (and, as mentioned before, the 7), IF the count is NOT negative — if high cards or Aces are NOT depleted (when the dealer would likely score well).

Splitting for the Advanced Player

OK, CHART 5 was easy! Now, CHART 6 (on page 209) differs from Basic Strategy CHART 3A surprisingly enough in that it is largely *more conservative!*

Take a moment now to peruse this chart. You will undoubtedly notice that you will be doing LESS splitting as an advanced player than you did with *Blackjack The SMART Way* Basic Strategy!

As I suggested before, most players think that being an advanced player means taking more risks. Where appropriate, that's great, but it's just as useful and profitable to cut back where you can on possible losses, to end up with more winnings when the day is through. As indicated in Chapter 5, those options can often prove to be the casino's friend, not yours.

Think about it. It's the hands where you split and double down that can lead to your biggest setbacks; you've got more money on the table. If you don't exercise proper caution, you'll end up chasing deficits instead of building gains.

Re-Think Splitting Against The Tricky 2s

The dealer's **Tricky 2** is reason for caution when you are considering doubling or splitting – moves that require you to increase your bet.

You should still split your 8s, because my research shows that splitting your 8s will do better for you than either hitting your 16 or standing on it. Keeping the two 8s together as a hand of 16 is NOT a good option in this case.

However, you will want to become more cautious with your pair of 2s. In a negative count, or when high cards have been depleted, simply HIT your 2s. You will save yourself the extra money you'd probably lose if you split your 2s. You're unlikely to win here either with your unsplit deuces or your split hands of 2 in that situation, when the dealer's 2 is less likely to bust.

There's another instance where you should play it safer – if you have a pair of 5s, in moderately negative territory. Instead of doubling here, HIT those cards if the count is **–4** or lower, or if **Card Observation** tells you low cards are overdue. In fact, doubling on any 10 point hand is no picnic if low cards are coming in large numbers. You're then likely to draw a stiff when the dealer's 2 is likely to draw to a winning score.

You will also want to play it safer with your pair of 9s. *STAND on your pairs of 9s if the count is negative, or* **Card Observation** *tells you that high cards and Aces have been played out more than other cards.* The 9s – with a total of 18 – provide a good score. No need to risk splitting them and placing more money on the table when the dealer's 2 becomes even stronger and your chances of drawing strong winning hands with the split 9s are not very good.

When You Should Play It Safer Against the 3

As mentioned above, the dealer's 3 acts more like the dealer's friend than the player's once the count is –4 or lower or when **Card Observation** tells you that low cards are coming. So you shouldn't take on more risk (as in putting more money on the table to double or split) if you think the 3 will give the dealer a winning total.

So DON'T split your pairs of 2s or 3s in that situation. HIT them. There's no advantage to splitting these cards if the dealer's 3 isn't likely to bust.

And HIT your pair of 5s when the count is moderately or strongly negative as outlined above — don't double down. As we saw earlier, you don't want to double your money on your 10 point hands when your hit card is likely to produce a stiff and the dealer's 3 looks like a winner.

A More Lucrative Possibility With Your 4s

For some psychological reason, when you hold a pair of 4s it isn't immediately apparent that they should be treated simply as a hand totaling 8 points, but this is the smartest thing to do! As a general rule, you NEVER split them. Because 4-point hands are most often losers. They behave just like the dealer's 4. So in cases where you intend on drawing to a 17 or better, you'll bust 43% of the time! No, a hand of 8 points is much better starting hand.

So, along these lines, against the dealer's 4, 5 and 6, you are not going to want to hit your pairs of 4s, as you did in Basic Strategy; you will want to double down if conditions are favorable, just as you did with your other 8 point totals (see pages 190-1). Since you know now that those weak dealer up cards are only dangerous in negative territory, the wise thing to do is to double down on your pair of 4s when the count is firmly positive: **+5** or higher. If you're using **Card Observation**, you should double on the 4s if it tells you that high cards (especially 9s, 10s and Aces) are due. Otherwise, HIT.

Something You Should Know About The 4, 5 and 6

Somehow, the dealer's up card of 6 has gotten the reputation of being the best card for the player. In fact, I am going to pop this balloon, as I have popped many others in this book. (We'll see justification for my saying this in much greater mathematical detail in my second book, *Cutting Edge Blackjack*.)

For instance, when the count is positive, the dealer's 5, and then the 4 are the two best cards for the player, causing the dealer to bust more than the 6. When the count is neutral, the dealer's 4 causes the dealer to bust more than the 5 which causes the dealer to bust more than the 6. When the count is negative, however, look out. These up cards are to be respected during moderately to strongly negative counts, when they bust a lot less than they normally do, and can even achieve busting rates lower than the dealer's 10, depending on the card imbalance. In fact, you'd be smart to treat them like the dealer' 10 once the count descends to **-8**, especially at a single or double deck game. At that point, for instance, DON'T split your 3s or 6s - or do any move you wouldn't do against the 10, using Basic Strategy.

When To Respect The Silent 7

There's one change you should make in your approach to the dealer's 7 from Basic Strategy.

Once the count gets down into fairly negative territory, simply HIT your pair of 5s. Use the same criterion we used earlier in this chapter with your hard hand of 10, which is really what you have here.

A Word About The Dealer's 8

Now we won't radically change our card pair strategy with regard to the dealer's up card of 8. But it won't scare us, either.

The 8 most often causes the dealer either to reach a point total of 17 or 18, or to bust. Since 18 points is a fairly weak winning total, you will often outscore the dealer (with a 19, 20 or 21), push, or win because the dealer busts. (We will look at this in much greater detail, in *Cutting Edge Blackjack*. You will actually beat the dealer's 8 a tiny bit more than you will lose to it!)

Therefore, when the dealer has an 8 as the up card, you should NOT throw in the towel. To the contrary, you should feel fairly lucky. How do you use this information?

We've already taken that into account, in deciding to double on your totals of 10, which includes your pairs of 5s. *Hit* your pairs of 5s however when the count gets down to moderately negative territory, **-4** or lower, or when **Card Observation** tells you that Aces, 10s and 9s have been depleted.

Where Does That Leave The 9?

The dealer's 9 is no weakling. That is definitely a heavyweight contender. And yet you can now consider doubling down on your pairs of 5s against this card as you did with your hard totals of 10. You will want to wait however until you really have the edge here, where the odds make this an obvious move. That would be when the count is strongly positive, or **Card Observation** tells you that the one extra card you'll be given will be a high card, or an Ace, producing a strong, winning hand.

You Mean I Should Sometimes Surrender Pairs of 8s?

Now my advice regarding your pairs of 8s is going to cause some controversy at the table among unsophisticated players, but as you saw in Chapter 5, it often makes total mathematical sense NOT to split them or see them as anything but pariahs. I won't repeat everything I said in Chapter 5, but it doesn't hurt to remind you how weak this hand often is.

Do NOT split them when your card analysis skills tell you that are very likely to get hit cards of 4 through 9 as your second cards. Those will put your 8s in a position where your loses due to busting will be severe. Always SURRENDER your pairs of 8s against the dealer's 10 or Ace under those conditions. If Surrender is not allowed, analyze the situation to determine if standing or hitting is your best move (treat them as you would any other stiff of 16 points). Losing 50% of your money (as in Surrendering) is actually the best result you can hope to achieve when you know your 8s will be married up with 4s through 9s.

When 10s and Aces are overdue, that might or might not be good news for your pairs of 8s. Against the dealer's 9 and 10, it could mean you'll wind up with hands of one less point than the dealer's. So beware splitting when you determine this is likely.

Now the 2s and 3s, when overdue, would be of help to your

split 8s. If those are depleted, however - especially if the 10s and Aces are as well - you know it's time to Surrender or play your 8s as any other stiff of 16 points.

And, as you saw in Chapter 5, no matter how you cut it, having a pair of 8s versus the dealer's strongest cards is a losing situation. The dealer's 10 and Ace, especially, will draw to very high winning totals – much better totals than your 8s will achieve.

You want to maximize your gains through a complete under-standing of the odds, the mathematics that rule the game, and sometimes that means going the path of cutting your losses. Therefore – although it will raise the hackles of those who have not read *Blackjack The SMART Way* – stand firm and make the correct moves. It's your money and you'd be foolish not to protect it if possible in a no-win situation.

You Mean I Should Sometimes HIT Pairs of Aces?

Now, HITTING pairs of Aces instead of ALWAYS splitting is another bugaboo among players, but, as you saw in Chapter 5, it is sometimes your smartest move. Remember: it's YOUR money.

How many times have you split Aces only to have them hang in the wind to certain defeat, when the one extra card each receives creates two stiffs? With the talents you have now, you can predict with good regularity when low cards and Aces are more likely to come than other cards. So, when the card count is **-4** at the pitch game tables, or **-8** at the 4- or 6-deck tables, or **-12** at the 8-deck tables, DON'T split your Aces, especially if you are facing the dealer's 9, 10 or Ace and Card Observation tells you that high cards have been played out disproportionately. Simply HIT them. You might even *win* that way!

But Don't Abandon Basic Strategy

OK, so now you're a lot wiser. But, you know what? There will be times where you still need to return to Basic Strategy!

When? When you don't know the count or it's neutral. Or you're momentarily confused (this mental block might occasionally occur when you're starting out). With **Card Observation**, it would be when the card flow is balanced. *Blackjack The SMART Way* Basic Strategy is your fall-back position, your port in any storm.

Now, when you're ready to take on *Cutting Edge Blackjack* and move to a higher level of play, or when you're ready to take one of my seminars, you'll find that great blackjack involves a lot more flexibility in making any move. But, for now, you're far better armed than any of the Old School players and you're well on your way to playing state-of-the-art blackjack.

Practice Makes Perfect

Now, study the charts on the following pages until they become second nature to you. You should know on sight, in a practice situation, what to do in every card situation. Practice, practice, practice! Plus *review your charts and notes at least an hour before you play to get your strategy down COLD.* Or if you just can't seem to do that on your own, you might consider obtaining my audio book, *Richard Harvey's PowerPrep Session*, which does the one-hour pre-casino review for you! It goes through every situation you'll need to remember, with fun quizzes at the end of both the Basic and the Advanced Strategy sessions.

But you're not done yet — in the next chapter, I am going to fill you in on something you need to become aware of: casino countermeasures and dirty tricks. You need to familiarize yourself with that chapter, so that you can avoid becoming victimized by the few dishonest dealers and casinos who are, unfortunately, still out there. (It's like anything else. When money's involved, you have to be careful.)

You are still not ready to enter a casino.

CHART 4:
HOW TO PLAY HARD HANDS
FOR ADVANCED PLAYERS

	2	3	4	5	6	7	8	9	10	A
4-6	H	H	H	H	H	H	H	H	H	H
7	H	H	H	D?/H	H	H	H	H	H	H
8	H	H	D?/H	D?/H	D?/H	H	H	H	H	H
9	D?/H	D?/H	D?/H	D?/H	D?/H	D?/H	H	H	H	H
10	D?/H	D?/H	D?/H	D?/H	D?/H	D?/H	D?/H	D?/H	H	H
11	D?/H	D?/H	D?/H	D?/H	D?/H	D?/H	D?/H	D?/H	D?/H	D?/H
12	H?/S	H?/S	S?/H	S?/H	S?/H	H	H	H	H	H
13	S?/H	S?/H	S?/H	S?/H	S?/H	H	H	H	H	H
14	H?/S	S	S	S	S	H	H	H	H	H?/Sur
15	H?/S	S	S	S	S	H?/S	H	H	H?/Sur	H?/Sur
16	H?/S	S	S	S	S	H?/S	H	H?/Sur	H?/Sur	H?/Sur
17+	S	S	S	S	S	S	S	S	S	S
BJ	S	S	S	S	S	S	S	S	S	S?/Even

207

CHART 5:
HOW TO PLAY SOFT HANDS
FOR ADVANCED PLAYERS

	2	3	4	5	6	7	8	9	10	A
Ace-2 & Ace-3	H	H	D?/H	D?/H	D?/H	H	H	H	H	H
Ace-4 & Ace-5	H	D?/H	D?/H	D?/H	D?/H	D?/H	H	H	H	H
Ace-6	H	D	D	D	D	D?/H				
Ace-7	S	D	D	D	D	D?/S	S	H	H	S
Ace-8	S	S	D?/S	D?/S	D?/S	S	S	S	S	S
Ace-9	S	S	S	S	S	S	S	S	S	S
BJ	S	S	S	S	S	S	S	S	S	S?/Even
Pair of Aces	SP	SP	SP	SP	SP	SP	SP	SP?/H	SP?/H	SP?/H

208

CHART 6A:

SPLITTING
FOR ADVANCED PLAYERS

	2	3	4	5	6	7	8	9	10	A
Pair of 2s	SP? H	SP? H	SP	SP	SP	SP	H	H	H	H
Pair of 3s	H	SP? H	SP	SP	SP	SP	H	H	H	H
Pair of 4s	H	H	D? H	D? H	D? H	H	H	H	H	H
Pair of 5s	D? H	D? H	D? H	D	D? H	D? H	D? H	D? H	H	H
Pair of 6s	H	SP	SP	SP	SP	SP	H	H	H	H
Pair of 7s	SP	SP	SP	SP	SP	SP	H	H	H	H
Pair of 8s	SP	SP	SP	SP	SP	SP	SP	SP	SP? Sur? H	SP? Sur? H
Pair of 9s	SP? S	SP	SP	SP	SP	S	SP	SP	S	S
Pair of 10s	S	S	S	S	S	S	S	S	S	S
Pair of Aces	SP	SP	SP	SP	SP	SP	SP	SP? H	SP? H	SP? H

CHART 6B:
SPLITTING WITH RESTRICTIONS
IF POST-SPLIT DOUBLING & SPLITTING NOT ALLOWED

	2	3	4	5	6	7	8	9	10	A
Pair of 2s	H	SP?/H	SP	SP	SP	SP	H	H	H	H
Pair of 3s	H	H	SP	SP	SP	SP	H	H	H	H
Pair of 4s	H	H	D?/H	D?/H	D?/H	H	H	H	H	H
Pair of 5s	D?/H	D?/H	D?/H	D	D	D?/H	D?/H	D?/H	H	H
Pair of 6s	H	SP?/H	SP?/H	SP	SP	H	H	H	H	H
Pair of 7s	H	S	SP	SP	SP	SP	H	H	Sur?*/H	Sur?*/H
Pair of 8s	S	SP	SP	SP	SP	SP	SP	Sur?*/SP?	Sur?*/SP?	Sur?*/SP?
Pair of 9s	SP?/S	SP	SP	SP	SP	S	SP	SP	S	S
Pair of 10s	S	S	S	S	S	S	S	S	S	S
Pair of Aces	SP	SP	SP	SP	SP	SP	SP	SP?/H	SP?/H	SP?/H

*SUR/SP means surrender if possible; otherwise, split.
SUR/H means surrender if possible; otherwise, hit.

A ♥

CASINO COUNTERMEASURES
&
DIRTY TRICKS

I felt it my duty to include this chapter in *Blackjack The SMART Way* after witnessing many things at casinos that can make playing hazardous. I decided that I couldn't in good conscience send you out into the treacherous modern casino environment without warning you about the few rogue casinos and dealers whom you must learn to detect and avoid.

Yet this issue is not one casinos want me to talk about. A talk show host in Vegas who'd been a huge fan and had me on his show several times suddenly became cold to me years ago, in a delayed response to this chapter. Perhaps someone spoke to him. "I wish you hadn't written that chapter," he told me curtly and then never spoke to me again.

That's a shame. Hopefully most casinos will understand that this chapter is not about them. If I believed cheating was the norm, I never would have written this book nor would I encourage anyone to play blackjack. I still feel the cheaters are in the minority, but, nonetheless, you will ultimately run into them, so you need to be aware of this issue.

I had long thought that some dirty tricks were going on at one or two casinos along my journeys, but it took me awhile before I figured out what was actually being done and what to look for, to spot the schemes. I decided to do some research to help me ferret out the cheaters, and I discovered that a number of other blackjack writers had talked about this subject. Their stories corroborated what I have experienced from time to time.

I Had Been Warned

Apropos of this; I had tried to interest an elderly friend into learning my system years ago but he surprised me by saying he felt all casino dealers were crooked. (So obviously, I didn't create the casino industry's image problem. They did. It predates me.) Well, let me say that while I still enjoy the game and do not agree with my friend's bleak assessment, my eyes have been opened.

The Bigmouth Bertha Who Opened My Eyes

I had nearly finished the First Edition of this book when I came across a dealer who forced me to rethink my approach, from start to finish, so that I would not send you into the clutches of such a dealer unaware that you might become a sheep to be shorn.

I had been field testing the blackjack system I am teaching you in this book at low stakes tables and had won well over a thousand dollars in 11 straight trips to various casinos, when I finally ran into a losing night. I was with a friend, and we kept running into awful tables. So we'd get up from those tables and move to other ones. Unfortunately, the casino had a limited number of tables. Not a single table was any good, and not a single player was winning. That was definitely a tip-off!

We moved to a 2-deck pitch game table where a middle-aged woman with a real bad attitude was dealing. As she shuffled, I politely asked a player in the second baseman's seat if he would kindly move to his right one seat, so I could watch my friend's cards and help him out with the difficult decisions.

"Awww," the dealer snorted in sarcastic baby-talk. "He wants to sit next to you."

I call these types of dealers **Bigmouth Berthas** (or, if the dealer is male, **Bigmouth Barneys**). I shot her a withering glance and ignored the remark.

Later when my friend – almost sheepishly – turned his cards over and told her he wanted to double down, she retorted: "I've worked as a dealer for 20 years; I know when a player wants to double down!" That was a totally gratuitous insult. My friend was only following casino rules. He had to tell the dealer he wanted to double.

Anyway, as my pile of chips sank below a $100 loss, I began to suspect that this dealer was not on the up-and-up. She was constantly drawing improbable streaks of great hands — 20s, 21s, and Blackjacks — and never busted. I was determined to ferret out what my sixth sense was telling me. It finally dawned on me: she had to use her hands to pull off any trickery she might be doing. So I decided to watch her hands very closely.

That's when I discovered she was peeking at the top cards! Whenever she found an excuse to use her right hand, to cash in a player's money for chips, or collect a player's busted hand and bet, *she would turn over the pile of cards she was*

holding with her left hand, pretending to scratch her chin. And while "scratching," she'd fan the top cards out and peek at them, while distracting the players with her right hand activity!!!

Then, having seen what cards she wanted to deal to the players (to bust them if possible) and herself (to avoid busting and draw to a high score), she'd deal with the cards held up toward her face at a peculiar 70 degree angle, so the players couldn't see the top of the cards. If she didn't want to deal the top card, she'd deal SECONDS: her left thumb would pull the top card back to expose the tops of the following cards, as her right thumb simultaneously pulled cards from under the top card!

This went on repeatedly. Yet no one else seemed to notice what I was observing, or sensed that anything was wrong!

Once I discovered this, I sat back and glared at her. She gave me a cocky look and, talking out of the side of her mouth, she nastily asked me: "Aren't you playing"? Her head shook with arrogance, and her eyebrows were raised as if she were hot stuff.

Livid, I shot her back a look that let her know "woman, I am on to your sleaziness," and pointedly responded: "No, I am waiting for the *next* dealer."

That's when she did something shocking. She immediately turned to her left, where another dealer was just standing, cooling his heels, made a clicking noise with her tongue signaling him to take over, and she then hastily made her getaway! Now – if you think I'm paranoid, YOU try to get a dealer to leave by simply telling them you are going to wait for the next dealer to arrive! Boy, that would be great if that were how it worked! You don't like a dealer, you just tell them so, and they leave! Fat chance!

I glanced at my watch to see that this Bigmouth Bertha HAD STAYED ON SEVEN MINUTES BEYOND THE END OF HER SHIFT. When have YOU seen a dealer do that? That was the confirmation I needed. They had left her in longer than dealers normally stayed, so she could work her "magic," as a **card mechanic**. That was one case where I truly felt the casino was in on it. For, there was that dealer who eventually took over for her, standing right next to her, ready to take over, but he did not make a move, nor did any casino boss tell him "hey, buddy, get to work!"

He waited for her signal, and that was OK with the pit boss and the floor managers.

When have YOU seen a dealer WANT to stay beyond her shift? When have YOU seen a dealer NOT working, just hanging out by the side of your table, waiting for your dealer to signal them? No, there's a protocol, executed with regularity. Any change in that protocol — look out!

Of course, I will never play at that casino ever again. I left with $125 in losses, which, although manageable for a losing day, was egregious in that it came at the hands of a cheating casino. It was a lesson I will never forget. I swore right then and there I would get the word out in this book.

That Wasn't The First or Only Time

In fact, that casino had long been suspect in my mind. I'd seen a dealer attempt to palm a card there. She was so clumsy that the card she was palming got stuck in the creases of her left hand when she tried to be slick and use it to win her hand. She wound up having to put the card FACE DOWN on the table before being able to flip it over! She even laughed when the card got stuck! I looked at the other players, who were busy chatting and didn't notice a thing!

Another dealer I suspected was cheating there got very nervous and clumsy with the cards when I focused my eyes directly on his hands at all times. Suddenly he couldn't shuffle without spilling cards and making a mess of it. Why did I make him so nervous? I caught yet another dealer there only *pretending* to shuffle the cards properly. As she distracted the players by making small talk, she was actually just dropping clumps of cards from the halves she held in her hands rather than intertwining the two decks. She was keeping the (bad) order of the cards intact!

Low Cards Runneth Over

My first concrete encounter with dirty tricks happened many years ago, at a large Atlantic City casino. I'd long thought that there was a smattering of some cheating or unfair practices going on, but I couldn't figure out how it was being done.

215

I was playing at a 6-deck shoe game table, and it quickly became obvious to me the shoe was unnaturally heavy with 2s, 3s, and 4s while being short on high cards, especially 10s. This made the dealer's busting rate virtually zero. It also led to player losses through unsuccessful doubling attempts. They'd get awful low cards and the dealer would beat them, never busting.

Because my cousin refused to leave, I was there for three hours, during which I proved the fact that the cards were crooked, to the satisfaction of all of the players at that table. I got cocky after awhile, hitting 17s and 18s to prove my point, saying loudly, "Well, I'm not supposed to do this, but something tells me I'm gonna get a low card here," and I'd pull to a 20 or 21 every time. I NEVER BUSTED DOING THAT! It was ridiculous how lopsided the shoe was with low cards, but, until I pointed it out repeatedly and loudly, NO ONE ELSE NOTICED!

I'd pull cards with a 14 against the dealer's 5 or 6, and always improve my score. Of course, the parade of dealers who dealt at that table over the course of the three hours I was there were always getting winning totals, too, usually with hands that ran to *six or more cards!* (The average hand contains three cards.) They never seemed to bust! It was obvious to me the shoe had been rigged. If you didn't notice it, and continued to play according to your normal strategy for an honest table, you would certainly lose much more than normal.

The players laughed at first, but then they started leaving the table when they realized I was right. They left grumbling about "all the low cards." My cousin foolishly then starting counting the number of 10s out loud, and everyone joined in. I was a bit embarrassed, because this was undoubtedly a practice that was not allowed by the casino, and I had prompted it.

Nonetheless, the other players determined that I was right. It was a crooked shoe, with too few 10s and too many low cards!

Finally, I offered to buy the cards for $50.

"No, sir, I can't sell you the cards," replied the dealer.

"OK," I said, "I'll give you $100!" I was up to $200 when the dealer called over a pit boss and two burly types who refused to sell me the cards and warned me they'd throw me out physically if I didn't stop talking about the cards.

"You're scaring the players," said the pit boss.

It was stupid of me to have made such a show of it. Number one, that draws too much attention to you — you want to remain anonymous. Number two, you never know with whom you're dealing. So, my advice to you is: If you catch a dealer or casino doing something wrong, simply leave. Don't say anything.

Other Dirty Tricks

I am now on guard for anything unusual that might be suspect. For example, not too long ago, I noticed a dealer doing something funny as she picked up her cards after the round was finished. She had these cards:

Then, instead of taking her cards in order, *she slipped the players' cards she'd picked up under her 2 and flipped it over her 8, on top of her KING (see the illustration below)!*

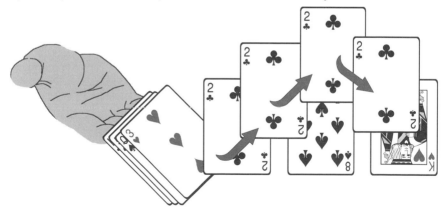

She then gathered the cards with her right hand, this time with a more understandable right to left sweeping motion, slipping

217

the 8 under the KING on the table!

She was interspersing l0s between lower value cards!
When dealt later, the high-low-high-low sequence causes a very bad flow of cards to develop (especially with even numbers of players). It also makes dealing seconds that much easier, because the dealer then knows which of the two top cards to deal to players he or she wants to bust, not to mention the card the dealer wants as his or her hit card, to make a winning hand.

There's just one standardized way dealers are SUPPOSED to collect the cards, at each casino. (One reason for this is that, if there's a dispute — as I had once with a dealer — management can then have the dealer recreate the round and determine who's right and who's wrong.) Leave the table if this is not the case.

Casino Countermeasures

I have also been targeted at times for **casino countermeasures** that — although not illegal like the out-and-out cheating I described above — are certainly not what I would call fair play.

For example, at a small stakes table at a New Mexico casino 15 years ago, I went up more than $100 in 20 minutes, and during that time the pit boss brought in TWO new dealers! To do this without alerting players too much to the unusual frequency of dealer changes, she created a ruse. She pretended to find fault with the first dealer, a nice woman who, to me, was obviously dealing properly and professionally. The pit boss then replaced that dealer — outside of the normal shift change time — commenting to the dealer in an exasperated tone, "No, you're doing it *wrong!*" The new dealer she brought in was a Quick Rick type, who threw the cards at us at the speed of light, the cards sometimes winding up on the floor. I guess the pit boss suspected I was card counting and that speeding up the game would hurt me.

Nope. I kept going up. The dealer then began to make "mistakes". He tried to take my bet when I beat him with a 21. "Ah, ah, ah! Isn't that a 21?" I asked him. He apologized and paid off my bet. But he continued to make "mistakes." He hit my pair of deuces when I wanted to split them. Although he apologized, he also told me he could not take back his error. I had to play my 2s unsplit. I lost that hand. Another thing he was doing was reshuffling after only about 35% of the cards had been dealt! That's very unusual and very suspect. I kept winning, however, and so I kept playing.

That dealer didn't last but 5 or 10 minutes before another dealer was brought in. I suddenly turned around from a conversation and noticed that *they were bringing in new cards too!* I was up about $300 by that time and knew it was time to leave!

Jealously Guarding Those Chips

On another occasion, up about $150 after 15 minutes, I decided to pocket some of my chips and move to a new table. The action had become rocky at the table at which I'd been playing. All of a sudden, the dealer at that new table was immediately replaced by a female dealer, OUTSIDE THE NORMAL SHIFT CHANGE TIME. It was odd because the other dealer's shift was not over. Casinos have dealers at the table for regular shifts. Depending on the casino, that could be 20, 30 or 60 minute shifts, which change like clockwork. It should never vary.

The new dealer was another one of those Quick Rick types, chucking the cards at high speed haphazardly all over the place. Some were hitting the floor, because she was not talented enough to deal at the speed at which she was apparently ordered to deal. (Casino bosses must think a quick dealer throws good players off. That's ridiculous. It only spoils the game for their customers. It's not fun.) Anyway, she suddenly singled me out – after not saying a word to any of the other players – and asked me: "How are you doing?"

"Not very well," I responded, lying. "I'm down."

"Oh really?" she said. "You must have gotten more cash from the money machine then!"

It was stupid of her to be so brazen! She could have tried some small talk first, to hide her purpose! I was shocked. It was now obvious to me what was going on. And it wasn't right. I ask you: HOW did this new dealer know how much I was up? I had pocketed many of my chips from a prior table, and only put a small amount out on her table BEFORE she arrived. I had never seen her before, and she had never seen me.

The conclusion is inescapable. Some casino boss sent her to my table to try to win back my winnings. She was told EXACTLY HOW MUCH I WAS UP IN WINNINGS, THUS EXPLAINING HER RESPONSE WHEN I TOLD HER I WAS DOWN. This was one of the first times I achieved confirmation that I was being targeted for countermeasures, simply for being a winner.

I picked up my chips and left. In fact, I did not return to that casino for well over a year, when a friend told me the action had become more honest there. I refuse to play at casinos that play unfair. I only like to play when it's fun and the action is honest.

One thing that surprised me about this incident was that I was not up a huge amount when they resorted to countermeasures! Since then, other players have confirmed that some casinos jealously guard every chip that goes out the door with a winner.

Beware the Shill

For many years, I suspected I'd been victimized on occasion by casino employees who were pretending to be players, who, I surmised, were sent to my table to louse up my game. I later found out that I was right, and that these phonies are known as "shills." I found a reference to them in "Jimmy the Greek's Crash Course on Vegas" in the July 1975 issue of Playboy. He wrote:

> "Finally, a word about shills. They are not, contrary to general opinion, designed to lure you into anything. The casinos know that a lot of gamblers don't like to play head to head with a dealer, so shills provide the social framework for a game."

Others disagree. John Scarne, in *Scarne On Cards* talks of shills who are what he calls "**anchormen**" who facilitate cheating by the dealer. The dealer peeks at his topmost cards, and signals to the shill whether he wants the shill to take a card or not. The dealer might, for instance, place his right hand, palm up, on the table to signal to the shill to take a card, or palm down, to pass. In that way, the dealer gets the card *they* want, to get a great score. This practice is said to be done by dealers who are not slick enough to deal seconds.

And Edward Thorp, in *Beat the Dealer,* informs us:

> "Shills generally follow "shill rules;" i.e., they never double down, split pairs, or insure, and they stand on hard totals of 12 or more. If the shill does not follow a fixed strategy he may be helping the dealer and/or house to cheat the players."

The Incident That Woke Me Up To Shills

Earlier in this book I spoke of **One-Hand Harrys and Harriets** who come to your table, mid-play, play a few hands and then leave. They often make stupid moves and louse up the card flow. Well, one day, one of these **One Hand Harrys** made the mistake of tipping me off that he was a casino employee.

I was up about $200 shortly after arriving at a casino where I always found the employees to be very unfriendly. The pit boss sent over a new dealer who was apparently instructed to be a Quick Rick. She sped up the game in an apparent attempt to hurt my winning cycle. I nearly laughed out loud, however, as she clumsily sent cards flying off the table, to the wrong players, all over the place – she just wasn't skilled enough to pull it off.

Suddenly, a guy in a suit sat down in the third baseman's seat. (I'd essentially been the third baseman until that time. No one had been to my left.) He looked out of place from the start. No one at this casino wore anything but casual clothes, and HE WORE A DARK, PIN-STRIPED SUIT WITHOUT A TIE! I immediately recognized this as his attempt to "fit in" and look like the rest of us. It didn't work.

He was looking right at me with a malicious grin as he placed his small bet of a chip or two. Still looking at me with his peculiar smile and not even pretending to look at or care about his cards, he casually hit the table, indicating to the dealer to hit his 16, a totally wacko move, because the dealer had a 6. The guy busted and the dealer "miraculously" beat us all with a 21. Still glaring at me, he placed a second bet, made a similarly stupid move (I forget what it was, but only a fool would have made it), and the dealer again drew to a strong winning score and beat all of the players at the table.

He was intentionally playing stupidly, with confidence and without hesitation. *And he did not care that he lost both bets.* And he never even pretended to look at his cards; he kept looking at me!

After those two hands, he promptly got up to leave, staring at me with his evil smile every inch of the way. It was kind of a "take that!" smile. He had given himself away. I instantly knew he was a casino employee, perhaps a boss, who came to spoil my winning streak (which he did), in cahoots with the dealer. But he was a fool, because he revealed himself to me. And, in so doing, he convinced me of what my sixth sense had told me long ago about shills and their true purpose. I left the casino.

A Strange Pair

Some years ago, I had another uncomfortable experience which I believe also involved shills. I was in a rather empty, small casino, midday, the same casino, in fact, where I'd later catch that Bigmouth Bertha dealing seconds. I was up about $50 within 10 minutes, when the two players who'd been playing at the table, a young couple, decided they had to leave.

Suddenly, two guys came from nowhere, two loud jerks, and they sat down on either side of me! I was on alert right away. That was too strange! And they kept looking at my cards, *leaning their heads over my shoulders (I found myself leaning back to avoid contact).* As if that weren't bad enough, they passed chips between themselves, their hands going right over my pile of chips! (Naturally, I watched their hands closely to make sure they did not take my chips, but I don't believe all of the chip exchanging that they did was what it seemed. I think their real purpose was to create a distraction to take my eyes off the dealer, so that the dealer could manipulate the cards, or peek at the cards, to spoil my winning streak. I say this because I now know that cheating goes on at that casino. The guys were definitely interested in knowing what my cards were, that's for sure.)

And indeed the cards started turning in favor of the dealer with the arrival of these clowns. He went on a super winning streak, pulling great cards every hand. Before very long, I knew something was wrong and so I left the casino.

But as I began to walk away, one of the two jerks I strongly suspect were shills or anchormen urged me to keep playing!

"C'mon, why are you leaving?" he asked, as if we were buddies. Would a real player do that? I couldn't WAIT to leave!

My Experience Is Not Isolated

My experiences have been echoed by a number of other blackjack authors who, like myself, are regular players. There has been ample documentation about this subject. The one new development in recent years has been the advent of hidden video cameras, which have supplied us with undeniable documentation of the shady practices of rogue dealers.

In fact, recently, there have been a spate of excellent cable TV documentaries, in which they have aired some excellent examples caught on tape by casino surveillance cameras. Some of the footage involved cheating and thievery by players. But some of it involved cheating by dealers.

Making Blackjacks

I have to share an incredible scam with you which was caught on videotape by a casino's eye-in-the-sky camera and then shown in a wonderful documentary on The Learning Channel. Get this. The male dealer involved was so good at manipulating the cards that the show's host had to pause the video several times to show how the sleight-of-hand dirty trick was pulled off!

Here's how the scam worked: the dealer had an Ace as his up card. He then curled up the edge of his hole card, to peek to see if he had a Blackjack. The camera caught him exposing a 6, giving him a weak score of 17. That was legal. However, he was simultaneously squeezing the undealt cards in his left hand, bending the top card and peeking at it! The camera clearly showed what the dealer then saw — that the top, undealt card, was a face card. In a flawless motion worthy of the best magician, he then indicated he had a Blackjack by immediately turning over the hole card. That is, he PRETENDED to turn over the hole card. Here's what he REALLY did: with blinding speed, he picked up his Ace and the hole card with his right hand. He then slipped the 6, the hole card, onto the top of the deck of undealt cards in his left hand! In a fluid motion, his left thumb then skillfully held the 6 apart from the face card, the former top card which was now below the 6, releasing it. Then, quickly snapping his left wrist, he flipped the face card over, face up, onto the table, as if he were revealing his hole card. Voila! A Blackjack!

THE DEALER WAS MAKING HIS OWN BLACKJACKS OUT OF LESS THAN PERFECT HANDS! (The key to detecting this scam, by the way? The dealer dealt the hole card with his left hand!)

The Card Clumpers

Interestingly enough, there's a whole school of players who believe that most every casino is crooked, and have fashioned a system that is meant to deal with that perception. I'm referring to the "card clumpers," as I think they call themselves.

Their theory, apparently, is that casinos routinely rearrange the cards into "clumps" of high and low cards, thus making it very hard to win. (I say "apparently" only because I have not read any of their books. I have just read their promotional literature, on the Internet.) They say the dealers arrange the cards in this way by incomplete shuffling.

This can be done. But I disagree with them on two counts, based on my wealth of experience. I believe most casinos are honest. And I've found that those that are not cheat in many ways, not just through shuffling "tricks." In fact, although I *have* encountered shuffling trickery from time to time, it appears to me to be the least likely cheat you'll ever face.

I have witnessed situations where many of the 10s have been grouped together, followed by wicked strings of low cards. When low cards are grouped together, it spoils players' efforts to win when they double down (leaving players with low, losing totals) and it tends to give the dealer a winning hand. So, if you see a dealer constantly winning by pulling 5 or more cards, yes, it could be a sign that the 10s were shuffled into groups so that there would be protracted streaks of damaging low cards. Or it could be symptomatic of other scams, such as ones I described earlier in this chapter.

That being said, I disagree totally with the approach these "clumpers" are apparently taking. They are altering their card strategy to anticipate just one possible unfair casino practice, whereas there are many other ruses to beware of. Plus, there *are* honest casinos worth playing at that do NOT engage in shuffling tricks or other improper behavior and THERE, their practices will hurt their chances of winning. And, if they truly do believe all casinos are dishonest, it's crazy for them to encourage anyone to play blackjack! My advice instead is: LEAVE at the first sign of trouble! (You'd think the casino industry would realize they have an image problem based upon the card clumper Internet sites! But they continue to lend credence to even the wildest theories by their antagonist attitude toward winners!) You have to become very discriminating about where you play. That's essential if you want to push your winning rate up to the max.

Other Authors Have Been Victimized

Lawrence Revere, author of *Playing Blackjack As A Business*, spoke of having been cheated by a dealer in a downtown Las Vegas casino. (Interestingly enough, he says he later found out that the dealer had previously been discovered cheating at a Northern Nevada casino!) He wrote: "As the dealer picked up the cards from the previous hand, I saw him "peek" at the top card on the deck. He then dealt four "seconds" and took the ace of clubs for himself. (In dealing a second, the dealer slides the top card back, then deals the next card, keeping the top card for himself.)"

Revere complained to the casino management but he says they did nothing. He later downplayed this incident, though, saying that it was a rare occurrence "at a large casino": "Word gets out whenever a casino is cheating or "Running Flat," and it is only a short time until the casino is closed by Nevada authorities."

The authors of 1980's so-called *World's Greatest Blackjack Book* also contained accusations they'd encountered cheating, although they offered no details or proof.

And If You Need Further Proof...

Both Edward Thorp's *Beat the Dealer* and John Scarne's *Scarne on Cards* are good resources if you want to read more about others' experiences at the hands of crooked dealers.   In fact, Thorp estimated back in the 1960's that a blackjack player would run into a cheater 5 to 10 percent of the time. He stated though, that there are definitely casinos that are entirely honest. (In my experience, the percentage of honest casinos depends on what state or country you're in.)

Regulated Vs. Unregulated Casinos

...Which brings me to another very important point.   On my nationwide book tours, I am always surprised that players don't seem to know whether the casinos in their area are regulated or not.   Nor do they know what being "regulated" means!

In Atlantic City -- the most honest place I've ever played -- there's a state gaming commission that oversees every casino and keeps them honest.   They place an investigator in a promi- nent place on the floor of every casino and occasionally confiscate cards to make sure they're not marked or rigged. Yet I read years ago that many casinos there had been caught using marked cards! Nevada, too, has a state gaming commission, whose job is keeping the casino industry clean. And they do crack down on cheaters from time to time. So I have greater confidence when I play in regulated towns like that; I know that most action is legit.

Many areas, however, even today, do NOT have proper gov- ernmental oversight.   While my home state is one such area and I do play in some unregulated casinos, my advice to you is: be more careful in places where no one's watching what's going on.

Countermeasures Vs. Cheating

Thorp's system was so successful against the fully-dealt, 1-

deck blackjack games of his day, by the way, that casinos changed the way the game was played (a reaction not documented again until the publication of my books, I might add, which have spawned changes of a similar nature)! Many of those changes became standardized, such as the practice of reshuffling the cards well before they have been completely dealt.

Casinos also instituted all kinds of unfair countermeasures to deal with winning players who were unfazed by the game changes. And in the decades since Thorp's book first appeared, casinos have only gotten better at these practices, and so it's important for you to understand what you might experience in this regard.

First, let me make this distinction: countermeasures are different than out-and-out cheating, or what I call dirty tricks. *Countermeasures* are legal but unfair. They are often detrimental to your game, and they are certainly *meant* to be. *Casino cheating*, however, refers to serious offenses that are *illegal* and, if documented by local gaming officials, could cause a casino to be shut down. Cheating will ALWAYS be detrimental to your game.

Edward Thorp reported that more than 20 Las Vegas casinos had been put out of business in the first five years of the Nevada Gaming Commission's existence alone, for playing dirty. One of those casinos had been caught removing a significant number of 10s from the deck and increasing the number of low cards. Another had instructed dealers how to cheat players.

Thorp himself discovered many irregular practices, as a player — decks that had too many cards (one 1-deck game featured 58 cards), a shoe that dealt seconds (and when he moved to a different table, they moved the shoe to his table), shills that followed him from table to table, and dealers who peeked at their top cards and then dealt "seconds."

He then went on a trip to Reno and Las Vegas with card experts in tow to see how much cheating he would uncover. He wrote: "There was cheating at large plush casinos, as well as smaller out-of-the-way places. There was cheating at all betting levels, even for 25¢!!"

He spoke of a situation at the hands of a crooked dealer where he'd lost 22 out of 24 hands, the probability of that happening by chance, he said, was TWO MILLION TO ONE! He later discovered the dealer was rearranging the cards in a high-low-high-low sequence when he picked up hands that had been played out (just like the dealer I saw flipping the 2 onto the 10, which I illustrated earlier in this chapter) that created a bad flow of cards.

And It Goes On From There

And there have other well-known authors who have documented their experiences of having been cheated in the decades since Thorp and Revere's books first came out. A much more recent book, *How To Detect Casino Cheating At Blackjack* by former Nevada Gaming Commission official Bill Zender, is excellent in this regard. He gives details on cases he pursued, along with helpful photos demonstrating each cheating scam he encountered as a Gaming Commission enforcer.

Now, whether or not the rare case of cheating you run into is sanctioned by a particular casino or simply the work of one crooked dealer working for his or her own benefit is beside the point. It affects you in the same way; it poses the same threat to your hard-earned money. So I felt an obligation to catalog everything I and others have witnessed so that you will be less likely to be victimized. By having the tools to spot and avoid the few places where such activity is going on will also prevent you from becoming soured on the game.

By now you should see that you're sometimes not just playing against the *game* itself. You're sometimes also playing against interfering casino employee, who, misguided as they might be, make things difficult. A minority of times, yes, but often enough and at enough casinos that you must learn to spot their intrusion and know how to react.

Speaking of which, do you know what a "**sizz**" is? If you hear the pit boss or floor managers talking about a **sizz** while you're playing, look out! That's the casino bosses alerting each other that a player — maybe you — is on a winning streak (which they call a **sizz**). If they're using this codeword, it's likely they're considering instituting countermeasures against that player. Pay attention, because that player might be YOU! Leave immediately if you confirm that suspicion.

How To Alter Your Approach to Avoid the Cheats

Now some forms of cheating are done only when a player places a large bet, so it might not be a constant factor you would notice all the time. Be on your guard! And here are some things you can do to avoid being victimized:

♥ *Use my **6-Unit Cheat-Proof Rule** (in Chapter 7): If you lose 6 Units while making 1-Unit minimum Basic Bets, within a dozen or so hands of arriving at a table or with the arrival of a new dealer or new cards, leave the table. (At a $5 table, this would stop your losses at $30 maximum; at a $25 table, you would apply this rule after going down a maximum of $150.)* You might or might not have been victimized, but, then again, moving saves you both from victimization *and* a table where the cards are breaking badly, so it's smart in two ways.

♥ *Pay attention to any changes or distractions going on at your table* – dealer changes, the dealer dropping a card, card changes, shift time changes, player changes, commotions, noises, objects falling off the table, annoying players, etc.

♥ *Find out when dealers are supposed to change shifts and then check your watch to make sure this regular pattern is not being disrupted, which would be a telltale sign.* Any unusual change might reveal the presence of a **card mechanic**.

♥ When approaching a new table, ask players how the table's been doing, and if there have been any winners lately. If the answers are "bad" and "no," don't play there.

♥ *Watch the dealers very closely.* Watch their hands, how they hold their cards, their eyes, how they shuffle, how they pick up the cards. Watch for dealer "mistakes" in paying off your bet or playing out your cards.

♥ Be on the lookout for **shills** and the use of an **anchorman** or **anchorwoman** (see page 222 or the Glossary).

♥ ***Remember the faces and names of the dealers you lost against and avoid them in the future.***

♥ *Remember the faces and names of the dealers you've won against, and seek them out in the future.*

A player has powerful ways to respond to casino dirty tricks and countermeasures – lower your bets, leave a table, or leave the casino. If cards are being shuffled when you raise your bet (the casino assuming you'd only do so when the cards are favorable), raise your bet whenever the cards are BAD. Then, the dealer will shuffle them away! A player can respond to nasty dealers by withholding tips and, finally, leaving their tables. *But you must be alert to possible trouble, and then be quick to react to factors that turn against your favor.*

Beware First Base Scams

By the way, the worst seat at the table, first base (the player with the first turn), is also the seat most targeted by cheating dealers. I happen to know of one or two dirty dealer tricks that specifically target the first baseman. Those particular scams depend upon the top cards being prearranged to deal the first baseman a bad hand.

It's easier to prepare a scam targeting the first baseman during a lull in action than it is to target other players, where more sophisticated sleight of hand tricks are required. So either be on guard when you sit in that seat, or, if you're like me, you will avoid sitting anywhere near it.

The Ultimate Countermeasure

I thought I'd also relate something that happened years ago at a small town casino that seemed to get upset immediately if you were winning. After having won $112.50 in less than 15 minutes, a new dealer was brought in. Suspecting a countermeasure to relieve me of my winnings (such as they were), I asked the new dealer to color me in after losing the first hand to her. As she was exchanging my stacks of red $5 chips for two black $100 chips, a very pretty floor manager suddenly showed up.

"What's your name?" she asked. The table was packed, but she ignored everyone else to pick me out. I noticed right away she was holding a pad with a pen ready to write my name down. Oh boy, I thought, someone wants to know who I am.

"Why do you ask?" I responded, politely.

"I just want to know," she retorted. That didn't make any

sense. Most people have a *reason* for asking such pointed questions. And she certainly seemed anxious to get my name.

"I'd rather remain anonymous," I blurted out, not prepared at the time for such a blunt approach. Realizing I might have raised a red flag, I added, "but *you* can call me Joe," and I placed my hand on her arm in a friendly fashion as I walked away.

"Joe what?" she shouted.

"Joe Sample!" And I smiled. Obviously, one of her higher ups sent her over to find out who I was.

Later that night she sidled up to me and asked me where I was from (a friend of mine was still at the casino). "Santa Fe?"

"No, locally."

"Oh, I thought you were from Santa Fe," she said. Yeah, right! How would she know if she'd never met me? She was just fishing for an answer to the question someone wanted answered. "I think I've seen you here before," she continued. Ah ha. Someone had taken note of the fact that I was a regular winner.

I related this story to a friend of mine, a former blackjack dealer in Reno, and his reaction was "They're starting a file on you. But isn't that ridiculous? It's OK if the casino wins *your* money but you're not supposed to win from *them!*"

I'd been identified as a smart player. Many casinos don't like smart players. They jealously guard every chip that leaves the dealer's tray and actively work against winners once spotted.

You probably have also heard about the Griffin "book" or "Griffin Gold" software promulgated by a Vegas security firm to alert casinos of players suspected of being card counters, cheats, and simply smart system players. You've also undoubtedly heard about the facial recognition software many casino use to see if any players who frequent their tables are in the "book." It's a sad day. You can be barred from a casino just for being a good player! There have been court challenges to these insidious practices, but so far the courts in most jurisdictions have ruled in favor of the casinos (not so in Atlantic City; it's illegal to bar players there, by state law). Griffin was the company that followed and harassed the MIT team players. That kind of behavior, I think, is unfortunate, and gives the industry a black eye. (They were just good at playing a game offered by the casinos. How did that become an offense?)

On the flip side, I consider it an **honor** that my play is considered so "strong" as to inspire fear when I enter some casinos. It certainly is a strong endorsement of my system, in a way!

Passing The Bar Test

But we don't want the badge of honor of getting barred if we can avoid it. So here are some tips to prolong your playing career:

- ♥ Remain anonymous at all costs. Give a phony name if asked.
- ♥ Never, never seek comps. That requires you to give the casino your name, and instantly garners you close scrutiny.
- ♥ Never play in tournaments. You'll draw too much attention to yourself. They'll get your name and see how good you play.
- ♥ Never fill out entry forms for drawings or contests. They'll get your name, and it's often a ruse used in barring you.
- ♥ If you've drawn the unwelcome attention of a casino boss, avoid playing during his or her shift.
- ♥ Never seek to become friends with dealers or bosses. That blows your anonymity; plus, casino higher ups might suspect you're in collusion with their employees to cheat the casino.
- ♥ DON'T play with a regular bunch of friends. That will raise a red flag. Casinos are on the lookout for both unscrupulous cheaters, who often come in pairs, and teams of players.
- ♥ Practice my methods at home until you can pull them off with finesse, without being noticed.
- ♥ Play a shoe game if you've gotten too much heat playing pitch games. Pitch games are scrutinized more than shoe games, because those are the games smart players prefer.
- ♥ Radically alter your appearance each time you play, especially after you win big. Study the art of disguises.
- ♥ Don't wear out your welcome. Play at a variety of casinos.
- ♥ Take a hiatus from casinos where you've drawn "heat."
- ♥ Play at a variety of times; don't become too familiar to any one shift.

I broke one of the rules above a few years back after winning big at a high stakes table at a major Strip casino, and I paid the price. I crossed the street to another casino and sat right down at a single-deck blackjack table. My gut told me they were waiting for me. A new dealer arrived at the table as I sat down. He seemed focused on me in spite of the others at the table and after a few minutes of suspect action, I'd lost five hands in a row. I got up to leave and that's when my suspicion was confirmed.

"There are some days you wished you never got outta bed, huh buddy?" the dealer said, his tone cutting, not hiding his puzzling dislike of me. We'd never met before. But I believe the casino at which I'd just won big spread the word, possibly passing a camera image of me to other casinos (through Griffin?). He taught me a lesson: take a break after winning big!

The Present And Future Of Blackjack

Since first writing this book, I can say I've not been barred from all casinos but there are certain casinos at which I know I am not welcome. One off-Strip casino, for instance, had a security guard follow me around and stand between me and any table in which I showed an interest. Another had my name paged repeatedly on the loudspeaker and shouted by floor managers the minute I arrived. At another, a pit boss followed me around and then shoved aside the dealer of the table at which he thought I would sit. Grabbing the cards, he glared at me, ready to deal to me, himself! I'd never seen that before! (I left.)

That's testimony to the power of my system. There have also been a few more serious incidents over the years. I was followed out of an Atlantic City parking garage (which led to a high-speed highway chase) after I questioned the legitimacy of a set of cards at a shoe game. (This was years before I wrote any books.) My cousin was with me at the time. I managed to ditch the car following me, but I that made me realize the foolishness of having voiced my opinion - a mistake I've never repeated.

More recently, I was followed out of a New Mexico casino by two carloads of guys who chased me for miles (even when I went way below the speed limit). A cell phone and crafty driving got me out of that one. I'm not sure, too, if there wasn't a connection to an attempted carjacking incident on the border of Arizona and California, a trip that began with a suspicious event in a casino parking lot. I would hope that's not the case, however. I do have a heightened sense of security, though. I take precautions.

There was also a strange incident at a Borders book signing event I (foolishly) did in Henderson, Nevada some years ago. A dealer with a heavy Brooklyn accent who said he worked at a Strip casino (which he mentioned by name) interrupted my event to tell me "they" killed blackjack great Ken Uston. "They say he died of a heart attack, but they put a bag over his head and suffocated him." I don't know whether that was a threat or even if he was telling the truth, but I thought I should put it out there. In this day and age of "corporate" casinos, one would hope that kind of thing would never be contemplated. It certainly would hurt the industry if they were connected to the seedy ways of the past. I think they're too smart for that.

That being said, I can still play at many casinos. But it does irk me that, unlike the golf world, where Tiger and Phil and the other greats are celebrated, I have to remain anonymous to protect and preserve my playing career. And I cannot appear on TV, for fear that it would ruin my playing career. In the long run, this isn't good business, making the best players feel unwelcome.

Hopefully, someday, the best and brightest of that industry will recognize this and turn it all around. Players and casinos need not be adversaries. And winners should not have to fear for their safety, or be chased and harassed by security people or others.

Other writers have been more pointed. Former MIT team leader Semyon Dukach has called the casino industry "evil," a term also used by Old School blackjack stalwart Arnold Synder in his last book. Obviously the industry has a lot to do to repair the casino-player relationship. I don't personally think the industry is evil, however. If I did, I'd tell you, publicly, not to play blackjack.

I still have a set of favorite casinos at which I love to play. They're honest, friendly, classy and a pleasure to frequent. I'd even consider doing endorsement deals for them under the right circumstances (if that were the way things worked in blackjack), because I truly recommend them to my friends.

Look. It's like anything else. You have to be choosy. That's what this chapter is all about. And by the way, poker players are no different. We all know which casinos the big names choose to play at in Las Vegas. They're choosy too.

I continue to hope that one day smarter, cooler heads, people with a head for business, will realize that if you offer winnable games like blackjack, you have to allow for winners. It's good business. The sight of winners makes the game attractive to others. So someday winners and experts like myself won't have to remain anonymous or hide in the shadows. Perhaps the casino industry will learn from the example of Tiger Woods, who's done more good for golf off the course than on (and that's a tall task), as an ambassador for the game. And, hey, poker didn't have its recent spike in popularity without a big PR campaign with big poker names. (They've tried doing that by placing phony blackjack "experts" on TV but it hasn't worked. Everyone knows they're not real players - and most of them have admitted to that.)

I mentioned earlier that my books had put a scare in the casino industry and caused them to institute new game changes...One change that is undeniably due to me is the introduction of new tables with fewer betting spots - six and sometimes five! I had to laugh when I saw the first 5-player table, at Binion's in downtown Vegas. I knew they'd read *Cutting Edge Blackjack* (which re-vealed that a player's likelihood of winning goes up with each additional seat at the table). Why else would they restrict the number of customers they can seat? These tables will hurt an Old School blackjack player's bottom line; us, not so much. But you should still seek out the 7-player tables, if possible.

I also mentioned (in Chapter 3) the lower Blackjack payouts and attempts at randomizing the cards with shuffling machines - changes that can be attributed at least in part to the new preci-sion I've brought to the game. (And, again, you should avoid the shuffling the machine tables and seek out the 3-to-2 Blackjack payouts if you can find them.) I take all of the changes meant as a countermeasure against my system as a supreme compli-ment. And fortunately, they've done little to hinder me.

FYI: There's a lot to absorb in this chapter, so I've distilled the information into two easy-to-use charts following this chapter.

Countermeasure	What To Do
The cards are shuffled more frequently than normal.	Leave the table if your winning streak has now becoming a losing streak or if the cards have become erratic.
A Quick Rick dealer has been brought in, greatly speeding up the game.	If you start losing, leave the table. Don't tip Quick Ricks. Move to a table where a dealer you like is dealing.
A new deck of cards has been brought in at an odd time.	You should get to know when cards are supposed to be changed. Leave the table right away.
A new, nasty dealer has been brought in.	If you start losing, leave the table. Never tip these types. Move to a table where a dealer you like is dealing.
The new dealer puts the shuffle marker very high up in the cards, so that players will only see 40 percent or less of the cards.	Leave the table.
A pit boss suddenly shows an interest in you, asking your name, or telling the dealer to shuffle up more, or changes dealers unusually frequently, or tells the dealer not to allow you simple things like coloring up some of your chips while you're still playing.	Leave the casino and slack off on your visits there for a month or so.

Countermeasure	What To Do
You think a shill is at the table.	Leave that table.
The dealer shuffles up whenever you place a higher bet.	This one is wonderfully easy: only place a larger bet than normal if the cards are BAD! That way, you'll get neutral or good cards, and can force the dealer to shuffle if the cards are bad.
The dealer singles you out from all the players and either seems too "interested" in how much you have won, or makes nasty comments. It seems as if they were told to do so, to ruin your concentration.	Leave the table.

Dirty Trick	Tip Off	Confirmation
The dealer is dealing the second card from the top of the deck. This is otherwise known as "dealing seconds."	The dealer holds the cards up at an angle so you can't see the tops of the cards (at a pitch game). The dealer always seems to win, even with the weakest up cards, scoring 20s, 21s and Blackjacks more than is likely. Often the dealer holds the cards very tightly, with the index finger held along the shorter end of the cards, at the top. This is known as a "mechanic's grip." A less-skillful dealer might fumble in attempting to pull this off. Look for one or more times when the dealer "accidentally" deals more than one card at a time to a player.	Watch the dealer very closely. He or she might peek at cards on the top of the stack, either by turning the cards upside down, or by "bubbling up" the top card, or by fanning the top card out a bit and peeking at its reflection in a mirror or shiny object lying on the table, or in any number of other ways, at a pitch game table. Also, *their thumbs never leave the top card.* At shoe tables, there are crooked shoes that have a mirror--like device that lets the dealer peek at the top card. Or, marked cards might be used (usually with braille). The dealer would then raise the top card deftly, and deal you the second one.

Dirty Trick	Tip Off	Confirmation
The deck(s) are rigged with too many low cards, especially 2s to 4s, with some 10s, and perhaps other high cards, such as 9s, removed. The number of cards might actually be less or more than there should be.	The dealer rarely busts, and often draws winning hands consisting of 4 or more cards with weak up cards. You, on the other hand, are losing whenever you double down, getting weak hit cards.	Over time, from shuffle to shuffle, this will become apparent, if you are observant. Watch the cards carefully. If cards have been added, they're bound to show up — for example, you might see three 4s of the same suit, in a 2-deck game! If no cards have been added but 10s are reduced in number, you might try simply counting the number of 10s (silently) that appear between shuffles, and see if the number appears to jibe with the right proportion you'd expect. This is hard to confirm, however. The flow of cards will mimic the same symptoms as with another scam, the shuffling away of the 10s.

Dirty Trick	Tip Off	Confirmation
Shuffling away the 10s.	The 10s don't show up very often, or in the correct proportion, from shuffle to shuffle. The higher proportion of low cards that then are dealt results in fewer busts for the dealer, and a higher number of dealer winning scores than normal.	This can only be confirmed at the time when new cards are brought in and first shuffled. This is done when the cards are fanned, face down. Most often, it is done by the dealer separating the cards in the very middle of the arc of cards from the rest, and then arranging it so that they wind up on top of the cards to be cut by a player. Most players will put the shuffle card in the middle of the pile, and those 10s on the top will therefore not find their way to the table.
The cooler deck: the cards are rigged in a specific order, to guarantee players will lose to the dealer's total.	The cards come out often in a sequential order, according to card values, with the dealer beating the player(s) by one or two points each time.	This is usually only effectively used against players who newly arrive at a table. The dealer has already "shuffled" the cards before you arrive. Hard to confirm, but the 6-Unit Cheat-Proof Rule will protect you.

Dirty Trick	Tip Off	Confirmation
The cards are marked. The dealer then sometimes will deal players cards other than the ones they should have gotten in an honest game, in order to cause them to bust; and deal themselves cards other than the ones they should have gotten in an honest game, to draw to a winning score.	With a sophisticated dealer, there's no easy tip off, except that the dealer wins way too much, and players (especially those who are winning, and/or who are making big bets) are busting more than should be expected.	This is very hard to confirm, with the clever markings in use. (Plus, shoe-game-table players never get to see the backs of the cards closely.) While you can casually look for any flaws on the backs of the cards with a pitch game, they would be hard to detect. Basically, your protection here is in watching the dealer's hands closely, to detect the dealing of seconds, or any dealing of improper cards in general (cards other than the top one).
The selective up card.	This is easy to spot. Watch which of the cards the dealer turns over to become the up card. In most casinos, it should be the first one dealt. It should be the same one each time.	Always watch the dealer's hands to confirm that the right card has been turned over to be the up card.

Dirty Trick	Tip Off	Confirmation
The cards have been "stacked" in a high-low-high-low etc. sequence.	The cards break unusually. Once you notice something is wrong, this cheat is perhaps the easiest to spot, now that you are aware of it. Just watch for the sequence of the cards as they are dealt.	The cards may have been pre-arranged, but, often, you'll *see* the dealer re-order cards as they are picked up, as described in Chapter 11. This is clearly improper.
The cards have been "stacked" so that the 10s are grouped together, as are the low cards.	The cards break unusually. The predictability of the cards seems gone.	This one might have been pre-arranged or done through clever shuffling. The confirmation that the problem exists is through observation — the 10s seem to come together in just one round, separated by devastating rounds consisting primarily of lower cards.
Making blackjacks. The dealer, in a pitch game, switches the hole card to give themselves a blackjack.	Hard to detect with a dealer who's good with sleight-of-hand tricks, although the dealer will get more blackjacks than is probable.	Watch the dealer's left hand; if it's the one that turns over the hole card, look out! Watch also for for dealer peeking at the top card.

Dirty Trick	Tip Off	Confirmation
The dealer is a "card mechanic" (a term for someone with sleight-of-hand skills like a magician), but it's not immediately apparent how they are scamming the players.	Card mechanics typically deal fast. They often act as if they know they're going to win. They continue to deal, although their shift is over; or, they are brought in before the prior dealer's shift was over. They win way too often, beating all the players in numerous rounds. Someone might be overhead to say "I never win against this dealer!" All of the above is circumstantial evidence and not proof.	Although the best are hard to uncover, watch them very carefully, especially their hands. Watch any funny behavior, such as continual scratching while turning over the cards (at a pitch game table). Pay attention to when they are brought in, and if they continue to deal beyond their normal shift. See if you can catch the dealer peeking improperly at their cards.
There's a shill at the table.	Watch for players who join the table when you're ahead; they typically have just a few chips and make stupid moves. Watch for players who don't seem to care they're losing.	Watch for a new player who makes stupid moves, while the dealer gets great totals (especially if the player sits in the third baseman's spot). Watch for new players who are overly eager to see your cards.

Dirty Trick	Tip Off	Confirmation
There's an anchorman or woman at your table working in cahoots with the dealer to cheat players.	The player in the third baseman's seat is winning a lot, while frequently making what seem like irrational moves.	Watch for any subtle signaling going on between that player and the dealer. If the dealer is using marked cards, this might go on undetected, but, if not, look to see if the dealer is peeking at the top cards. Beware of any distractions that might cause you to take your eyes off the dealer.
Palming cards. The dealer has chosen a card he or she wants, either to bust a player, or to improve their own hand, palming it in their left hand, to turn the trick later. (Used more at a pitch game table.)	The dealer uses his or her left hand to flip over a card that either busts you, or "miraculously" gives the dealer a great score.	Watch the dealer's left hand. The dealer should be dealing cards with the right hand.

A ♠ PRACTICE, PRACTICE, PRACTICE

Now that you've completed your first read-through of *Blackjack The SMART Way*, you're probably very eager to put all the information to good use!

How To Practice

To get a full command of the skills you've acquired in this book, you absolutely have to practice them first, at home. You have been handed an awful lot of material to digest, much of which was entirely new to you. All of that doesn't fully sink in until you've played a good number of blackjack hands, and your decisions become flawless and quick.

At first you will find you are having trouble remembering some of what you thought you had down pat. It's better that you have your moments of uncertainty at home, where you're not under the gun to make the right move and make it quickly, with your money on the line. With all of the distractions you'll face at the casino, you don't want to be struggling to remember your strategies and methods under that kind of pressure.

You have a lot to memorize, initially, above and beyond the *Blackjack The SMART Way* Basic and Advanced Card Strategies.

Study up on the **3-Level, Notch-Up, Notch-Down Bet Management System** and the **X Factor** (which work together), until you understand exactly how to apply both of those at the table. Practice card counting, with the idea in mind that you'll need to be able to keep up with the fast pace of any Quick Rick dealer that is sent to your table. Practice **Card Observation** until you can analyze the cards on the table speedily, remembering all the **Card Observation Questions** you need to ask yourself, and then using the information properly in making your move.

There's an especially important reason why you need to have your playing skills down pat before entering a casino. Because once inside, you will need to keep track of more than just the cards. You must keep a watchful eye on the dealer, to make sure everything is on the up and up. You'll want to pay attention to the pit boss and the floor managers, casually, to make sure there are no countermeasures in effect. You should pay attention to anything unusual at your table – players who might be shills, any distractions that might be staged to divert your attention from the dealer, and so on. You won't be able to do all of this if your head is filled with confusion about how to handle card strategy and implement the *Blackjack The SMART Way* system components.

The Advantages Of Practicing With Cards

Now, here's what you should do. If you don't already own a good set of cards, go to the store and buy a dozen decks of good-quality cards like the casinos use. (If a casino is near, you can usually buy inexpensive decks that had been used at their tables. Or you can find quality cards at a discount price at those huge warehouse stores.) If you have some spare cash, buy yourself an inexpensive blackjack layout, either on a large piece felt or a roll-up mat. Gambling supply stores typically have these for between $15 and $35, depending on the materials used. Buy some inexpensive betting chips, too, so you can practice your betting system. (FYI: Keep an eye on blackjacktoday.com; I'm eventually going to create a practice game product of my own.)

Nothing substitutes for practicing with cards. Software simulations do not present you with real-world conditions so you cannot pick up on all the factors you'd master when using real cards, with all their repeating phenomena. Also, the action is slower using cards, and you will tend to notice things you do not when you're whipping through hands with a super-fast computer program.

Now take those 12 decks you've purchased and deal rounds with various numbers of players using, alternately, one and two decks. If you plan on playing at multi-deck tables, work on up from one to two to however many you plan on playing against. Play all of the players' hands until you have the strategy charts down cold. Place bets on each of the hands, and play according to your **3-Level, Notch-Up, Notch-Down Bet Management System**, while applying the **X Factor**. When you are ready, try your hand at card counting and **Card Observation**.

Then, see what you might learn from patterns that tend to

make themselves apparent as the cards unfold during each round.   Really study the cards.   (And replace the decks with new ones periodically; each mix of cards has its own personality.)

FYI: There's A Companion Audio Book

I also recommend you obtain my Compact Disc audio book, *Richard Harvey's Blackjack PowerPrep Session.* You need to review your game just before you play but unfortunately few players do so. This fabulous 70-minute CD audio book does the job for you, so reviewing becomes fun and almost effortless. You can order it online at www.blackjacktoday.com or by sending $14.95 plus $3.95 S&H to: Book Orders, c/o Mystic Ridge Books, 222 Main St., Suite #142, Farmington, CT 06032.   (Or you can special order it at your favorite bookstore.)

What's Next?

Once you've integrated everything you've read in this book and have used it to great success, you'll probably hunger for more information on becoming yet a smarter player and bigger winner. At that time, you can take your game to an even higher level with *Cutting Edge Blackjack.* It contains the powerful and profitable results of my latest research projects.   My third book *NEW Ways to Win MORE at Blackjack* offers additional tips from my columns, on an entry-level basis.   Also visit **blackjacktoday.com** regularly for free advice, blogs and updated book and seminar information.

You are now armed with enough information to become a very good player.   If you have studied, practiced and perfected your skills, then it's time to go to the casino!   I wish you the very best.

But, most of all, have <u>fun</u>.   To become a really great player, you really need to have passion for the game.   And along these lines, you'll know when you're really ready to take on the house when your mind says: *Bring it on!*

You have now completed your entry-level introduction to my system.   Now please go back and reread this book (taking notes) until it becomes second nature to you.
...See you at a seminar perhaps?

Glossary
Of
Terms

Glossary of Terms

(Note: Terms starting with numbers are listed under the *letter* that starts the alphanumeric spelling of those numbers.)

Advanced Strategy Charts: A diagram showing suggestions as to how the Advanced Player might play his hands in every card situation. They sometimes contain two or more suggestions per situation, if judgment needs to be exercised according to the card count or Card Observation.

Advanced Strategy: What Advanced Players use in deciding how to play their hands. It's arrived at by these players, through the use of the Advanced Strategy charts, in combination with their application of card counting and/or **Card Observation**, the realities regarding the behavior of the dealer up cards, the **X Factor**, and advanced players' understanding of the mathematical probabilities they face in every card situation.

All-Inclusive Counting System: The *Blackjack The SMART Way* card counting system which takes into account every one of the 13 possible cards. (See Chapter 8 for details.)

Anchorman or Anchorwoman: A shill or buddy of the dealer's, who, sitting in the third baseman's seat (or, simply to the left of all the players), works in cahoots with the dealer to cheat players out of their chips. Most often, the anchorman or woman is told by the dealer, through the use of signals, whether or not to take a card, so that the dealer might draw the card he or she needs to achieve a high, winning score.

Barring a Player: The controversial practice in which a casino bans a player from playing there anymore. The courts have ruled in favor of the casinos so far in allowing this practice to continue (except in New Jersey, where state law forbids it). Casinos bar players for being cheats, counters, system (or "advantage") players or simply winners.

Basic Bet: The name I give to the minimum bet you want to play, whatever Level you're at. If you're at Level 0 or 1, the Basic Bet is 1 Unit. If you're at Level 2, the Basic Bet is 2 Units. If you're at Level 3, the Basic Bet is 3 Units. At no point during play at any Level will you place a bet that's lower than the Basic Bet.

Basic Strategy: An approach in which each type of player hand is given one recommended move versus each dealer up card, as dictated by the Basic Strategy charts. Invented in 1953, this approach is outdated and is recommended for beginners only.

Basic Strategy Charts: The diagrams or spreadsheets which dictate to Beginners and Intermediates how to play their hands in every card situation. These diagrams contain only one suggested move per situation.

Betting Spot: The place on the table, in front of your seat, denoted by a circle or square usually, where you must place your betting chips.

Bigmouth Barneys & Berthas: The nickname the author gives to dealers who are verbally abusive and/or insulting.

Blackjack: When your first two cards contain an Ace and a 10-point card, for 21 points. It pays a bonus of either 50% (3-to-2) or 20% (6-to-5) depending on the casino. (unless you tie with the dealer, in which case you win nothing unless you've chosen to take Even Money or Insurance; if you've chosen one of those options, you're paid an amount equal to your bet). **Also known as a natural.**

Burning A Card: After shuffling, the dealer usually discards the top card into the discard rack. That's referred to as "burning" a card. It means "to discard." Some casinos burn as many cards as there are players, before the dealer starts dealing from the newly shuffled stack.

Bust: To go over the maximum allowed point total of 21 when drawing a card. If a player busts, he or she loses instantly. If the dealer busts, all players who have not busted win.

Card Counting: The practice in which cards are assigned either a positive or negative number, and counted as they are played, in order to keep track of the proportion of low and high cards played, so as to predict what cards might be dealt next. The concept dates back to the 1950s or earlier, when players were known to be quietly plying this trade; the first published method was the Hi-Lo system in 1963. This Old School approach is now outdated.

Card Mechanics: Veritable magicians who employ sleight of hand tricks to cheat players out of their bets. They possess specialized skills beyond the ken of the average dealer. *(Nor is the average dealer crooked.)*

Card Observation: A card analysis method to determine your correct card move. Much more accurate than card counting and one of the author's innovations, this practice enables the player to figure out what cards are due and therefore what the dealer's hole card and your hit cards are likely to be. It's based upon mathematical probabilities and is easier to implement than card counting.

251

Card Observation Questions: Five questions in using the author's Card Observation card analysis method that help you identify the dealer's hole card and your most likely hit cards. (See Chapter 8.)

Casino Countermeasures: Moves made by casino bosses and dealers to win back the money won by players. Often unfair, these moves include bringing in new cards, frequent reshuffling, speeding up action, and changing dealers.

Cashing out: Taking your chips to the cashier's window (found off to the side somewhere in the casino) in exchange for their cash value.

Charts: The diagrams in which suggested moves in particular card situations are displayed.

Chips: The colored "coins" you use instead of money to place your bet. Although the colors of the various denominations — $5, $25, $100, $1,000, $5,000 on up – are usually the same from casino to casino (red, green, black, pink and "chocolate"), the graphics and writing on each coin is peculiar to each casino, and always contains the name of that casino.

Circle of 13: A learning tool found in the author's second book, *Cutting Edge Blackjack*, the audio book *Preparing YOU To WIN,* and seminar material. It's an introduction to how to ferret out the mathematical probabilities in analyzing the cards and making the smartest moves.

"Color me in": What you say to the dealer to exchange your lower denomination chips for easier-to-carry higher denomination chips. Low stakes table players - who play with red $5 chips - typically exchange those chips for green $25 chips. How to do this: Wait for the dealer to finish post-round card collecting or shuffling and then place your chips on the table just beyond the Insurance circle and say "color me in, please." The dealer will then make the exchange. The reason this is done is the casino doesn't want the table to be depleted of the most commonly used chips.

Cooler Deck: Cards that have been secretly prearranged in a certain order before being dealt so the dealer beats all of the players at the table.

Coupon Charlies & Charlenes: The name the author gives to players who come to your table, with newspaper coupons in hand, only to play one or two hands to use their coupons and then leave. They are often not even blackjack players – they are often slots players who play simply because they've received coupons. They usually play poorly and louse up the action. Take note of their arrival and moderate your bet.

Cutting the Cards: After the cards are shuffled, the dealer offers the shuffle marker to a player who then pushes that marker into the cards wherever they choose, thereby cutting the cards in two. The cards above where the player places the marker go to the bottom of the stack; the card directly below the marker becomes the top of the stack (and that card is "burned," or discarded by the dealer; the card below that one usually is the first card dealt).

Dealing Seconds: When rogue dealers cheat players by either peeking at the top undealt cards or using marked cards to decide which card they want to deal - the top one or one below it. They use this illegal selection process in order to bust your hand or to make their hand reach a great total (a tip off is how frequently they reach totals of 20 or 21 points). To deal a card below the top one in pitch games, they typically hold the cards at an angle toward their bodies so you cannot see the top cards; their left thumb pulls back the top card and their right one pulls out a lower card to deal. In a shoe game, they push up the front card while yanking out the next one to deal.

Double Down or Double: Placing an amount of chips besides your original bet equal to the amount of your original bet (although you can place less) in exchange for the restriction of getting just one more card. You can say "double" although most dealers don't need that verbal cue. In traditional blackjack games, you may do this only immediately after having been dealt your first two cards. (Some specialized games allow you to double after receiving any number of cards.) You only want to do this when you have a point total that won't bust with the taking of an extra card. Recommended only when the dealer's likely to bust or you're highly likely to outscore the dealer in taking just one hit card.

Even Money: When a player who has a Blackjack asks the dealer to be paid off right away in even money (chips equal to your bet, without the normal Blackjack bonus) when the dealer's up card is an Ace. To do this, you say, "Even money," when the dealer inquires if any players want Insurance. It's equivalent to taking Insurance but it's a better move; it's quicker and it helps prevent possible payout confusion later on.

Eye In The Sky: The collective term for the many cameras focused on your table and all casino surveillance activity in general. It refers to the security employees in surveillance monitoring rooms who continually watch and record all activity in a casino to identify cheats, card counters and big winners. If they identify a cheat, they initiate an arrest. If they identify a big winner, they notify the pit boss to initiate countermeasures or bar the player. Betting disputes are sometimes resolved with the recordings made.

253

Face Card: A Jack, Queen or King. Sometimes referred to as "paint."

First Baseman: The player who sits in the seat by the dealer's left hand, who has the first turn (see DIAGRAM A, page 55).

Floorman or Floor manager: The casino boss directly under the pit boss who supervises a number of tables from the floor (outside the Pit).

Flow of the Cards: The author's term for the order in which the cards you're analyzing were dealt. The **Flow of the Cards** is of concern to you when you are using the practice of **Card Observation**. (See Chapter 8.)

Good Outs: The specific hit cards that would give you great scores, preferably of 21, 20 and, to a lesser extent, 19 points.

Hand: The first two cards you or the dealer receive. Secondary meaning: all the cards you eventually receive in one round at one betting spot.

Handmakers: The hit cards, by type (of the Aces through 10s), that would give you great scores of 21, 20 or, to a lesser extent, 19 points. You especially want to know if they're available when doubling or hitting stiffs.

Hard Hand: Any hand that does not contain an Ace.

Hard Total: Any total that does not contain an Ace or where the Ace can only count as 1 point.

Hit: To ask the dealer for a card.

"Hit Me": What players sometimes tell the dealer when asking for another card (even though a hand signal is required and the verbal expression is unnecessary).

Hole Card: The card dealers deal themselves facedown. The "mystery" card you won't see until you've played out your hand. With *Blackjack The SMART Way*'s Card Observation techniques, a player can determine, with good probability, what this important card is likely to be. Antiquated books wrongly tell the player to assume the hole card is a 10, but overall that occurs less than 31% of the time; so they're wrong 69% of the time!

The House: Another way of saying "the casino."

Insurance: When the dealer turns up an Ace as the up card, he or she will ask, "Insurance?" At that time you can make a side bet (that costs half your original bet) that pays off 2-to-1 if the dealer indeed has a Blackjack. Only a smart move for skilled state-of-the-art players who can tell when the dealer's highly likely to have a 10 in the hole.

Money Management: How you handle your bets. Secondary meaning: a host of procedures to manage your money in order to become a winner and maximize your gains.

Negative Count: When the card count is in the minus numbers. That tells you that more high cards have been dealt than low cards. The higher the number, the more likely it will be that low cards will be dealt.

One-Hand Harrys & Harriets: The name the author gives to players who come to your table in the middle of ongoing action and play just one or two hands, often lousing up the flow of the cards. They are either bad players, they might be shills (see below) or they might have read Stanford Wong's books, which recommend this practice (which has become known as "wonging"). Pay attention to their arrival and moderate your bet because they can spoil the predictability of the flow of the cards to your betting spot.

Outs: The specific hit cards you need to either achieve a winning score or at least not bust you. **Also known as handmakers.**

Personality of the Cards: The author's term for the peculiar character-istics of each set of cards being used. It includes the consideration of whether the cards are "Great," "Good," "Neutral," "Bad" or "Horrible." It also refers to repeating patterns that extend from shuffle to shuffle. (See Chapter 9). It's set in motion by the first shuffling of new cards and persists, through repeating phenomena, for many tens of shuffles and sometimes throughout the life of that mix - when shuffled in the exacting way it's done at the casino.

Personality of the Dealer Up Cards: The author's term for the behav-ior of each of the up cards, each of which has its peculiar tendencies in leading the dealer toward a particular winning total or busting.

Pit: The rectangular or circular floor space surrounded by a bunch of blackjack tables, in which dealers and the pit boss work.

Pit Boss: The casino manager who works in the Pit and is in charge of the dealers and lower casino bosses (floormen) who directly supervise the tables surrounding the Pit.

Pitch Game: Single and double deck games. They got this nickname because the dealer PITCHES the cards to each player (facedown). The players then pick up their cards (in one hand) to play out their hands, placing their cards facedown under their bets when they decide to stand.

Placing a Bet: The act of putting the amount of chips you want to wager on the upcoming round, in your betting spot.

Positive Count: When the card count is in the positive zone (as indicated by a "+" symbol). This tells you that more low cards have been played than high cards. The higher the number, the more likely that high cards will be dealt.

Push: When your score ties the dealer's and you neither win nor lose. You keep your bet. (The dealer typically knocks lightly on the table to indicate that you've both achieved a tie.)

Quick Ricks: The name the author gives to dealers who are brought in by management to unduly speed up the game to a ridiculously fast pace.

Round: The period of play from the first player card dealt to the playing out of the dealer's hand.

Running Count: A card count you get by simply adding each card's count value as it appears in the course of the game. This is what you use with the **Blackjack The SMART Way All-Inclusive Counting System.**

Second Baseman: The player that directly faces the dealer, in the middle of the table (in the fourth of seven seats).

Shoe: The tray that holds the undealt cards in a blackjack game with 4, 6 or 8 decks. (But 4-deck games are all but extinct.)

Shoe Game: The alternative to the pitch game, where the cards, usually 6 or 8 decks, are dealt face up from a plastic or wooden tray called a "shoe." The players are not allowed to touch their cards.

Shuffle Marker: A plastic marker in the shape and size of a card, of various colors, that's used by a player (chosen by the dealer) to cut the cards and then by the dealer to push into the stack of newly-rearranged cards as a reminder to reshuffle the cards when the marker is reached later (shuffling being done at the completion of that round).

Silent 7: The nickname the author gives to the dealer's 7, because, while the current wisdom is that it is a strong card for the dealer, it actually is the player's fourth-best dealer up card.

Stiffmakers: The hit cards that would give you a stiff total (12-16 points).

6-Unit Cheat-Proof Rule: One of the stop-loss methods in *Blackjack The SMART Way*, which tells you to *leave the table* if you've lost 6 or more betting Units after a dozen or less hands immediately after arriving at a table or with the arrival of a new dealer. Whether the result of rogue dealer cheating or simply bad cards, it's time to leave the table. Invoke this twice in any one session and you should leave the casino.

Sizz: The term casino floormen and pit bosses use to alert each other to a player who's on a big winning streak.

Soft Hand: Any 2-card hand that contains an Ace, or one where the Ace can count as either a 1-point or 11-point card, at the player's or dealer's discretion.

Soft 17: When a score of 17 is made with the aid of an Ace. In other words, a combination of an Ace and a card or cards totalling 6 points. Most casinos have dealers stand on soft 17s. Some casinos require dealers to hit these poor totals, hoping to improve them to beat the players but that policy also causes the dealer's busting rate to increase.

Soft Total: A final point total in a hand that contains an Ace where the Ace is counted as 11 points.

Splitting: When you are dealt two like cards and you divide those cards into two new starting hands (after putting down an extra bet equal to your original bet). You tell the dealer "split" when it's your turn, while you place extra chips equal to your original bet to the right of your betting spot. The dealer then plays each card as a new hand, giving you as many cards as you'd like on each card with the exception of Aces (you get just one extra card upon each Ace and you usually cannot resplit them if you receive another Ace upon the original split cards).

Stand: To decide not to take any more cards.

Stiff: A bustable hard hand (of 12 to 16 points).

Surrender: You're essentially folding your hand (because it's lousy or you realize your likely score will lose to the dealer's likely score). You get to keep half your bet. A great option for savvy state-of-the-art players. Upon saying "surrender" (at your turn), the dealer takes half your bet (leaving the other half in your betting spot) and discards your cards. (First offered in 1958 in the Philippines, this is not allowed at most casinos, although increasing casino competition has seen this option increase in availability since the mid-1990s.)

Table Winning Percentage: The author's term for the approximate number of hands you win, in percent. You can do it through exact mathematics, dividing the actual number of times you've won by the total number of hands you've faced, and then multiplying the result by 100. Or you can keep track of your Winning Margin, which is easier (see Chapter 7). Or an approximation is nearly as useful (see Chapter 9.)

Ten-pointers or 10s: Cards that either say "10" (the "pips") and the face cards, all of which count for 10 points in blackjack.

Third Baseman: The player who sits in the seat dealt to last by the dealer, by the dealer's right hand (see DIAGRAM A, page 55).

3-Level, Notch-Up, Notch-Down, Bet Management System: A 3-tiered betting system developed by the author, to better time bets such that increases and decreases come when it's mathematically most wise.

Tip: Chips or money you give to the dealer, as in tipping a waitress. **Also known as a toke**.

Tip Slot: The slot where the dealer deposits tips. Dealers typically tap the tips (usually chips) loudly on the metal slot first, to alert the floor managers to watch them as they take some chips off the table. This is a check against dealers stealing chips they should not be taking.

Toke: A tip for the dealer.

Tray: Where the casino's chips are kept on each table (the chips they use to pay off winning bets, collect losing bets, color up player chips, and provide chips to players who want to buy more).

Tricky 2s: The nickname the author gives the dealer's 2. While the current wisdom is that the 2 is a player-friendly card, it actually is a neutral card. When it scores, it draws to high winning totals. Using the Old School methods, you miss out on many winning opportunities versus this tricky card because you stand too often with stiffs against this up card (which has the lowest overall busting rate of the low dealer up cards, 35%, and busts a lot less at times - when 10s, for instance, are not in the hole).

258

True Count: A card count you arrive at by taking the running count and dividing it by the number of decks of cards that remain undealt. (With some systems, the running count is actually divided by fractions of decks!) It's very impractical. Few players can do division in their heads, with fractions, in the heat of action.

Unit: The absolute lowest bet you will play. With beginners, it coincides with the minimum at the table. If you're at a $5 minimum bet table, a $5 chip will be your "unit." At a $10 table, two $5 chips will be your "unit" (there are no such things as $10 chips). And so on. This designation is a way to simplify your betting calculations.

Up Card: Of the dealer's first two cards, the one that's dealt face up. The dealer's up card tells the player a lot of information. Good card strategy begins with an accurate read on the dealer up card's strengths and weaknesses - specifically regarding the card imbalances of the moment.

Winning Margin: The number of rounds you've won versus those you've lost, expressed simply as one number (positive or negative) that indicates your margin of gain or loss. A positive number tells you that you've won more rounds than you've lost, the number itself indicating how many more wins you've had than losses. A negative number tells you the reverse.

X Factor: The name the author gives to a variety of factors that tell you how well your betting spot is doing and how well the dealer is doing. This is an entry-level means of getting in touch with repeating phenomena detailed in *Cutting Edge Blackjack*. A series of questions reveals what the **X Factor** *is* at any one time; the answers indicate how you should play your bets and whether you should stay at the table or leave (see Chapter 9). They also tell you whether the table is "horrible," "bad," "neutral," "good," or "great." In addition, the **X Factor** enables you to determine what the **personality of the cards** is, to spot any useful repeating patterns from which you might profit. This information also helps you to determine how to handle some of your card situations.

X Factor Indicators: Any one of a number of signposts that alert you as to how good or bad the table is for you. Some point you toward making higher bets and moving to a higher Level or Step within your **3-Unit, Notch-Up, Notch-Down Bet Management System**; other indicators tell you it's time for you to leave that table.

X Factor Questions: The questions that lead you to an understanding of what the **X Factor Indicators** are telling you.

Index

Symbols

A

B

E

F

G

H

I

S

U

W

X

273

TAKE A SEMINAR!

Mystic Ridge Books is the proud sponsor of Richard Harvey's nationally-acclaimed seminars. Many have flown *hundreds of miles* to attend. *One player drove 4,000 miles round trip and it was his* third *seminar!*

But now *only New Books Club members who have purchased the latest Editions of Blackjack The SMART Way and Cutting Edge Blackjack (at or near retail price) may attend* (see the following pages for details). To make your seminar experience worthwhile you need to have read Richard Harvey's latest books. They are your textbooks and seminars would suffer if attendees were not up to date. You will be required to show these books at the door; book contents will be referred to during the seminar by page number and you'll need to have them on hand in order to keep up with the presentation.

Once you're a New Books Club member, send your request to be included on our seminar waiting list (with your name, address, phone number and email address) to: Blackjack Seminar List, Mystic Ridge Books, 222 Main Street, Suite #142, Farmington, CT 06032. Include a **check for $9.95 made out to Mystic Ridge Books** (a onetime nonrefundable processing fee) along with a **self-addressed stamped envelope and a photocopy of your driver's license,** whose address must match the address on your check. (The fee helps defray expenses for the screening process to come and mailings.) Also send proof of non-casino employment. Seminars take place on weekends, so please let us know what dates you can or cannot attend for the next 6-12 months so we can best coordinate the seminar dates with those on our waiting list!

Seminar tickets currently cost up to $495 depending on the location. Please consult blackjacktoday.com for any price increases. *You must be willing to travel to attend. Seminars are held infrequently and at locations convenient to Richard Harvey. To attend, you must agree to follow all screening requirements (including proof of non-casino-related employment and a photo ID at the door) and abide by all restrictions or you may not attend. You must also agree in writing* not to record the seminar; not to pass along the location to anyone prior to or during the event; *and* not to give seminar-related information to the casino industry. Those accepted to the seminar waiting list will be eligible to attend for two years; any who have not taken seminars after two years will be removed from the list.

Richard Harvey's *Table-Intensive* Blackjack Seminars include his popular card demonstrations; practice games with one-on-one attention; and tabletop instruction in Precision Betting, shuffle tracking, Strategic Card Analysis, probability assessment, identifying the dealer's hole card and determining the dealer's outcome, End Game Strategy, and other state-of-the-art techniques.

What's better than learning the ropes from the world's top expert? Ken H. of California, a past seminar-goer said, "I thoroughly enjoyed it! You understand the game far better than most so-called experts. I do believe you are on to something (big)." Mark L. said, "I flew from California to attend this seminar. Given the quality of the material, I would not hesitate to repeat the process." Jim S. of Rio Rancho said, "Since attending your outstanding seminar, I realized just what a novice I was. Now I have been winning *consistently!*"

Unfortunately, so long as casinos bar winners, those working directly or indirectly for casinos or related security firms are not eligible to attend, nor are their relatives, friends or associates, so as to protect the playing careers of all concerned.

ABOUT THE AUTHOR

Richard Harvey began his blackjack career in Atlantic City after being a victim of corporate layoffs. The system he used, which he'd developed in the two years beforehand, sprang from a love of cards (he was a member of a New York City Bridge club at the time) and math (he'd minored in theoretical math and statistics in college).

His decision to create his own blackjack system was born out of frustration at his lack of success using others' methods, in computer tests. University-trained in conducting scientific and mathematical research, theoretical math, computer science, and statistics, his background provided the perfect qualifications for achieving success in doing what no one else had done in more than 50 years: producing a new and better way to beat the house, with an unheard-of precision. Although his approach has been greatly refined over the years, even his early experiences at the blackjack table were highly profitable. He went on an immediate tear in Atlantic City, and hasn't looked back since.

The spark for his first book, *Blackjack The SMART Way* (now a bestseller in its Fourth Edition) was a request from his friends that he write an instructional manual for them. (They'd witnessed how often he won at blackjack.) His latest monumental blackjack, shuffling and card behavior research project (spanning more than three years) resulted in many more awesome break-throughs, as well as his second book *Cutting Edge Blackjack*, hailed by many insiders such as Las Vegas gaming expert Howard Schwartz for blazing "new territory!"

Mr. Harvey has been on more than 100 talk shows and he's received innumerable glowing newspaper and magazine write-ups. He continues to play blackjack, do research, write syndicated columns and books, and give seminars. He says he is especially proud of the fact that so many readers have gone on to great success using his unique approach to the game.

FOR MEMBERSHIP IN OUR NEW BOOKS CLUB:

First purchase the Third Edition of *Cutting Edge Blackjack* or the Fourth Edition of *Blackjack The SMART Way new* at the cover price of $21.95 (or at a discount of no more than 20%) *from a recognized bookstore*. (Books bought on the Internet, from resellers or used book outlets *do not qualify*.)

Then mail the following to Mystic Ridge Books, 222 Main Street, Suite 142, Farmington, CT 06032:

① The form below completed legibly with your *real* name and *home* address. No P.O. Box or mailbox store addresses please.

② A onetime processing fee of $4.95 by check made out to Mystic Ridge Books. Your check must have your name and address printed on it (not handwritten). No money orders will be accepted. Please consult blackjacktoday.com for future club price increases.

③ Your *original* bookstore receipt with the *book title* and *price* circled. No handwritten, photocopied, questionable, or illegible receipts will be accepted. *(Send proof of purchase for BOTH books if you want to join our seminar waiting list.)*

④ A legible photocopy of the *back cover* of the qualifying book.

⑤ A self-addressed stamped envelope.

Once approved, you will receive a Club orientation packet, with information on how you may access all Club benefits. You may then apply to be added to the Richard Harvey Blackjack Seminar Waiting List (see requirements on page 348). You must have access to the Internet to enjoy some Club benefits. But if you're not yet online, tell us and we'll send you special brochures to order the special booklets that will be made available only to Club members.

Mystic Ridge Books reserves the right to reject without response or explanation applications that flagrantly violate the requirements listed above.

MYSTIC RIDGE BOOKS **NEW BOOKS CLUB** APPLICATION FORM

NAME: ———————————————————————

HOME
ADDRESS: ————————————————————————

————————————————————————

PHONE: ————————————————————————

EMAIL ADDRESS: ————————————————————

ENJOY SPECIAL BENEFITS AVAILABLE ONLY TO THOSE WHO BUY OUR BOOKS <u>NEW</u>

Mystic Ridge Books is now offering *rewards* to readers who buy the Third Edition of *Cutting Edge Blackjack* and/or the Fourth Edition of *Blackjack The SMART Way* <u>new</u> at the retail price of $21.95 (or at a discount of no more than 20%) at recognized bookstores. Doing so makes you eligible to join our New Books Club whose members enjoy many unique benefits worth many times the cover price of the two qualifying books listed above. (If you want to join our seminar waiting list, you must present proof of having purchased *both* books listed above, at or near retail price. They are your seminar textbooks.)

If you qualify for membership (by properly completing the procedure explained on page 349), you will enjoy these benefits (and more to come):

① *Only Club members will be allowed to attend future seminars.* The reason for this new policy is that we want seminar-goers to be up-to-date on Richard Harvey's latest methods. This is also our way of rewarding those who do the ethically and morally correct thing (only books bought *new* compensate the author and publisher for their work and without new book buyers these books and future titles would become impossible to publish). See restrictions on page 348.

② *Only Club members can purchase new strategy booklets* at a nominal price, such as the mind-blowing "Stealing Winning Betting Spots (for BTSW)" booklet, *with information not currently available in any current book.* Three will be released in the months following the release of this book and more will follow. You will be given a special URL address to to purchase these online when available.

③ *Only Club members will now be given access to Richard Harvey's two free advice blogs on our web site www.blackjacktoday.com.* The URLs for these will be revealed only to Club members.

④ *Only Club members can purchase upcoming special learning tools and receive special discounts periodically for products offered on blackjacktoday.com.*

And there will be even more special advantages only Club members will enjoy, to be announced soon. See www.blackjacktoday.com for updates.

Sweet! Now, once you've purchased one of the qualifying books mentioned above, new, at or within 20% of the retail price (as marked on the back cover), simply follow the instructions on page 349 to apply for membership.

Mystic Ridge Books reserves the right to reject any membership application that does not meet the requirements listed on pages 349-350. We will help those who make honest mistakes but *we reserve the right not to respond to applications that blatantly violate the rules.*